Growing Wildflowers

MARIE SPERKA

Growing Wildflowers

A Gardener's Guide

Drawings by Charles Clare

HARPER & ROW, PUBLISHERS
NEW YORK, EVANSTON, SAN FRANCISCO, LONDON

FIRST EDITION

Designed by Lydia Link

Library of Congress Cataloging in Publication Data

Sperka, Marie.
  Growing wildflowers.
  1. Wild flower gardening. I. Title.
SB439.S63   635.9'676   76–156553
ISBN 0–06–013959–5

21651

Contents

Perennial Wildflowers for Permanence

Foreword

The native flora of our prairies, mountains, and woodlands are a living part of the American heritage, as valuable and irreplaceable as any we have. But daily our wilderness and woodlands are vanishing, and with it the plants they nurture. Unless we act quickly, our wildlings will disappear.

Wildflowers, ferns, and other native flora have been my lifelong interest, and in this book I would like to share with my readers my experience in growing and propagating them. Although the cultivation of wildlings is in no way a substitute for their preservation in their natural habitats, it does give to the care of the amateur gardener, the expert, and the nurseryman a small piece of the American wilderness and keeps before us living treasures of our natural heritage.

Please note that many of the flowers I list here are already becoming rare; some are on protected lists. Before you acquire a rare plant, make sure that you have the proper conditions for its growth—and never pick the blooms before they have scattered their seeds if the plant is on the protected list in your state.

The cultivation and propagation practices discussed in this book are those that I have developed and used over years of successful wildflower and fern cultivation, first for my own pleasure and then later as a business. My nursery, Woodland Acres Nursery, is located in the Nicolet Forest area of northeastern Wisconsin. Most of the land there is uncultivated: forest crop or wilderness, a network of lakes and streams, stretches of reforested areas, prairie land, and rolling hills. The climate is severe. Summers are hot and often dry, and in winter the temperatures can drop to thirty degrees below zero and even lower.

Yet I have found that, with care, even in such conditions, it is often possible to grow wild plants in an environment entirely different from their native habitat. In the text of this book I have given detailed instructions on how to cultivate various species. Should any readers know of better methods or have different results to report, I would be very interested in hearing from them.

I would like to thank everyone who encouraged me to put my experience into book form so that I might share the knowledge and satisfaction I have gained from my years of working with wildflowers and ferns.

Marie Sperka

Crivitz, Wisconsin
Winter, 1973

Growing Wildflowers

Some forty years of watching wildflowers grow in the woods and on the prairie, along streams and lakes, among rocks and boulders, and in my nursery, have taught me what I know about their requirements. Their needs in most instances are few, but they are extremely specific and must be followed exactly if the plants are to be grown successfully. Although it appears that wildflowers and ferns thrive under conditions that would kill most cultivated perennials, most of them have, in fact, very particular requirements for soil, sunlight, moisture, and nutrients, and are at least as demanding as domestic plants in these respects.

In this section of the book, general techniques and principles are given for preparing the soil and surroundings so that you may cultivate a lovely wildflower area under varying conditions.

There are two main types of wildflowers. Those that have a root or bulb system that enable the plant to live for many years and faithfully reappear each spring are called the *perennials*. Those that bloom, set seed, and die in the same year or in two years are called the *annuals* and *biennials*. Most of them are grown directly from seed. Mature perennials, planted while dormant, are the mainstay of an established natural garden. The annuals and biennials provide a ready means of naturalizing a large open area, and they are also used to fill in the bare perennial beds until the perennial plants can take over.

The annuals and biennials are treated individually in the section starting on page 27. Perennial plants are discussed in the section starting on page 41.

Both the botanical name and common name are given for each wildflower. Common names, of course, vary from area to area, and sometimes a plant is known by several names at once. The botanical names are given by family, genus, and species according to *Gray's Manual of Botany* (Merritt Lyndon Fernald, 8th edition, 1950, corrected printing, 1970). Certain wildflowers, which have been imported from foreign lands, will not be found in *Gray's*.

PREPARING THE SOIL AND SURROUNDINGS

Reclaiming Barren Earth

Rebuilding infertile soils to make them productive can often pose a real problem, but with a little patience, energy, and planning, wonders can be accomplished. Sandy hillsides, gravelly or gritty soils, barren earth, and even blow sands—any land of low fertility—can be greatly improved and conditioned.

More than fifteen years ago I reclaimed two small plots of land, one of a desert type near where we now have our garden pool and the other a barren excavation next to our house. They could not have seemed more hopeless.

The first plot was a deep hole that I filled with the earth dug out to make the pool. The fill consisted of sand with a mixture of grit and a small amount of clay; humus was nonexistent. For a whole year the area lay bare but was kept free of weeds by frequent hoeing.

Finally the long process began of making the soil suitable for growing something. A layer several inches deep of compost and small leaves was strewn over the entire area. (This was before I had come upon the method listed below for reclaiming soil.) Here and there I made pockets in the earth and filled them with fertile soil, mixing some of the barren earth with it, and planted a few hardy wildflowers. I also planted a seedling birch and a small balsam fir, about twenty-five feet apart. At first the tiny trees seemed too far apart, but as they grew the span closed and today I see that this was the right spacing. The birch is now about twenty-five feet tall, and the balsam fir about twenty feet.

Over the years I have continued to add small leaves, old marsh hay, and weathered straw to the sandy soil. Now hepaticas, bloodroot, and *Trillium grandiflorum* flourish beneath the white birch. They have multiplied, indicating that organic matter has built up sufficiently to grow the woodland wildflowers.

Some half-ton boulders were brought in to create a realistic woodland setting. The untrimmed branches of the balsam fir now sweep the ground.

4

In sunny open spots, prairie-type wildflowers have taken a firm hold. The entire problem area has been transformed from an arid waste into a spot of natural beauty.

The other barren plot was a hollow filled with earth excavated from the basement of my house. A ten-foot strip along a walk was marked off for a perennial flower bed, and the remaining filled area was readied for a lawn.

The key to working up a fertile soil is the humus: the type, the amount, and the way it is scattered on the soil or combined with it. I call this method of reclaiming barren areas "A Dozen Steps to Success."

1. Start with an area of about 1,000 square feet (for example, a plot 20 by 50 feet). Remove any unwanted growth and all debris.

2. Spread six bushels of peatmoss—it must be damp or wet—over the entire area, and over this spread six bushels of good compost or well-decayed, weed-free manure. (The more life-giving humus material you add, the better will be the finished soil, so add more if it is available.)

3. Ten to twelve bales of combined, weed-free oat straw are needed. Combined straw is preferred as it has usually been exposed to the weather for several weeks before baling and is easier to handle. Old clean straw or weathered hay may be substituted. Spread five bales of the straw evenly (about a half bale for every 100 square feet). Loosen the pads as you spread the straw. This is important. As you walk over the straw while spreading it, some will settle.

4. When the entire area is covered with the five bales of straw, sprinkle on twenty pounds of 10-10-10 commercial fertilizer.

5. Over this, sow one-fourth bushel of clean, weed-free oats.

6. Now spread the remaining five bales of straw as you did in step 3.

7. Thoroughly wet down the entire area and roll with a lawn roller or tamp down to settle the straw and flatten the surface. Wetting the straw is not absolutely necessary, but it hastens the germination of the oat seed and dissolves some of the nutrients in the fertilizer.

8. To keep the straw from blowing away, it is desirable to peg the plot down until the oat plants are several inches tall. Place one-inch-square stakes or strong sticks one foot apart along all four sides of the plot. Tie one end of a ball of strong twine to the bottom of one corner-stake and walk back and

forth with it the entire length of the plot, looping the twine around each stake. Now do the same along the width of the plot. This will form a pattern of one-foot squares outlined in twine. In a windy area it is especially important to keep the straw down until the oats have grown tall enough to anchor the straw.

9. As soon as the oat crop is a few inches tall, remove the twine. (It may be saved and used again.)

10. If the project was started in the spring, the oats will be ripe by mid-summer. Now it is time to repeat the enriching process. As soon as the oats have ripened and before the birds can steal the seeds, roll the entire area to flatten the stalks to the earth. The ripened seeds will resow the plot.

11. Sprinkle the plot with ten pounds of 10-10-10 commercial fertilizer again, plus ten pounds of bonemeal. Bloodmeal may also be added, but I find that where dogs run loose this is a poor practice—dogs like to dig wherever bloodmeal is spread.

12. Cover the area with another five to six bales of combined straw, as in step 3. Repeat steps 7, 8, and 9.

The second crop of oats will not ripen, but it will make a good mulch that will be winter-killed and then laid down by the weight of the snow.

The next spring repeat the process beginning with step 4, using more commercial fertilizer if you wish. The addition of fertilizer depends on what you wish to plant when the soil is brought back to good fertility level. Follow through with the remaining steps. This process may be repeated another year in cases of extremely barren soil. Woodland flowers, most perennials, and good lawns need fertile soil. Very few soils will be ready for planting at the end of the first year. Usually it is best to treat a plot for two years or longer.

The poorer sun-exposed soils are best suited for planting the prairie type of wildflower or the sun-lovers of lean meadows, such as butterfly flower, hoary puccoon, bergamot, and ox-eye daisy. When the wildflowers are planted, the coarse mulch should be pushed aside and the rich humus worked into the earth in a circle three to four inches deep. A little extra compost may be added. After planting, return the coarse mulch around the plants. When planning a prairie garden, grasses of the prairie type may be left to grow in tufts here and there for a more natural effect.

Beware of quack grass (also called couch grass) and wild oats. Should they or any other creeping grasses appear, uproot them at once and add more mulch to that spot. The remaining roots will eventually come to the surface as they cannot tolerate deep mulching. Quack grass will literally work its roots right out of the soil if enough mulch is applied.

Where you plant the woodland wildflowers, rather than the prairie type, you must provide shade and continue to build up the soil with humus, as these plants require a rich, fertile soil and protection from intense sunlight. Consider your newly acquired earth a step in good conservation.

When the soil has been enriched to a good depth by decaying mulch and by the addition of humus in planting pockets, you are ready to grow a variety of woodland wildflowers—hepaticas, bloodroot, trilliums in variety, Dutchman's-breeches, mertensia and wild blue phlox, as well as many of the wildflowers of drier woodlands. Continue to mulch your plot until the trees grow their own mulch, and then let the falling leaves take over. It is important to water in periods of drought, but do not water trees after the first of August.

Time and effort go into reclaiming barren earth, but the beautiful and natural results are well worth it.

Reclaiming Overgrown Lands

Woodland wildflowers require uncultivated soil that contains a lot of decaying humus and abundance of fungi. Large areas of wild land can be reclaimed, and your woodland garden expanded, with the simple method given below.

In your selected site, mark desirable wildflowers with a stake so that they will not be accidentally destroyed or smothered. Now dig out all the undesirable wild shrubs, leaving only the fine hair-roots interlaced with the mycorhizal fungus that are beneficial to the growth of lady's-slippers. Remove young trees and saplings where there is crowding; be sure to cut the stumps even with the ground, and remove the bark down to at least three inches below the soil level to prevent new shoots.

The soil in the entire area should not be disturbed any more than necessary. Since fertility is not a problem, all that remains is to smother undesirable grasses and plants. It is best to do this in spring, especially after a heavy rain. Here is my method.

First, spread newspapers, three to five sheets thick, over the entire site. Cardboard can also be used, but it does not deteriorate as quickly. On paths and trails, magazines can be used. Then, spread a generous layer of old straw and marsh hay over all the paper. Finally, scatter a generous amount of 10-10-10 commercial fertilizer over the entire area to hasten the decay of the mulch and newspaper.

If you are laying the newspaper on a hillside, always start from the highest point and work downward (the reverse of shingling a roof). You want to absorb the rain as it falls rather than have it run downhill.

Next spring, if plant life beneath the newspaper has not died, repeat the mulch and fertilizer process. The fertilizer will have leached before planting time in the fall.

Pull back the mulch when you are ready to set plants in the new plot. If any newspaper remains, remove it to the compost heap. Do not spade! Disturb the soil only enough to remove any coarse lifeless roots that remain— and perhaps a few unwanted living ones. Now carefully insert wildflowers into the new soil, spreading the roots and then pulling the mulch up around the stems. Add more mulch where needed, as you would in a garden plot. This type of reclaimed area is an excellent home for all woodland wildflowers and ferns.

Even quack grass will give up under a heavy layer of newspaper and mulch. Quack grass roots need air to grow and cannot stand smothering with a heavy mulch. The roots will grow toward the top, and you will be able to lift them out.

By this method I reclaimed an old chicken yard that had grown up in quack grass; it took several years, but it was worth the effort. The reclaimed area is a very fertile piece of land in the shade of some large oak trees. In open spots I planted a few birch trees. I had always envisioned the yard as ideal for growing lady's-slippers and woodland ferns, and it has indeed proved to be wonderful. The ferns grow luxuriantly. The lady's-slippers thrive, continually growing new roots and multiplying—many two-crowned plants now send up five to seven flower stalks.

Steep Banks, Hillsides, and Rugged Slopes

There are many ways to plant steep and rugged areas that have a tendency to erode. The quickest method is to plant a groundcover suitable to the terrain. The groundcover should have strong spreading roots, which will hold the soil in place. This method is satisfactory if the soil has not eroded and is fertile enough to support the plants you have selected.

Rather than planting steep areas with groundcover, I prefer the method outlined below, even when the soil is fertile. To me it seems wiser to lay down a cover of natural mulch before planting.

1. Lightly rake the selected area and sprinkle with ten pounds of 10-10-10 commercial fertilizer for every 100 square feet (for example, 10 feet by 10 feet). The fertilizer is used only to grow more luxuriant oat plants and will have leached considerably before it is time to plant the wildflowers.

2. Sow broadcast some clean oat seed over the area.

3. Mulch moderately to lightly with clean straw or old marsh hay. The latter is preferred.

4. Sprinkle the area thoroughly with water, being careful to avoid letting the surplus run down hill and cut tiny rivulets that can later contribute to the soil's washing away.

5. Roll the entire area with a lawn roller or tamp down with a board. Unless the area is windy, it is not necessary to peg down the straw until the oat seed germinates.

In a short time this area will be covered with a good stand of oat plants, the roots of which will hold the soil on the slope. The plot should not be disturbed any further, except to push aside the mulch to insert the desired plants.

The oats are best planted in mid-August. The plants will grow only six to ten inches and not set seed. In late fall, the oats will winter-kill and then be packed down by the snow. Plant only oats and not rye, as rye will live over winter and continue to grow the following spring when you will want to insert the plants.

Let us assume that the plot is fertile and in the shade. Woodland wild-flowers with strong roots will furnish support to the soil and flourish here. Among these are mayapple, wild ginger, Greek valerian, foamflower in patches, hepaticas in clumps, wild geraniums in drifts, and large colonies of wild violets (except birdfoot, which is for sun only). At the bottom of the slope some of the taller woodland ferns will adapt themselves readily.

In such a shady area it is desirable to continue to add some mulch, unless there are enough leaves each fall to take over naturally. As added fertility builds up the soil, you can add many of the wildflowers that need humus. Trilliums planted in colonies among bloodroot make an appealing picture.

Suppose that the plot is in full sun. It will then need no further mulching, unless weeds are a problem. The addition of tufts of nonspreading grasses will add interest. Suitable wildflowers are butterfly flower, hoary puccoon, gray goldenrod, black-eyed Susans, *Phlox pilosa*, *Liatris scariosa*, and *Monarda fistulosa*. Ox-eye daisies for an early splash of white can take over a whole area. In open sandy spots an addition of drifts of birdfoot violet will spread a wave of blue across the slope in late May and early June.

Clay Soils

The addition of organic matter to clay soils will help to make them porous and easier to work. The method outlined below should give good results. Let us start with a plot about 1,000 feet square.

1. Remove any unwanted growth or debris from the area before starting your project. If large rocks are present and can be moved to one side, it will make for easier tilling or spading later.

2. Over the entire area spread an inch or two of coarse sand or gravelly earth with sand.

3. Over this, spread six bushels of rich organic compost, preferably coarse, or spread some strawy manure. Also spread a bushel or two of damp peatmoss. The more organic matter you add, combined with a balance of sand, the better the condition of the new soil will be. Leafmold from an old leaf pile is also desirable.

4. Sprinkle on ten pounds of 10-10-10 commercial fertilizer.

5. Sow broadcast one-fourth bushel of clean, weed-free oat seed. Cover the oat seed by raking or add some more compost.

6. Wet down entire area thoroughly to hasten germination of the oat seed.

As soon as the oats crop is about seven inches tall, it should be turned under. In a large area, it may be necessary to till several times for best results. Small plots can be spaded by hand. When the vegetation is turned under, it decays and adds the much-needed humus to give texture to the clay soil. With liberal amounts of humus added to clay, the soil will not be as gummy nor bake as readily during periods of drought.

The process may have to be repeated until the desired soil texture is obtained.

Mucklands

Most heavy mucklands require tilling or ditching to drain off the excess moisture that would otherwise stand. In this type of soil, organic matter is usually very abundant and no more need be added. But the addition of coarse grit or sand is advisable in some cases to make the soil less pasty and sticky.

Plants that flourish in mucklands, provided there is no stagnant water, are turtlehead, Joe-pye, boneset, red and blue lobelias, and other plants native to moist areas. The wild calla is one wildflower that will grow in stagnant water.

If I had such an area to work with, I would try making a pool not more than two feet deep at the lowest end. In it I would plant cattails in a container (or they will claim the whole area); at poolside *Iris versicolor* in clumps. I have noticed that these plants can survive undamaged even when the water around them freezes. Around the edges of the pool I would place some large rocks at intervals and in groups. Between the areas where the pool and land meet, fern would make good groundcover and would prevent any silt from washing into the pool during heavy rains. Royal and cinnamon ferns do very well in partial shade.

Highly Acid Soils

Under conifers there are usually bare spots with exposed gnarled roots. Also, the soil is very acid but lacking in the type of humus found under trees in the deciduous woodland.

The soil under spruce trees is usually toxic, and most of the needles should be removed before spading in organic matter. It is a good practice to reserve other evergreen needles for mulching only; that is, for acid-loving plants. Leafmold, damp peatmoss, and organic matter worked only a few inches into the soil among the tree roots will greatly improve the overall condition for planting shallow-rooted, acid-loving wildflowers such as wintergreen berry, goldthread and bunchberry. These make an excellent groundcover requiring a minimum of moisture.

For very acid soils rich in humus, with sufficient shade and ample moisture, select galax, pyrola, pink lady's-slipper, potted bunchberry, clintonia, and painted trillium. Bunchberry, goldthread, and wintergreen will also thrive here. The oakfern quickly forms colonies in this type of soil and adds a note of interest to the wildflowers.

Rocks, Trees, and Fungi

A woodland garden is at its most distinctive when you incorporate into the surroundings the natural elements they grow among in the wild. It will also ensure the success of some of your flowers.

ROCKS. Rocks in a garden recall hills, outcroppings, and ledges as well as fieldstones. When you are landscaping or planning a garden, rocks also mean materials with which to build terraces, stone walls, tree wells, paths, or pools with fountains. Besides lending interest to the landscape, rocks also conserve moisture for the plants growing near their base. Many plants take on an air of elegance when planted beside a large rock or among a group of medium-sized rocks, and some plants, especially the showy lady's-slippers, like to run their roots under the rocks, where they are assured of extra moisture.

A drive down a winding country road often provides lessons in rock positions. At first glance the rocks along the fencerow seem to lie haphazardly, but a closer look reveals that many of them lie at interesting angles and in groupings. A camera or a pad and pencil will aid in making notes about a spot you may want to duplicate later.

Formerly, road builders and farmers had a knack for placing rocks in the most interesting positions. Lacking power equipment, they pushed rocks along the fence lines, glad to have the bigger ones out of their immediate way. Today roadways are made clean, and farmers hire bulldozers to bury the rocks.

Old rocks that have weathered for a considerable time are more interesting than freshly unearthed ones—but use the fresh rocks if you have them. They will take several years to age. Rocks lying in the shade age faster than those exposed to full sun, possibly because shade promotes humidity, which in turn fosters the growth of small fungi. After some years, the flat limestone around our pool is beginning to show a flush of green, adding a touch of permanence to the area. With age, rocks acquire a distinctive beauty and character.

In the woodland garden it is best to use mostly granite rocks of all sizes, up to those that have to be brought in by heavy machinery. Woodland ferns especially thrive when planted among rocks where humus stays and roots are kept cool. The rocks also help to keep the winds from sweeping through. Granite rocks contribute to the acidity of the soil over a long period of time, but rarely is it enough to be measurable.

In the prairie garden I prefer the odd-shaped limestone with rough, weathered textures. Its light color is better suited to the open sunlight. Limestone will make the soil in the immediate area less acid. But this, too, is negligible, unless the limestone is crumbly.

Another rock, found only occasionally, is to all appearances a piece of brownish-red sponge over which glitter has been sprinkled. It is an excellent rock to use in shade, where an aged look is important. When it is used in a moist shady nook, mosses soon grow over it, covering the entire surface. It is very desirable in the woodland garden among small plants such as starflowers, oakferns, clintonias, Canada mayflower, and bunchberries. Sprinkling a little soil from the woodland where mosses are present will hasten growth.

If you are fortunate enough to find rocks with small ledges and indentations, plant mosses and dainty ferns in them. This creates a very natural formation. Common polypody fern (*Polypodium vulgare*) does well in rocky crevices, even if there is only a small opening in which to tuck a bit of humus on which the fern can anchor its root.

One can learn much by studying the wildflowers and ferns that grow among the rocks in the wilderness. You will find long stretches between rocks, and small outcroppings, yet a continuous growth of vegetation. When you place rocks in your own landscape, you will be able to tell whether they look natural.

TREES. If you would like to plant a tree among wildflowers, consider a white birch, which is easy to grow. Select a young tree that is only two to four feet tall and has not yet peeled its bark. Lay aside the coarse mulch and dig a hole one foot deep and three feet in diameter. Shovel some old compost or humus-rich garden soil into the bottom. Woods soil is the best if it is available. (No manure should ever be put into the hole when planting a tree or any other plant: in the process of decaying, the manure will generate heat and burn the roots.) Put the tree into the hole and spread the roots. Fill the hole with soil and replace the mulch, adding more if needed.

A nursery-grown dormant birch tree has a much heavier root system than one dug from the wild and will adapt more readily to the rugged environment of reclaimed soil. By the time the birch has grown seven to nine feet tall, it will usually peel its dark-colored bark and show the much desired paper-white bark.

FUNGI. Mushrooms and toadstools often spring up in areas of a woodland garden where the humus and leafmold are plentiful and moist conditions encourage their growth. A scattering of fungi in a woodland garden lends a note of realism. Huge fungi found growing on old stumps are often gorgeous. Even the rare poisonous fungi lend a beauty all their own to a little spot where they reign a short while and die.

If fungi become too plentiful, simply remove them. (They should be sealed in a plastic bag so that spores cannot ripen and spread before they are disposed of.)

The threadlike mycorhizal fungus and mycelia of other fungi literally web the humus-rich earth of the woodland as they form a lacework on the fine roots of shrubs and trees. These fungi are beneficial to some acid-loving plants, wildflowers, and ferns that flourish best in woodland soil. This type of environment is especially necessary for the successful growth of pink lady's-slippers (see Appendix II, Successful Lady's-slipper Cultivation).

Mulches

It has already been made obvious that no gardener, especially the wild-flower gardener, can do without mulches. They are used to kill unwanted

14

growth, to hold moisture in the soil, to protect plants from severe winter cold, and to provide nourishment to the soil. Below is an assortment of mulches for various purposes.

MARSH HAY MULCH. The finer marsh hay is preferable, but I have used hay that contained a considerable amount of cattails and found it satisfactory for mulching larger plants. Marsh hay does not decay as quickly as straw and it lies flatter. It has a neater appearance and does not blow away as easily.

STRAW MULCH. Because it is easier to handle, I prefer oat straw that has weathered for a week or more and then has been baled. During weathering the straw loses its high gloss; I have found that the gloss is detrimental to plants when used as a mulch during the summer, when the sun is stronger.

LEAF MULCH. White birch, soft maple, willow, mountain ash, and other small leaves are preferable to the coarser oak leaves. The small leaves turn to humus more quickly and do not smother the smaller plants as readily. All oak leaves except those of the white and bur oaks make a good mulch for the coarser and more robust wildflowers and ferns. For a coarse mulch that will not blow, run the lawnmower over oak leaves that the wind has swept into rows. The bur and white oak leaves, when shredded, are excellent for mulching in paths and rows of larger plants. Decay is slow. When run through a one-inch screen in a compost grinder, oak leaves and other woodland litter, even dead branches, make an excellent all-round mulch. It is best put down in fall: the snows and spring rains will settle and moisten it thoroughly.

GRASS MULCH. You are fortunate, indeed, if your lawnmower is equipped with a bag to catch grass clippings. The clippings make an excellent mulch for lady's-slippers, especially the showy lady's-slippers. Each time you mow your lawn, add a light dressing of fresh grass clippings to your lady's-slipper bed. Over the years the grass clippings will build up a rich humus.

EVERGREEN NEEDLE MULCH. The needles of the white pine and Norway pine are excellent for mulching acid-loving plants—for example, pink lady's-slipper, clintonia, bunchberry, Canada mayflower, goldthread, and wintergreen. I have never used needles of the balsam tree, but I noticed that in the wild the goldthread and wintergreen berry flourish beneath the balsams. The needles of the spruce tree are supposedly toxic; in yards and woodlands where the large spruces grow, you rarely see plant life beneath their branches.

15

STALKS AND BRANCHES AS MULCH. Disease-free flower stalks of New England aster, blue false indigo, goldenrods, and other tall flowers make a good coarse, airy mulch if you remove their seed heads first. Lobelias usually come through the winter retaining their fall foliage if protected with such mulches. Balsam branches also offer an airy mulch, especially for bearberry vines.

COARSE-SCREENED GRAVEL MULCH. Gravel is a good mulch for the wildflowers of the dry prairies. Gravel mulch helps retain moisture and holds down weeds. Screen gravel through a half-inch mesh, then use a smaller screen to remove the fine sand. Very coarse gravel is also used for mulch. Butterfly flower and blazing star especially flourish when these mulches are used. Hoary puccoon does well with a mulch of fine screened sand.

PEATMOSS MULCH. Damp peatmoss is very beneficial. It is best used next to the earth and then covered with a mulch of hay, straw, or small leaves. As a top mulch, peatmoss dries out and prevents rain from penetrating to the soil. Beneath other mulches, the damp peatmoss retains its moisture and lets other moisture through readily.

SPHAGNUM MOSS MULCH. Like peatmoss, this is best used as an undercover mulch. Both peatmoss and sphagnum moss are long lasting.

COMPOST MULCH. When vegetable matter has decayed to an unrecognizable point, it, too, can be used as mulch. Unless it is very coarse, it should be used as an undercover mulch.

ROCK MULCH. Flat rocks make good mulches when they are laid among plants to cover most of the area. Some cracks should be left, however, so rain can get through. Screened gravel may be used in the cracks. Rocks will offer no enrichment to the soil other than a small amount of minerals. For this reason, I prefer to lay down a compost or other humus-rich mulch before putting down a permanent rock mulch. With a rock mulch you may let falling leaves remain to hide some of the surface. In a prairie garden, rocks will settle somewhat and spreading grasses will eventually hide them.

WOODCHIP AND ROTTED SAWDUST MULCH. I have used sawdust only sparingly. Very old sawdust is excellent. Woodchips are also excellent for woodland paths among coarser plants.

OTHER MULCHES. The list is endless, but I have named those that are easiest to obtain. Any organic matter that decays over a period of years makes good humus. I sometimes use old newspapers and magazines in pathways among large plants where the soil is rich in humus (magazines are slow to decay and should be covered with other mulch to keep the area neat). And several layers of paper of any kind makes a good mulch to kill unwanted growth.

MAKING THE WILDFLOWERS GROW

PERENNIALS. Perennials are almost always planted from dormant stock—that is, from roots, rhizomes, stolons (nodes), or bulbs. Left in the ground, the root system will spread and the plants will reappear each spring. Some perennials may be grown from rootstock bare of sod (bareroot stock) and some must have fresh sod clinging to the roots. Some may be transplanted in their entirety provided they are past their period of bloom. It is usually best to start with stock from mature plants.

Perennial stock can be ordered from nurseries or gathered from the wild. The nurseries either grow the stock from plants they have cultivated (nursery-grown stock) or they collect stock from plants that have good qualities of size, bloom, and hardiness (quality collected stock). When you plan to collect your own stock from the wild, find plants with good quality, mark them with a stake, and dig them up later when they are dormant. Specific instructions for each plant are given in the section devoted to perennials.

Some very attractive perennials have vigorous spreading root systems that have discouraged gardeners from growing them for fear that they might crowd out other plants. For years I have been burying bottomless containers of various sizes to restrict some otherwise aggressive plants. A bottomless gallon container buried at soil level will enable you to grow interesting plants that would otherwise choke out their neighbors. When plants become crowded in the container, remove them and fill the can with new soil. Then replant some of the new shoots of the original stock. Blossoms of such plants should be cut back as they fade to keep them from setting seed.

The fine and small perennial seeds often germinate readily, but the larger seeds are usually slow to germinate and many years are required to bring them into bloom. This is especially true of the fleshy rooted and bulbous types. Cuttings or divisions are more desirable than seeds if you already have stock with which to work. I certainly recommend for the beginner plants large enough to bloom.

Fall planting is best for all early-blooming perennials, especially those with heavy roots. For the woodland flowers, a shady border in the garden or a place under high open shade is best. The sun-loving wildflowers will do well on a leaner, drier soil. Whatever your selection, be sure that the plants are suited to your environment.

ANNUALS. Annual wildflowers are grown from seeds, usually sown in early spring or left to self-sow. These flowers bloom, set seed, and die in the same year.

Biennial wildflowers require two years of growth to bloom. Then they, too, set seed and die.

Often the annual and biennial wildflowers can be used to fill in bare spots until perennial wildflowers mature. As well as being interesting and useful, they are an inexpensive way to naturalize a large open area.

With a little special attention and care, most of the annual or biennial wildflowers listed in this book can be grown easily from seeds. Seeds scattered after the plant has bloomed will usually germinate at the proper time. An open area where grasses are sparse is an ideal spot, as most of these wildflowers need sun to complete their short life-spans.

Divisions and Root Cuttings

Dividing large clumps of plants is one of the easiest methods of propagating wildflowers, although it is not always advisable (for example, it is not wise to divide plants that have been recently shipped through the mails). A better method is to grow the plants for at least a year before making the divisions. The best propagating times are early spring, late summer, or fall, depending on the species.

To make a division, carefully break up the clump either by pulling it apart or by cutting it. Each rooted portion may be planted separately, and in one to three years you will have several adult plants.

The division of forking rhizomes is another method that often gives good results. Solomon's plume and bluebeard lily are examples of plants that propagate successfully with rhizome division.

Many plants with very fleshy roots will grow new roots and buds when cut into pieces. Among these are butterfly flower, spikenard, and ginseng. Each root portion is planted separately and is regularly watered to encourage it to form a new plant. When planting pieces of root, remember that the side facing up will grow shoots and the side facing the soil below will grow roots. To prevent accidentally planting the root upside down, cut the top of the piece straight across and cut the bottom at an angle. Special instructions for propagation are discussed under the species name.

Most lily bulbs can be reproduced from scales as well as from seeds and bulbils.

The liatris family, among others, propagates well by the division of corms. All liatris tubers may be cut into pieces as one would cut potatoes, leaving one to two eyes or buds on each piece. Let the pieces dry a little before replanting. Spring is the best time to plant by corm division.

Seeds and Seedlings

Growing perennial wildflowers from seed can be a great challenge, but it is definitely not for the person who expects quick returns. Many wildflower seeds are slow to germinate, and once sprouted, are slow to mature.

Most wildflower seeds are best planted in the fall so nature can do the job of stratification. The hard-shelled seeds, such as baneberry and blue cohosh, require two or more years to germinate. You can file a nick into large seeds to hasten germination, but this is a tiresome task. I have had bearberry and horse gentian remain dormant for four years; germination was then very uneven. Do not be too quick to discard a flat because the seeds failed to germinate in the expected time. Trilliums, for instance, can be very slow at times.

The seeds of trillium and bloodroot must be planted as harvested or they will not germinate the next spring. If the bit of white matter (caruncle)

19

that is attached to a fresh trillium or bloodroot seed is left to dry out, the seed usually takes two years to germinate. The caruncle helps the freshly planted seed to absorb moisture and therefore plays an important part in germination.

For potting soil, one third should be composed of damp peatmoss and sharp sand (or vermiculite), and two parts each of rich compost and woods soil (or garden soil). Thoroughly mix these ingredients before putting them into flats or pots. Make certain that all containers have good drainage. Some seeds may also be sown in a protected woodland area; those for sunny areas may be sown in the garden.

Mix dust-fine seeds with a teaspoonful of fine sand and scatter them on top of the soil without covering. If seed-flat soil is a little uneven, the seeds will settle. It is best to water these fine seeds from the bottom. After planting, the fine seeds should be dusted lightly with a bit of sharp sand.

The medium-sized seeds should be covered with one-quarter inch of sharp sand. The sharp sand prevents damping off as seedlings emerge.

A general rule for seed flats and seed beds: All plants that grow naturally in damp soil will need more moisture than those that require only constant moisture when growing in a permanent location. Therefore, the containers with seeds for damp areas should be watered a little more often. But under no condition should any of the seed flats or seed beds be allowed to dry out, even for only an hour. Seeds in the germination stage are very tender and quickly killed.

When seedlings have developed their second or third set of true leaves, they may be successfully moved to small pots or flats if handled with care. Early August is a good time to transplant seedlings, when they still have time to make considerable growth while the weather is favorable. Unless seedlings have made exceptionally good growth, it is best to winter them in a cold frame. Protect them from mice. After the plants have filled their pots with roots, they are usually ready to be moved to their permanent location.

Water all transplants regularly and mulch very lightly. A little Rapid-Gro in a weak solution helps to prevent transplant shock in both the seedling stage and the well-developed stage when the plants are moved to their permanent sites.

Most seedlings that have fibrous roots usually bloom the first year after transplanting. The seedlings with fleshy roots often do not bloom until the third or fourth year, and some require many years to bloom. Dog-tooth violets take about the longest.

Stem Cuttings

In most of the colder northeastern areas, the period from late June to late July is the most suitable time to make stem cuttings from propagating wild-flowers. This is usually before the plants have set any buds.

The soil mixture used for stem cuttings is made up of one part of sharp sand or (preferably) vermiculite, one part of fine compost, one part of damp peatmoss, and two parts of good garden soil or fine woods soil. Add a half cup of bonemeal for every ten quarts of the mixture. Mix all thoroughly and moisten a little if necessary. Use a 2¼-inch plastic pot for each cutting.

For propagation, select a mature healthy plant with good qualities, remembering that the plants grown from stem cuttings will inherit all the characteristics of the parent plant.

Each stem cutting should have four joints, two above the soil and two below.

Clip the leaves carefully from the two lower joints. Avoid destroying the axillary buds hidden in the axils of the leaves. These buds are responsible for sending new growth above the soil when the cutting shows signs of life.

Nip out the terminal leaf bud to prevent continued upward growth and to promote root growth and new growth from axillary buds.

Dip the lower two joints from which the leaves have been removed into the rooting compound and insert the cutting in a little hole made in the rooting mixture in the pot. Fill the hole with sharp sand.

Firm the soil and continue to treat all the cuttings in the same manner.

Set the pots containing the treated cuttings in a pan of water until moisture shows on the surface of the pot soil.

Remove the pots to flats for easier handling, and then put the flats in a propagation frame or in a cold frame with windows.

Cover the frame closely and keep the inside moist by spraying occasionally with a fine sprayer. Humidity must be maintained within the frame at all times.

A spot with filtered sunlight is ideal for a frame for propagating purposes.

Most cuttings will root in about four weeks. Bottom heat hastens rooting. When roots begin to come out of the bottom of the pot, the flat can be removed from the frame and placed in a sheltered, partially sunny area to harden. Gradually bring the flat into stronger sunlight until the new plants can tolerate full sun. Water carefully at all times.

The hardening process usually requires two weeks or gradually moving the rooted cuttings to stronger light every few days. When cuttings are fully hardened, they may be planted in their permanent location and treated as you would young seedlings.

Immediately after transplanting, give the new little plants a weak liquid fertilizer. I prefer Rapid-Gro. It will not burn foliage or roots if used according to directions. Later in the fall, when the ground is slightly frozen, it is wise to mulch the young plants for winter protection.

Most cuttings are better left in the pots in the cold frame if they have not made good growth at the end of four weeks. Remove the windows, but mulch lightly. Gradually remove the mulch in spring. Some hardening in the frame without the windows is advisable.

In spring, the young plants are ready to transfer to the open ground. Water faithfully to establish them, and mulch those that require it. Diligent care will bring excellent results.

SHADE TERMS

The special names given to the degrees of light and shade required by plants are known as "shade terms." They are used throughout this book according to the following definitions.

Full Sun. Totally unshaded. At no time during the day should the plant be in shadow, although shade after 4 p.m. is permissible.

Sun. At least eight hours of sunshine a day, preferably beginning early in the morning; do not count the time after 4 p.m.

Filtered Sunlight or Light Shade. A dappled light, such as spring-blossoming woodland plants receive through the young leaves of deciduous trees.

Open Shade. The plants may be shaded by buildings or nearby trees, but there should be no canopy of trees or extended eaves overhead.

Moderate to Partial Shade. As the sun moves, the plant receives both shade and light during the day, with brief exposure to direct sun.

High Open Shade. Trees with high branches let some light through, and some light comes from the slanting rays of the morning and late afternoon sun.

Deep Shade. Where evergreen trees grow or where deciduous trees stand close together, the shade is denser. Here temperatures will be several degrees lower and the moisture content of the air higher. Winds do not sweep through so readily.

Annual and Biennial Wildflowers
for Quick Color and Cover

CHENOPODIACEAE [Goosefoot Family]

Chenopodium capitatum • strawberry blite

ANNUAL

HEIGHT: 6 to 12 inches

Strawberry blite is suitable for either a moist sunny area or slight shade where the soil is humus-rich. The flowers are greenish and not pretty, but the plant is grown for its showy clusters of pulpy red fruits that are suggestive of lush ripe strawberries.

The seeds within the cluster are shiny black. Sow them in the fall. The strawberry blite self-sows.

PERIOD OF BLOOM: June–August.

PAPAVERACEAE [Poppy Family]

Eschscholtzia californica • California poppy

ANNUAL

HEIGHT: 6 to 10 inches

The California poppy has light blue-green, finely cut foliage and an abundance of four-petaled yellow or orange flowers. It blooms best on sunny days; the flowers close at night.

The seeds are offered in most garden seed catalogs; they are best sown in spring in full sun. California poppy is easy to grow. Seeds self-sow in the West.

PERIOD OF BLOOM: All summer.

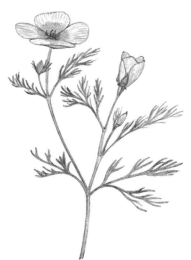

Argemone intermedia • prickly poppy

ANNUAL

HEIGHT: 2 feet

The stocky stem has prickly alternate foliage shaped much like that of a slender oak leaf. The blossoms are single 3-inch flowers in shades of yellow or white. The plant will grow in any soil in full sun. Sow seeds in fall or early spring. The prickly poppy rarely self-sows in my area.

In the West, where this poppy is native, it is considered poisonous to cattle, and ranchers battle to destroy it.

PERIOD OF BLOOM: All summer.

Corydalis sempervirens • pale corydalis

BIENNIAL

HEIGHT: 12 to 24 inches

The shiny black seeds of pale corydalis are planted in August and grow to dainty rosettes of blue-green fernlike foliage during the first season. The following season, in May, a single, many-branched stalk appears, bearing countless half-hearts of clear pink with a touch of bright yellow. The plant is quite ornamental in the fruiting stage, when each blossom is replaced by a long slender seed capsule.

When cultivated and given room, pale corydalis will attain the size of a bushel basket. In the wilderness the plants are straggly and not nearly so large.

Pale corydalis is often found growing in full sun among boulders and in the crevices of rocks.

PERIOD OF BLOOM: May into September.

Adlumia fungosa · Allegheny vine

BIENNIAL

LENGTH: 6 to 12 foot vine

The Allegheny vine has airy, bleeding-heart foliage and many pinkish hearts over a long season. It is native to the Allegheny Mountains but will grow in any spot where there is high open shade.

The plant readily self-sows, but I prefer to plant seeds each year as they ripen to ensure spring germination.

PERIOD OF BLOOM: June until frost.

GERANIACEAE [Geranium Family]

Geranium Robertianum · herb-Robert

ANNUAL

HEIGHT: 3 to 5 inches

Herb-Robert has delicate, fernlike green foliage, often with a hint of red later in the season. The dainty trumpet-shaped, rose-colored flowers persist all summer in shade in reasonably moist woodland. It is best grown where it can naturalize.

Herb-Robert sets seeds and disperses them in the same way as its larger cousin, the cranesbill: the pods open with a surprising abruptness and the seeds scatter far and wide, making them difficult to collect. Sow seeds as they ripen or in early fall.

PERIOD OF BLOOM: All summer.

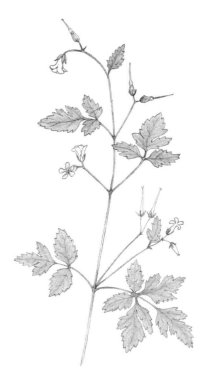

BALSAMINACEAE [Touch-me-not Family]

Impatiens capensis • jewelweed

ANNUAL

HEIGHT: 2 to 4 feet

The orange-spotted flowers of the jewelweed are as worthy of praise as an orchid. The many branches and large succulent stems are characteristic of the species. The entire plant is fragile and should be cultivated in close groupings or in protected areas. When a single plant can be grown to display its full development, the jewelweed is at its loveliest.

Jewelweed is found growing in moist, partially shaded areas, but in my gardens it volunteers almost anywhere. The roots are shallow and the plant is easily uprooted. A seed capsule will explode at the touch of a finger and send the seeds flying, hence the popular name touch-me-not. Sow seeds when ripe.

The juice of the jewelweed is often recommended as a treatment for poison ivy, but I have not found it effective.

PERIOD OF BLOOM: July until frost.

UMBELLIFERAE [Parsley Family]

Heracleum maximum • cow parsnip

BIENNIAL

HEIGHT: 3 to 6 feet

Seeds planted in fall send up several large leaves during the first spring. The leaves resemble those of the maple and are about the size of an outstretched hand.

The second spring, a stout but hollow leafy stalk appears, bearing two or three large flat-topped umbels, similar to but larger than those of the cultivated parsnip.

The plant, which has a strong odor of parsnip, is found in moist, shady thickets along creek bottoms. It is a fine plant for the bog garden but will grow equally well anywhere there is constant moisture.

PERIOD OF BLOOM: July.

Daucus Carota • Queen Anne's lace

BIENNIAL

HEIGHT: 1 to 3 feet

The leafy stem with its lacy foliage resembles that of its edible cousin, the garden carrot. The seeds are also similar to those of the carrot, but the Queen Anne's lace seeds have barbs which aid in spreading. When the lacy white flowers fade, the outer parts of the umbel curl inward to take on a shape like a bird's nest, and it is often referred to as the bird's-nest flower.

In some areas, Queen Anne's lace is found growing abundantly along fencerows and roadsides. Sow the seeds in fall. It self-sows readily.

The flower stalks are charming in dry floral arrangements. Pick them before the seeds fully ripen.

PERIOD OF BLOOM: June into August.

COMPOSITAE [Composite Family]

Anaphalis margaritacea • pearly everlasting

ANNUAL

HEIGHT: 8 to 12 inches

The willowlike leaves of pearly everlasting are sage green with a white blush. The crushed foliage has a lemon-lime fragrance, which can be used in sachets. The flowers are terminal clusters, and each flower head is round with a yellow eye encircled in pearly white. It is found in wastelands and along roadsides.

Pearly everlasting is an excellent flower for dry floral arrangements. Pick the flowers just as the yellow eye begins to appear. Hang it upside down in a dry place to cure.

The seeds must be sown in fall; in wastelands it self-sows.

PERIOD OF BLOOM: August to September.

Rudbeckia hirta • black-eyed Susan

BIENNIAL

HEIGHT: 1 to 2 feet

The foliage of the black-eyed Susan is mostly basal and hairy. The flowers have deep yellow petals and a prominent raised center of dark glossy brown.

The plant is often abundant in wastelands, old hayfields, and along roadsides where grasses are sparse.

If the blossoms are cut immediately after blooming, the plant often acts as a perennial and persists for several years. When cultivated, the black-eyed Susan is much prettier than when growing in the wild. Large expanses make a colorful display, and they are excellent for naturalizing in large areas.

Sow seeds as soon as they ripen. The plant self-sows freely.

PERIOD OF BLOOM: June to September.

Tragopogon pratensis • yellow goatsbeard

BIENNIAL

HEIGHT: 1 to 2 feet

The yellow goatsbeard, found along roadsides and in wastelands, has slender ribbonlike foliage and a partially leafy stem. Pale yellow-rayed flowers crown the stiff stalk.

The ripening seed forms a globe larger than that of the dandelion. The globes are excellent for dry floral arrangements and are much sought for this purpose. Pick the flower just as it is about to open, and place each stalk in a wire holder, spacing them well apart. When a full globe emerges, spray it with clear hair spray or spray paint (gold is usually chosen). Hold the spray can about 18 to 24 inches away from the globes so that the pressure will not destroy their fragile structure. Dust them immediately with glitter to add a touch of sparkle and color. The globes make interesting displays in bowls of harmonizing colors.

Sow the seeds as soon as they ripen.

In some areas this plant is on the noxious weed list.

PERIOD OF BLOOM: June to September.

CUCURBITACEAE [Gourd Family]

Echinocystis lobata • wild cucumber

ANNUAL

LENGTH: 6 to 12 foot vine

The leaves of the wild cucumber are shaped much like that of the ivy house plants, but they are thinner and lighter green. The vine anchors itself with tendrils as it climbs over fences and through thickets, where it is usually found.

The four-seeded burr resembles a tiny cucumber with spines. The seeds must be planted in fall or they will not germinate the following spring. The plant self-sows readily.

PERIOD OF BLOOM: All summer.

MALVACEAE [Mallow Family]

Abutilon Theophrasti · Indian mallow

ANNUAL

HEIGHT: 3 to 5 feet

A robust plant with large, heart-shaped leaves and single yellow flowers, the Indian mallow is usually found in legume crops, wastelands, and along fencerows.

Sow seeds in fall, preferably in fertile soil. The plant does not self-sow readily.

Because of its cup-shaped seed pod with a disklike pattern, Indian mallow is also called butter print.

PERIOD OF BLOOM: July to September.

GENTIANACEAE [Gentian Family]

Gentiana crinita · fringed gentian

BIENNIAL

HEIGHT: 1 to 3 feet

Fringed gentian is the most coveted and elusive biennial wildflower, and it has proved a trial to many who have tried to grow it from seed. Potted stock is easiest to transplant.

This wildflower needs no further identification than its distinctive fringed blossoms. It grows along still lakes where the damp shores are partly taken over by grasses. It also grows in wet roadside ditches, and I have even found it growing in a little patch of dwarf moss on the north side of a hill where scrub oak grew. As a rule it is quite scarce.

The small tan seeds are very light and are easily blown by the wind. Fresh seeds should be sown immediately, in peatpots or flats or directly where you are able to naturalize the plant. Place the seeds on top of the soil and cover them with evergreen branches. Remove the branches in spring as seedlings appear. Grow the seedlings in partial shade, never letting the soil become dry. The plants grow very little during the first year. The following spring, transplant potted stock in a damp meadow or any other suitable place. With care and regular watering the seedlings will grow to maturity, bloom, set seed, and die, completing their life cycle in the second year.

You will need to set out seedlings for two consecutive years if you want to establish a colony. If the plants are growing in an ideal location, they will self-propagate.

Make every effort to preserve this wildflower in its natural state, and try to establish new colonies where conditions are suitable.

PERIOD OF BLOOM: August to October.

Never pick this rare wildflower.

SCROPHULARIACEAE [Figwort Family]

Verbascum Thapsus • common mullein

BIENNIAL

HEIGHT: 3 to 6 feet

Mullein, also called "velvet plant," is often found growing in dry sunny wastelands. It forms a rosette of gray woolly leaves in the first year. In the second, it sends up a heavy spike with a raceme of small yellow flowers.

For dry floral arrangements, cut the spikes right after they bloom. The seeds are very fine and should be sown in fall.

PERIOD OF BLOOM: June into August.

35

Gerardia virginica • smooth false foxglove

BIENNIAL

HEIGHT: 2 to 4 feet

The leafy stem of the smooth false foxglove appears in the second year. At the top of the stem, the leaves are gradually replaced by yellow or occasionally white flowers growing like flared tubes in the axils of the smaller upper leaves. The plant is found in dry woodlands and thickets, but will grow in gardens in full sunlight.

Sow seeds in June or late fall. When the smooth false foxglove is in close proximity with other plants in protected areas of open shade, especially where leaves fall to provide additional protection, it often forms clumps and lasts for years.

PERIOD OF BLOOM: July into August.

Castilleja coccinea • Indian paintbrush

BIENNIAL

HEIGHT: 12 to 18 inches

The true flowers are yellow, but the red bracts give the Indian paintbrush its color. Flowers grow on the upper third of the stem. The plants tend to be parasitic and grow best in a soil containing some decaying humus.

Whole colonies often disappear for several years, only to reappear for long stretches again. I have known it to grow year after year on an old logging trail where shade is high and open.

The plant will grow in wet ditches among sparse grasses where the soil is lean but where decaying humus is present on the surface. The plant is not easy to establish. If you wish to naturalize it, select a spot where grass is sparse; or you can choose an open spot and scatter some oat seed, then cut the oats back, leaving about a six-inch stubble to shelter the seedlings. Scatter the fine seed as soon as it ripens and do not disturb the soil. Once established, the plant will reappear from time to time. Try growing this wildflower in a damp woodland trail in high open shade where the soil is damp most of the year.

PERIOD OF BLOOM: May into July.

Never pick this rare wildflower.

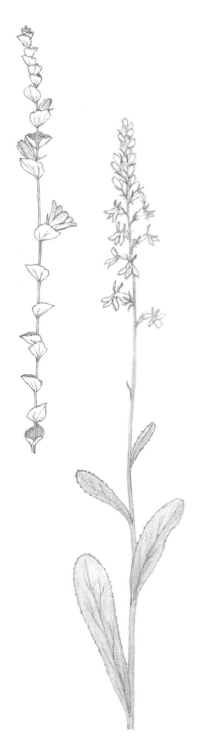

CAMPANULACEAE [Bluebell Family]

Specularia perfoliata • Venus's looking-glass

ANNUAL

HEIGHT: 10 to 20 inches

Each tiny rosette of Venus's looking-glass sends up a single spike bearing dainty starlike flowers of intense purple in the axils of the clasping leaves.

The seeds must be sown in fall for spring germination. Cultivated plants are huskier than wildlings, and small seedlings transplant easily. The plant also readily self-sows.

PERIOD OF BLOOM: June into August.

Lobelia spicata • spiked lobelia

BIENNIAL

HEIGHT: 2 feet

A single stem rises from a small rosette of basal foliage, bearing a slender spike of pale blue-lipped flowers. When growing in masses it is unusually pretty.

Spiked lobelia can be found along roadsides and in wastelands. It often volunteers in land that has not been cultivated for a few years.

Sow the seeds as soon as they are ripe. Where the soil is open, the spiked lobelia self-sows readily.

PERIOD OF BLOOM: June.

Perennial Wildflowers
for Permanence

TYPHACEAE [Cattail Family]

Typha latifolia • common cattail

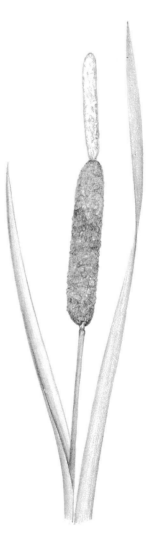

DESCRIPTION: 4 to 6 feet tall. The common cattail has 6 to 8 inch yellow or brown flower spikes, each supported by a solitary heavy stem. Ribbonlike leaves, as long as the stem, extend from the base. As the upper male portion of the flower withers, the lower female portion grows fatter, becoming the cylindrical spike we know as the cattail.

Cattails are found in wet open swamplands, along low lake shores, and often in roadside ditches where water collects in early spring.

PERIOD OF BLOOM: June into July.

SOIL: Neutral to acid soils that are always moist, or at least quite damp.

LOCATION AND EXPOSURE: Cattails are not suited to every wildflower garden because they demand constant moisture and because of their vigorous growth. Do not underestimate their power to reproduce; where conditions are favorable, they can take over large areas. However, they are ideal for naturalizing along a stream or lake shore or for planting singly in a container in a small pond.

PLANTING TIME: Spring or fall.

ROOT SYSTEM: A stout creeping rhizome with feeder roots that have a strong tendency to multiply in wet areas, especially once the plant has become established in sunny marshes. The rhizomes are edible. The Indians cooked the fleshy portions, which are rich in starch.

PLANTING DEPTH AND SPACING: Space about 1 to 2 feet apart. Set plants at the same level at which they previously grew, making certain to tuck in all the rhizomes and any stray roots.

PLANTING STOCK AND PROPAGATION: Few, if any, nurseries grow cattails for sale. Take your own quality collected stock by dividing the creeping rhizomes, preferably in spring in the colder climates.

COMMENTS: The leaves of cattails laid lengthwise among tall wildflowers furnish a long-lasting mulch.

For dried floral arrangements, the cattail spikes should be picked when only half grown or else the cylinders will break open into a mass of fuzz. When completely ripe, the cylinders may be loosened and used to stuff pillows. Be certain to use a fine quality of ticking.

ARACEAE [Arum Family]

Arisaema triphyllum • Jack-in-the-pulpit

DESCRIPTION: 15 to 30 inches tall. Brown-and-green hooded flowers rest above thrice-parted leaves. In August the plant produces bright red berries. Jack-in-the-pulpit is found in rich moist woods, wet swamps, or drier areas in high open shade where soil is rich in humus though of only moderate moisture content.

PERIOD OF BLOOM: Late May into June.

SOIL: Any humus-rich soil of moderate acidity, preferably a little moist, especially in spring.

LOCATION AND EXPOSURE: Deep to light shade. "Jacks" can be planted in small colonies among other woodland flowers, or they can be used effectively as bold accents when placed as lone "sentinels" in a well-chosen rocky spot. They are also outstanding when interspersed with maidenhair fern.

PLANTING TIME: Preferably fall, but it is also possible to plant in early spring when the plants are still dormant or have only slightly sprouted.

ROOT SYSTEM: A corm, increasing in size with age, has feeder roots on its upper side just below the new shoot. These roots seek nutrients from the soil and humus. The feeder roots are not present on dormant stock held in storage, but new roots develop in spring. Cormlets often appear at the upper and outer edges of larger corms.

PLANTING DEPTH AND SPACING: Planting depth is best determined by the size of the corms. Small corms up to the size of a nickel should be planted 2 to 4 inches deep, larger corms 5 to 8 inches deep. Depth also depends on whether or not the soil is heavy or humus-rich.

If you live in a colder region and have trouble with your "Jacks" coming up too soon and being cut down by frost, add some extra mulch as soon as the ground freezes in late fall. This will help to hold the frost in the ground and retard spring growth. Remove the extra mulch a few weeks later than usual.

PLANTING STOCK AND PROPAGATION: Plant nursery-grown corms or quality collected stock.

Pulp-free seeds may be planted in flats or in the woodland as soon as they ripen. Sometimes seeds do not germinate until the second spring. Seedlings usually do not bloom until the third year. Chipmunks are very fond of the seeds and cormlets and will often plant and replant them.

COMMENTS: The Jack-in-the-pulpit is a stately flower which has many uses in the woodland garden. Years ago the Indians cooked the corms for food, hence the common name Indian turnip. Uncooked, the corm is supposedly poisonous, at least for humans. I doubt that it is harmful to other animals, especially bears: One fall a mother bear and her cub uprooted our "Jack" bed, leaving behind a mess of half-eaten stalks and corms.

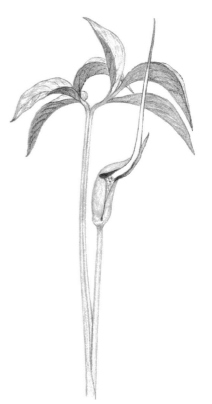

Arisaema Dracontium • green dragon

DESCRIPTION: 1 to 3 feet tall. A long, slender, green spadix extends from a greenish half-opened spathe above the fan-shaped compound leaves. The white flower is tinged or streaked with green. Orange fruits appear in early fall.

The green dragon is usually found in wet, rich woods and along woodland brooks, often interspersed with its cousin, the Jack-in-the-pulpit.

PERIOD OF BLOOM: May into June.

SOIL: Humus-rich, acid to slightly acid woodland soil.

LOCATION AND EXPOSURE: Green dragon grows best in cool open shade where constant moisture is available. It provides a bold accent in the moist wild garden. In damp shady areas I have seen it reach a height of 4 feet.

PLANTING TIME: Spring or fall, while dormant or only slightly sprouted.

ROOT SYSTEM: The corm has a prominent new shoot from which many white feeder roots penetrate the soil. This corm is very similar to that of Jack-in-the-pulpit. Sometimes the parent corm produces cormlets.

PLANTING DEPTH AND SPACING: Set small corms 2 to 4 inches deep, and larger corms 5 to 7 inches deep. Plant in small colonies or at random for best effect.

PLANTING STOCK AND PROPAGATION: Use nursery-grown stock. Quality collected stock is very scarce.

The offsets of large corms give quicker results than propagating by seed. Seeds sown when they ripen in fall take several years to become big blooming-sized corms.

COMMENTS: Green dragon is a novelty in the wild garden when planted beside a rock, along a path, or in a shady spot beside a pool where it can reflect in the water.

Calla palustris • wild calla

DESCRIPTION: 5 to 10 inches tall. Wild calla has fleshy, jointed prostrate stalks and medium heart-shaped leaves on upright stems. The flower is white with a hint of green, on a round spadix. It is held on 4 to 5 inch stems above the forking and creeping rootstock. The clusters of fruit are shaped much like pineapples, but are only about 1½ inches long.

Wild calla is usually found in lake indentations, bogs, and swales, in cool open shade where the water is still and shallow and apparently stagnant. Much of its rootstock shows.

One August I found a large colony of wild calla growing in a wet peat bog, with water several inches deep in places. The plants crept along amid fallen branches and wood litter; it was apparently an ideal location. Some plants had already set fruit that was turning reddish, while other plants were just coming into bloom.

PERIOD OF BLOOM: June into late fall.

SOIL: Slightly acid soil with constant moisture or where water is still and shallow. Wild calla cannot survive a dry spell.

LOCATION AND EXPOSURE: An excellent plant for naturalizing at the edge of a still body of shallow water in a cool shady spot. For

years I grew a few plants in an old five-gallon container that was buried in the ground to the top edge. I punctured several holes in the container to allow for slow seepage. The container was filled within two inches from the top with mucky soil from a nearby lake where swamp and water met. A generous handful of bonemeal should be mixed into the top few inches of earth. It grew in this container for many years, until one extremely cold, snowless December the plant winter-killed because of lack of cover. A light mulch might have saved it.

PLANTING TIME: Early spring or fall. Moves easily.

ROOT SYSTEM: A jointed, creeping rootstock with some feeder roots at nodes on the underside. The plant moves about as it grows, the old portion dying as new joints are formed to produce next year's growth and bloom. The cycle is continually repeated, and as the stalks fork the colony becomes denser and larger.

PLANTING DEPTH AND SPACING: Plant close together if you wish rootstocks to overlap. The roots that grow along the bottom of the rootstock should be anchored into the earth, but leave the creeping rootstock at soil level or barely covered. A winter mulch is suggested for very cold climates.

PLANTING STOCK AND PROPAGATION: Nursery-grown potted stock is much preferred, but you can use quality collected stock.

Cuttings taken in July and set into peat-muck rooting medium give fair results. Fill a container with a few inches of water, and place the peat pots in it. Then moisture will be constantly available.

Pulp-free seeds may be planted in muck or very wet swampy soil as soon as they are ripe. Seedlings will bloom in a few years.

COMMENTS: If you can meet the needs of the wild calla, by all means grow it. In general the plant is rather scarce, but I have been fortunate in finding some large colonies.

Symplocarpus foetidus • skunk cabbage

DESCRIPTION: 1 to 3 feet tall. Very early in spring, the greenish yellow spadix of the skunk cabbage appears, enclosed by a reddish brown spathe that is open at one side and looks very much like a dwarf's hut with the door ajar. As the flower in the spadix wilts, the green leaves unfold.

Skunk cabbage is usually found in swales and amid hummocks in grassy swamplands. At the Keshena Indian Reservation (now Menominee County) I have seen large colonies of skunk cabbage growing in full sun in grassy lowlands and along small brooks.

PERIOD OF BLOOM: April into May, often before the snow has completely thawed.

SOIL: Damp, humus-rich soil, neutral to slightly acid.

LOCATION AND EXPOSURE: Preferably a shady spot, unless the soil is very moist. Plant the skunk cabbage where you want it to stay, since a full-grown plant will have a bushel of soil adhering to its roots, and is next to impossible to move.

PLANTING TIME: Fall planting is best.

ROOT SYSTEM: A stout rhizome with long, stringy, white roots.

PLANTING DEPTH AND SPACING: Space plants several feet apart to allow for development. Set young dormant plants with the shoot just at soil level. Mulch heavily with forest litter or old marsh hay.

PLANTING STOCK AND PROPAGATION: Nursery-grown seedlings are best. Quality collected young stock with good roots will also do well.

To propagate from seed, sow the seeds when ripe in a peaty soil that is kept constantly moist. Seedlings require considerable time to mature.

COMMENTS: The bruised leaves have a foul odor which gives the skunk cabbage its name. The plant has no odor otherwise. Do not hesitate to grow skunk cabbage near the house if you have a suitable location. Its large quilted green leaves are handsome.

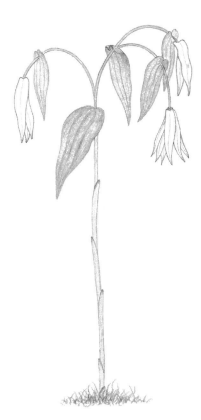

LILIACEAE [Lily Family]

Uvularia grandiflora • merrybells

DESCRIPTION: 10 to 15 inches tall. Merrybells have clear, lemon-yellow flowers and three-cornered green seed capsules. From forked stalks and leafy stems, sparse clusters of long, loosely bell-shaped flowers hang on arching stems.

In woodlands, on shaded slopes, large colonies of merrybells bloom each spring beneath the high branches of white birches and oaks. Here leafmold is deep and there is very little competition from other large wildflowers. Fringed polygalas and, when there has been a wet August, ghostly Indian pipes (*Monotropa uniflora*) are often found as companion plants.

PERIOD OF BLOOM: May into June, depending on location.

SOIL: Any humus-rich woodland soil that is slightly acid.

LOCATION AND EXPOSURE: Light, open shade where leafless trees allow the sun to filter through in spring but shut out its burning rays in the summer. Merrybell's bountiful foliage matures after bloom and makes a good groundcover for the bare spots left by mertensias, which bloom at the same time. The two combine well.

PLANTING TIME: While dormant in spring or fall.

ROOT SYSTEM: A pure white rhizome with stringy white roots, very similar to that of pink lady's-slipper but not as coarse.

PLANTING DEPTH AND SPACING: Space plants 1 to 2 feet apart. Give ample room, as each plant becomes a clump. Plant the short rhizomes about 1½ inches deep with the tip of the new shoot slightly below soil level. Spread roots carefully.

PLANTING STOCK AND PROPAGATION: Nursery-grown stock is huskier, but freshly dug collected stock may also be used.

Clumps may be divided for propagation by pulling them apart very carefully and planting each separately. To propagate from seeds, sow as soon as they are ripe. The plant often self-sows. Seedlings mature enough to bloom about the third or fourth year.

COMMENTS: Merrybells benefit greatly from transplanting. The plants will form clumps a few seasons after being moved, whereas plants growing in the wild stay much the same. A generous mulching of old straw, weathered marsh hay, or old leaves is helpful.

Another common name for the merrybell is bellwort.

Uvularia sessilifolia · wild oats

DESCRIPTION: 6 to 10 inches tall. Dainty 1 inch yellow bells are held jauntily above light-green, oval, tapering foliage. Later they are replaced by three-cornered green seed capsules.

This small type of merrybell is at home in moist woodlands where the soil is rich in humus. It has a habit of colonizing in groups to carpet the forest floor.

PERIOD OF BLOOM: May into June. The little flowers are long lasting.

SOIL: Neutral to slightly acid soil that is rich in leafmold and retains some moisture.

LOCATION AND EXPOSURE: High open shade where some sun can filter through to the forest floor. Because this merrybell is both dainty and small, it should be planted in colonies to give the best color effect. Wild oats are lovely when planted in patches alternating with small airy ferns.

PLANTING TIME: While dormant in spring or fall.

ROOT SYSTEM: A small white rhizome with stringy white roots.

PLANTING DEPTH AND SPACING: Space 4 to 6 inches apart, or plant at random in colonies of a dozen or more. Set the rhizome about 1 inch deep with the tip of the new shoot just barely below soil level. Mulch lightly.

PLANTING STOCK AND PROPAGATION: Use nursery-grown stock or freshly dug collected stock of good quality. When colonies become crowded, separate the rhizomes and replant at once.

Sow seeds as soon as they ripen; they are sometimes slow to germinate. Seedlings are slow to bloom.

COMMENTS: The wild oat is a dainty wildflower for a choice spot in your woodland garden. Its little bells are precisely shaped and droop gracefully above the neat foliage.

Allium cernuum • nodding wild onion

DESCRIPTION: 18 to 20 inches tall. A nodding umbel of loose florets and flat ribbonlike foliage. The florets are pale rose-lavender with a faint pinkish cast.

The wild onion is usually found in shaded woodland and rocky areas where the soil is humus-rich; it is also found in prairies.

PERIOD OF BLOOM: July into August.

SOIL: Neutral to slightly acid soil. (I use a sandy loam.)

LOCATION AND EXPOSURE: Although its native habitats are shady woodlands, the wild onion blooms more profusely in full sun.

Plant it in colonies or scatter bulbs among other wildflowers. It is very easy to grow.

PLANTING TIME: While dormant in early spring or fall.

ROOT SYSTEM: A white bulb with white basal roots, looking very much like the edible green garden onions.

PLANTING DEPTH AND SPACING: Set the bulbs 1 inch deep and space 3 to 5 inches apart. Or plant at random in a rock garden.

PLANTING STOCK AND PROPAGATION: Use nursery-grown stock or quality collected stock.

Divide clumps in very early spring. To propagate by seed, sow them in shallow soil in fall or very early spring. The plant rarely self-sows.

COMMENTS: I grew the nodding wild onion for several years before it established itself sufficiently for me to enjoy its beauty.

Lilium philadelphicum • wood lily

DESCRIPTION: 1 to 3 feet tall. Upright stems with willowlike foliage grow in whorls at intervals along the entire stem. Vase-shaped flowers grow one or two to a stalk, rarely three. They are reddish orange, with brown-purple dots from the center of the blossom to the throat.

The wood lily inhabits dry prairielike areas and open cut-over woodlands. Sometimes it is found growing in colonies, transforming a common grassland into a glistening sea of orange.

PERIOD OF BLOOM: June into July.

SOIL: Acid to moderately acid sandy loam. Good drainage is important.

LOCATION AND EXPOSURE: Full sun or very light open shade where the flower can benefit from the morning sun. Intersperse the wood lily with other prairie wildflowers. It does best where there is a groundcover of grasses and is, therefore, a fine plant for naturalizing in a meadow.

PLANTING TIME: While dormant in very early spring or fall. It resists transplanting.

ROOT SYSTEM: A scaly white bulb with lower fibrous feeder roots.

PLANTING DEPTH AND SPACING: Set bulbs 4 to 5 inches deep and space 8 to 12 inches apart; or plant them at random for a more natural effect.

PLANTING STOCK AND PROPAGATION: Nursery-grown stock is best. Quality collected stock may be dug up in fall—place a marker in summer because the plants go dormant in August.

This lily can be successfully increased by removing scales from the parent plant and planting them in flats or in large, squat pots. Use a humus-rich soil. Winter over in the cold frame. The following summer tiny new shoots will emerge and new bulblets will form. As soon as the bulblets are the size of small acorns, plant them in a permanent location to mature. You can expect excellent results.

Sow seeds as soon as they ripen. Seeds sown in flats produce only a single leaf the first year. Seedlings bloom in four to five years.

COMMENTS: The wood lily is on the protected list and is quite scarce. Flowers last only one day in a bouquet, and the blossoms are better left alone to set seed.

Lilium canadense • Canada lily

DESCRIPTION: 3 to 5 feet tall. The Canada lily has graceful, partially nodding flowers with large, slightly curved petals. The flowers grow in groups on arching stems. They are yellow on the outside, orange-colored with dark spots on the inside. Smooth, lanceolate green leaves grow in whorls along the sturdy, upright stalk.

The Canada lily haunts wet meadows and lowlands.

PERIOD OF BLOOM: June into July.

SOIL: Fertile, moist, slightly acid soil is best.

LOCATION AND EXPOSURE: The Canada lily can be grown in full sun in wetlands and in moist shade in open woodland. In areas where the soil is unshaded, a generous mulching will protect the plant and keep its roots cool.

PLANTING TIME: Early fall is best, but spring is satisfactory if bulbs are still dormant.

ROOT SYSTEM: A white scaly bulb with basal white feeder roots.

PLANTING DEPTH AND SPACING: Set bulbs 5 to 8 inches deep, depending on size. Space 1 foot apart in scattered colonies in meadows.

PLANTING STOCK AND PROPAGATION: Use nursery-grown stock or quality collected stock.

For propagation, scales removed from the parent plant right after bloom give the quickest results. Grow the scales in a humus-rich soil to which a considerable amount of sharp sand has been added. Grow them in flats or in a protected area for two years before moving the medium-sized new bulbs to their permanent location.

Sow seeds as soon as they ripen. It takes as many as five years to produce a bulb large enough to bloom.

COMMENTS: The Canada lily is truly a showy plant. It is best suited for a partially shaded woodland area or a damp-to-wet open meadow.

Lilium michiganense • Michigan lily

DESCRIPTION: 2 to 3 feet tall. The flowers of the Michigan lily are deep orange with brown spots and distinctly curved petals. The foliage is alternate on sturdy stems.

This lily inhabits wet prairies and meadows as well as moist woodlands and the thickets at river bottoms.

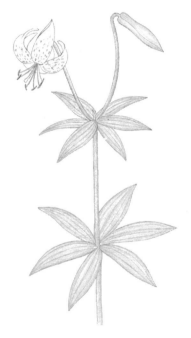

PERIOD OF BLOOM: July into August.

SOIL: Fertile, slightly acid to neutral soil with constant moisture.

LOCATION AND EXPOSURE: Grow Michigan lilies in full sun or in high open shade in moist woodland. Planted in a wet meadow with other wildflowers, they will provide a lovely contrast.

PLANTING TIME: Early fall is best.

ROOT SYSTEM: A scaly, pale yellow bulb with horizontal rhizomes which produce new plants to form colonies.

PLANTING DEPTH AND SPACING: Set the bulbs 4 to 6 inches deep, depending on size. Space 1 foot or more apart. Often this flower does not bloom until the second year after it has been moved.

PLANTING STOCK AND PROPAGATION: Nursery-grown stock mature enough to bloom is best. Quality collected stock may also be used.

To propagate, divide the clumps that are formed by new rhizomes (if large enough, these often bloom in the second year), or sow seeds in fall as soon as they ripen. Seeds do not always germinate the following spring or summer. Several years may elapse before seedlings will bloom.

COMMENTS: In my garden I have a colony of Michigan lilies in a spot which was once used as a burning pile and then as a compost heap. Here they grow in high open shade on a slope, mulched with marsh hay. Some of the older plants have flowers in clusters of eight to ten blossoms. These lilies have grown so well that I now believe compost and wood ash are helpful in promoting luxuriant growth. Although the Michigan lily is usually no more than 3 feet tall, mine grow to 5 feet in moist, partly shaded spots.

Lilium superbum • Turk's-cap lily

DESCRIPTION: 3 to 6 feet tall. The several orange flowers with their deeply curved petals and the stately stems make this a distinctive lily. The upper foliage is alternating, and the lower foliage often grows in tiers.

The Turk's-cap graces wet meadows and marshy lowlands with its elegance. Sometimes it is found in damp roadside ditches, accompanied by the fringed gentian.

PERIOD OF BLOOM: July into August.

SOIL: Fertile, loose, somewhat acid soil with reasonably good drainage.

LOCATION AND EXPOSURE: The Turk's-cap is a good plant for high open shade in moist woodland or for a sunny meadow. For best results, plant this flower in colonies in the meadow in full sun, and shade the roots by using a good mulch or companion planting.

PLANTING TIME: Early fall is best.

ROOT SYSTEM: A scaly white bulb with basal feeder roots.

PLANTING DEPTH AND SPACING: Set the bulbs 4 to 6 inches deep, depending on size. Space 1 foot or more apart. For naturalizing, plant in colonies. As with other wild lilies, Turk's-cap may not always bloom in the first year after transplanting.

PLANTING STOCK AND PROPAGATION: Two-year-old, nursery-grown stock is best. But also use quality collected stock.

Scales removed from the parent bulbs will produce new bulbs the following year and will be ready to be moved to a permanent location. Large bulbs usually give good results, but I find the scale method quickest.

To propagate from seed, sow the seeds in flats or in the open as soon as they ripen. Be sure to keep the seed bed area moist all through the year. There should be good germination the following spring and early summer. Seedlings are usually large enough to move the third fall.

COMMENTS: The Turk's-cap is very similar to the Michigan lily and may be confused with it. Turk's-cap is smaller and darker.

Lilium tigrinum • tiger lily

DESCRIPTION: 2 to 4 feet tall. Clusters of orange-red flowers grow at the top of a single stem; the curved petals are covered with dark spots. Leaves alternate along the length of the stem, with black bulbils forming in the leaf axil.

The tiger lily is an Asian garden lily that took kindly to our fields and thickets. It is often found in very old gardens and around deserted homesteads. Rodents carry the seeds away and help to spread it.

PERIOD OF BLOOM: July into late August.

SOIL: Ordinary fertile garden soil or humus-rich woodland soil. It is not demanding.

LOCATION AND EXPOSURE: Full sun or light open shade. It is excellent in a border planted among blue flowers for deep contrast.

PLANTING TIME: Fall planting is best.

ROOT SYSTEM: A large white bulb with white basal roots.

PLANTING DEPTH AND SPACING: Set the bulbs 3 to 5 inches deep. Space 10 to 15 inches apart or plant in small colonies.

PLANTING STOCK AND PROPAGATION: Nursery-grown stock or bulbs collected from old gardens or fencerows should grow well.

To propagate, plant bulbils ½ inch deep as they fall from the parent plant. These bulbils will produce only one true leaf the following spring. Young plants can be moved at almost any time of the year.

The tiger lilies in my garden never set seed.

COMMENTS: Originally grown only in cultivation, this is an excellent lily for naturalizing along a rail fence.

Erythronium americanum • trout lily

DESCRIPTION: 5 to 8 inches tall. The flared, bell-shaped yellow flowers are flushed with brown on the outside. They droop over the slender, leafless stems. There is also a rare white species with

an orchid-lavender flush on the outside, but it is rarely found in the same woodland.

The trout lily grows in rich, deciduous woods, in thickets, and in areas where the soil is heavy.

PERIOD OF BLOOM: May.

SOIL: A slightly acid soil that is humus-rich or fertile to a good depth.

LOCATION AND EXPOSURE: Light open shade in the woodland where the sun filters through or in partial shade among other wildflowers. Since it goes dormant after bloom, plant the trout lily among other small wildflowers that retain their foliage. Blue phlox or hepaticas are excellent for interplanting.

PLANTING TIME: While dormant in late summer or fall.

ROOT SYSTEM: Small, light tan, teardrop-shaped bulbs with white basal roots.

PLANTING DEPTH AND SPACING: Set the bulbs 3 to 5 inches deep; they will work down to their correct level. Plant at random for a natural effect. Often years pass before transplanted bulbs will bloom again. Trout lilies planted where early spring sun is at its fullest will bloom sooner than those planted in shadier areas.

PLANTING STOCK AND PROPAGATION: Nursery-grown stock planted in peat pots will give the best results. Set the peat pots 2 to 3 inches deep and cover with earth and mulch. Quality collected stock of good size may also be used. Because trout lilies grow deeper into the ground each year, old bulbs are hard to find.

Seed production is poor and germination is even poorer. It often takes eight years for seedlings to mature enough to bloom.

COMMENTS: I wonder if the speckled foliage accounts for the name of trout lily.

Camassia scilloides • eastern camass

DESCRIPTION: 10 to 15 inches tall. Pale blue (or, more rarely, white) starlike flowers grow in spikes above foliage resembling those of the leek.

The eastern camass inhabits damp meadows and very open woodlands.

PERIOD OF BLOOM: May into June.

SOIL: Neutral to slightly acid soil of good fertility.

LOCATION AND EXPOSURE: Naturalize in damp sunny meadows or plant in open woodland in patches among birches or other deciduous trees. Interplant with ragwort for color.

PLANTING TIME: While dormant in late summer or early fall.

ROOT SYSTEM: A white onionlike bulb with white basal roots.

PLANTING DEPTH AND SPACING: Set the bulbs 3 to 5 inches deep. Space about 6 inches apart. In an ideal location each bulb will soon become a clump. Mulch. Insert an identifying tag into the ground of planted areas since the eastern camass often goes dormant right after the seeds ripen.

PLANTING STOCK AND PROPAGATION: Nursery-grown stock of good size is best. Or use quality collected stock of good size.

As soon as seeds ripen, sow them in flats. They will produce one slender spear of green the following spring. Several years elapse before seedlings are mature enough to bloom.

COMMENTS: Many years ago some species of camass were used by the Indians as food, but other species are very poisonous.

Camassia esculenta • western camass

DESCRIPTION: 1 to 2 feet tall. Starlike flowers grow in spikes above grasslike foliage. The flowers are an intense copen blue, or (rarely) white.

Western camass forms a sea of blue in moist meadows and open woods along streams.

PERIOD OF BLOOM: June.

SOIL: Fertile garden soil or humus-rich woods soil. Mix in some sand for drainage, which is important during dormancy.

LOCATION AND EXPOSURE: Best planted in clumps among other wildflowers with good foliage that will provide color when the camass goes dormant. Excellent in colonies in damp meadows.

PLANTING TIME: When bulbs become dormant, or early fall.

ROOT SYSTEM: A white onionlike bulb with basal white fibrous roots and a tan paperlike covering.

PLANTING DEPTH AND SPACING: Set the bulbs 4 to 5 inches deep. Space 8 inches or more apart since each bulb forms a clump.

PLANTING STOCK AND PROPAGATION: Use nursery-grown stock or quality collected stock of good size.

Camass can be multiplied by removing offsets from larger bulbs and planting them separately. Do not plant small bulbs more than 2 inches deep. They often bloom in the second year.

Seeds sown when ripe or in early fall germinate the following spring and produce one spearlike leaf, which then becomes dormant about midsummer. Several years elapse before the seedlings mature enough to bloom.

COMMENTS: The intense blue of this camass is spectacular, rivaling other wildflowers that bloom at the same time.

Ornithogalum umbellatum • star-of-Bethlehem

DESCRIPTION: 5 to 8 inches tall. The waxy-white starlike flowers have a greenish tint on the outside. The leaves resemble those of the crocus; they are linear, with a white midrib.

Originally grown only in cultivation, the star-of-Bethlehem is now found in old fields and meadows among grasses.

PERIOD OF BLOOM: Late May into June.

SOIL: Ordinary garden or woodland soil. Not fussy.

LOCATION AND EXPOSURE: Very light open shade or a place where the morning sun shines briefly. A fine plant for the semishaded rock garden or along a woodland path. Excellent to naturalize in patches. Star-of-Bethlehem quickly becomes dormant after bloom.

PLANTING TIME: While dormant in spring or fall. Fall is preferable.

ROOT SYSTEM: A small white bulb with white fibrous roots.

PLANTING DEPTH AND SPACING: Set the bulbs 1 inch deep. Space 4 to 6 inches apart, since each bulb forms a clump.

PLANTING STOCK AND PROPAGATION: Use nursery-grown stock or quality collected stock.

Propagation by division of bulb colonies in early spring or fall offers a fast method of increasing stock. I have never noticed seeds.

COMMENTS: Star-of-Bethlehem is interesting planted among low groundcovers that retain their foliage.

Muscari botryoides · grape hyacinth

DESCRIPTION: 6 to 10 inches tall. An elongated cluster of neat little porcelain-blue bells clings closely to an upright spike. A rare white variety also exists. The foliage is ribbonlike.

At one time grown only in cultivation, grape hyacinth is now found in deserted gardens and along fencerows.

PERIOD OF BLOOM: Early May.

SOIL: Ordinary garden soil or rich woods soil that is neutral to only slightly acid.

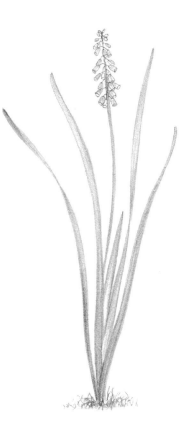

LOCATION AND EXPOSURE: There are many uses for this blue early-spring flower. I planted it along a sunny path to our pool and under a nearby birch among hepaticas, bloodroot, and white trilliums.

PLANTING TIME: Transplant after blooming when the foliage fades or anytime thereafter into the fall.

ROOT SYSTEM: A white onionlike bulb with white basal roots. It multiplies readily.

PLANTING DEPTH AND SPACING: Set the bulbs 2 to 3 inches deep. Space 3 to 6 inches apart. Each bulb will form a neat little clump. For naturalizing, plant at random, or tuck the plants in niches of a rock garden.

PLANTING STOCK AND PROPAGATION: Use nursery-grown stock or divide clumps if the grape hyacinth is already in your garden. Or use quality collected stock.

This plant rarely sets seed. Division of clumps is the best method of propagation.

COMMENTS: Wherever you choose to grow grape hyacinths they will be welcome bursts of heavenly blue in the early spring sunshine, but grow them where other plants will provide interest when the hyacinth goes dormant shortly after blooming.

Smilacina stellata · star-flowered false Solomon's seal

DESCRIPTION: 10 to 18 inches tall. This variety of false Solomon's seal is referred to as the star-flowered; a sparse plume of starry white flowers grows at the top of a leafy stem. The stem is arching and grows in a slightly zigzag fashion. Dark red berries appear in the fall.

The plant is often found in moist woods with good drainage and along sandy roadsides where there is some shade during the heat of the day.

PERIOD OF BLOOM: Late May into June.

SOIL: Fertile or sandy soil that is slightly acid. Good drainage is important.

LOCATION AND EXPOSURE: Partial shade where tree branches are high overhead. It is excellent for naturalizing or as groundcover in the woodland. If you wish to keep a few plants within bounds in a small garden, plant them in bottomless gallon cans.

PLANTING TIME: Early spring or anytime after dormancy until late fall.

ROOT SYSTEM: A pale, slender, creeping rhizome that frequently sends up new plants, forming large colonies that take over wide areas.

PLANTING DEPTH AND SPACING: Plant the rhizomes horizontally, 1 inch deep with the eye almost at soil level. Point each rhizome in a different direction since each will creep and fork to form a colony. Space at least 1 foot apart.

PLANTING STOCK AND PROPAGATION: Use nursery-grown stock or quality collected stock.

Fall is the best time to propagate from divisions. Divide rhizomes at the forks, leaving one newly formed shoot in each division.

Seeds sown in fall often do not germinate until the second year, and seedlings bloom several years later.

COMMENTS: In our area of the Nicolet National Forest this plant claims countless miles, growing in older Jack pine plantations.

Smilacina racemosa • false spikenard

DESCRIPTION: 1 to 3 feet tall. A leafy stem arching at the top bears a solitary white to creamy-white plume. Speckled berries appear in August and provide excellent food for grouse.

False spikenard is found in dry open woodlands where the soil is rich in humus. In our woodland the chipmunks have been carrying and burying seeds for some time now, and several colonies of the plant have been established as a result of their activities.

PERIOD OF BLOOM: May into June.

SOIL: Rich soil of moderate acidity.

LOCATION AND EXPOSURE: A fine plant for open woodlands or in the shade as a groundcover among shrubs. False spikenard is best grown where humus is deep. Planted in colonies under deciduous trees, it will spread after once becoming established. Mulch generously.

PLANTING TIME: While dormant in spring or fall.

ROOT SYSTEM: A coarse tannish rhizome with many rings and coarse white feeder roots. Newly formed eyes remain below the ground for a year before emerging.

PLANTING DEPTH AND SPACING: Plant the rhizomes horizontally, 2 inches deep, with the tip just below soil level. Space at least 1 foot apart since the rhizome forks as it creeps along.

PLANTING STOCK AND PROPAGATION: Nursery-grown stock has a heavier root system and thicker rhizomes, but quality collected stock from plants mature enough to bloom may be used.

Divide the rhizomes for propagation, preferably in fall. Seeds planted as soon as they ripen usually require two years to germinate and another five years to bloom.

COMMENTS: The false spikenard should be planted in its permanent home since it resists moving and often will not bloom the first year after transplanting. It is also known as Solomon's plume.

Clintonia borealis • bluebead lily

DESCRIPTION: 6 to 8 inches tall. Clusters of small, greenish yellow bells rise on upright stems above broad, glossy leaves. Steel-blue berries appear in August.

In cool, damp, deciduous woodlands and among evergreens, where the soil is humus-rich and mulch is plentiful, the bluebead lily grows in huge colonies among cinnamon fern, starflower, and bunchberry. In drier, shaded areas it grows among bracken fern, blooming before the ferns unfurl their fronds.

PERIOD OF BLOOM: Late May into early June.

SOIL: Humus-rich acid to slightly acid soil. Add a generous amount of damp peatmoss to the soil.

LOCATION AND EXPOSURE: The bluebead lily cannot tolerate the hot summer sun on its leaves. It is an ideal plant for deep shade, where many other wildflowers would fail.

PLANTING TIME: Fall planting is preferable, but plants can be moved in the spring while still dormant.

ROOT SYSTEM: A slender creeping rhizome that divides at the nodes to form additional plants. Collected stock has only a few feeder roots at each node, while nursery-grown stock has a vigorous root system.

PLANTING DEPTH AND SPACING: Place the rhizome horizontally about ½ to 1 inch deep with the new shoot-tip just about at soil level. Mulch with partly decayed oak leaves, weathered straw, or old marsh hay.

The clintonias are ramblers. When planting a colony, point the tips of the rhizomes in different directions so that they can spread outward. New rhizomes form, and these will fork also.

PLANTING STOCK AND PROPAGATION: Nursery-grown stock is far superior to collected stock in root system and vitality, but quality collected stock with ample roots may be used.

Division of rhizomes in fall is the quickest method of propagation.

Sow pulp-free seeds as soon as they are ripe or in early fall. Next spring, each seed that germinates sends up one tiny green spear. Each succeeding year the spear lengthens and broadens until a single leaf on each plant has almost reached maturity. Over the next few years some of the plants will produce two mature leaves. Blooms appear only when the plant has matured sufficiently to produce three or four leaves. A bluebead lily bed that I started from seeds about twelve years ago is finally displaying some plants with three leaves that should grow to full size this year. Next year I hope to be rewarded with some bloom.

COMMENTS: I know of no other wildflower that takes as long as *Clintonia borealis* to grow from seed to the flowering stage. But the glossy foliage is like a carpet of green velvet in shaded forest nooks, and it is one of the few plants that retains its quality of foliage throughout the growing season.

Disporum maculatum • nodding mandarin

DESCRIPTION: 1 to 2 feet tall. Nodding bells grow on a forked stalk with alternate, ovate, quilted leaves tapering to a point. Flowers are cream-colored to yellow with brownish-purple speckles.

This mandarin is a native to shaded woodlands where there is a carpet of deep humus.

PERIOD OF BLOOM: May into June.

SOIL: Neutral to slightly acid, rich woods soil. It must have constant moisture if it is to set seed.

LOCATION AND EXPOSURE: A fine, showy plant for naturalizing in a colony in open shade.

PLANTING TIME: While dormant in spring or fall.

ROOT SYSTEM: A white rootstock that forms a clump to develop new plants. Very much like that of merrybells.

PLANTING DEPTH AND SPACING: Space the rootstock 1 to 2 feet apart, to leave room for clumps to spread. Set 1 inch deep and mulch.

PLANTING STOCK AND PROPAGATION: Use nursery-grown stock, or quality collected stock where available.

Divide rootstocks while dormant in spring or fall. Seeds should be sown when ripe. They are slow to germinate.

COMMENTS: The nodding mandarin is an excellent plant to grow in colonies because of its showy flared bells and its distinctively textured, deeply veined foliage. Other disporum flowers are not as showy as those of the nodding mandarin.

Maianthemum canadense • Canada mayflower

DESCRIPTION: 3 to 6 inches tall. The Canada mayflower looks very much like a miniature lily of the valley and is sometimes called false lily of the valley. It has fragrant, tiny white flowers in an oval spike and bright red berries from August into September.

Canada mayflower covers woodland floors, where it grows among clintonia and bunchberry. On drier wooded hillsides it is found among wintergreen and pyrola. It also tends to form colonies around fallen logs of evergreen trees and stumps of the white pine, sending its rhizomes through the decaying wood.

PERIOD OF BLOOM: Late May into June.

SOIL: Humus-rich to slightly acid soil. But I have also found it growing in fire furrows in pure sand where it was mulched by falling leaves. Plenty of mulch will help this plant to spread more quickly.

LOCATION AND EXPOSURE: A good groundcover for partial or deep shade. Grow it among pink lady's-slippers or clintonias. Canada mayflower is very neat and easy to cultivate.

PLANTING TIME: While dormant in spring or fall. Potted stock may be planted anytime.

ROOT SYSTEM: A very extensive and forking rootstock consisting of slender, jointed, white rhizomes that creep at about 1 inch below soil level.

PLANTING DEPTH AND SPACING: Plant bareroot stock horizontally, cover with 1 inch of earth, and mulch. If you are planting stock grown in peat pots, sink to soil level and mulch lightly. Space either stock 6 to 12 inches apart. If planting sods, sink to soil level, space 1 foot or more apart, and mulch lightly.

PLANTING STOCK AND PROPAGATION: Nursery-grown stock in peat pots is best and gives the quickest results. Freshly dug bareroot stock may be used; unless sods are large, many of the eyes will be severed from the parent rootstock.

Sow seeds in the fall in individual pots. Later, set the pots in their permanent location. Propagating from seed is slow, and it takes several years for the plants to bloom.

COMMENTS: The Canada mayflower is one of the best ground-covers to grow among lady's-slippers and other acid-loving wild-flowers. It spreads surprisingly fast when mulched with leaves of soft maple and white birch. Old weathered straw and partly decayed marsh hay also make an excellent mulch; they must be put down in fall so that snow can settle the mulch.

Streptopus roseus • rose mandarin

DESCRIPTION: 1 to 2 feet tall. The dainty, drooping bells in the axils of the upper leaves are dull rose to pink. The leafy, twisted stalk has ovate leaves which taper to a point. Red berries appear in the fall. The plant grows in colonies in deciduous woods that have plentiful leafmold.

PERIOD OF BLOOM: Late May into June.

SOIL: Humus-rich, neutral to slightly acid soil. Moist but not wet.

LOCATION AND EXPOSURE: Plant rose mandarin in deep to open

shade or among rocks and stumps in a woodland garden. Or grow it in colonies to serve as groundcover.

PLANTING TIME: While dormant in spring or fall.

ROOT SYSTEM: A matted rhizome that divides at frequent intervals to send up new plants.

PLANTING DEPTH AND SPACING: Set the rhizomes horizontally, 1 inch deep, and spread the fibrous feeder roots carefully. Mulch.

PLANTING STOCK AND PROPAGATION: Use nursery-grown stock or quality collected stock.

Divide rhizomes while the plant is dormant. Sow seeds as soon as they ripen or in the fall. Germination is slow, and the plant will take several years to bloom.

COMMENTS: The rose mandarin, also known as rosy twisted stalk, is a showy plant, especially suited for groundcover in forest areas with high open shade. It can be planted in small groups or in large colonies.

Polygonatum biflorum • Solomon's seal

DESCRIPTION: 1 to 3 feet tall. Tiny, elongated pale yellow or greenish bells hang in pairs in the axils of the leaves on arching stems. Dark blue berries, flushed with white, appear in the fall. Solomon's seal grows in moist woodlands, in deep shade where the soil is humus-rich. I found it growing among rocks along a shaded river bank where the mulch had accumulated in pockets.

PERIOD OF BLOOM: June into July.

SOIL: Slightly acid, humus-rich soil retaining some moisture.

LOCATION AND EXPOSURE: Plant in light shade or even in high, open, deep shade among rocks, on hillsides, or in colonies along with *Trillium grandiflorum* and *Trillium cernuum*. It contrasts nicely with medium-sized ferns.

PLANTING TIME: While dormant in spring or fall.

ROOT SYSTEM: A twisted, heavy white rhizome that forms a shoot at each node. The shoot branches off to start a new plant.

PLANTING DEPTH AND SPACING: Plant the rhizome horizontally, 1 to 2 inches deep, with the tip just below the surface of the soil. Space 1 foot apart or intersperse with other wildflowers.

PLANTING STOCK AND PROPAGATION: Nursery-grown stock is more heavily rooted, but you can also use quality collected stock of good size.

Divide rhizomes in spring or while dormant. Sow seeds as soon as they are ripe. Germination is uneven and seedlings are slow to mature, but I found that when freshly gathered seed was planted next to a shady stone foundation germination was much better, possibly due to even moisture.

COMMENTS: This excellent groundcover is especially handsome under large trees or among shrubs. When the berries turn blue they have a blush like Concord grapes.

A coarser version of Solomon's seal is the great Solomon's seal (*Polygonatum commutatum*). It requires more moisture. A lone specimen turned up in my garden and grew to a height of 6 feet. But because there was a dry spell that summer it did not set seed.

Medeola virginiana • Indian cucumber

DESCRIPTION: 1 to 2 feet tall. Above a whorl of light green leaves, the Indian cucumber displays an umbel of small, greenish yellow drooping flowers with curved petals. The flowers are replaced by green berries that turn black in the fall.

Indian cucumber grows naturally in moist woods where the soil is humus-rich and the earth is reasonably moist throughout the growing season. It can also grow in shade on rocky hillsides.

PERIOD OF BLOOM: May into June.

SOIL: Moist, slightly acid, rich woods soil.

LOCATION AND EXPOSURE: Ideal for naturalizing in deep to moderate shade in deciduous woodlands. Plant in colonies, or among smaller ferns or low-growing wildflowers for contrast.

PLANTING TIME: While dormant in spring or fall.

ROOT SYSTEM: An odd-shaped oblong and fleshy white tuber that tastes like cucumber.

PLANTING DEPTH AND SPACING: Plant the tubers horizontally 1 to 2 inches deep. Space 6 to 8 inches apart.

PLANTING STOCK AND PROPAGATION: Use nursery-grown stock or quality collected stock.

Divide tubers, preferably in spring. Seeds sown when ripe may germinate the following spring, but it takes several years for seedlings to mature.

COMMENTS: Indian cucumber is an unusual and worthwhile addition to the wild garden if you can meet its requirements. I find it demanding at times, but not always. In fall, as the berries ripen, the leaves take on a maroon flush which makes an interesting contrast with evergreen ferns.

Trillium luteum • yellow trillium

DESCRIPTION: 10 to 15 inches tall. A whorl of three brown-mottled green leaves grow on a sturdy stalk. At the top, just above the leaves, is a solitary, pale-yellow to clear-lemon-yellow flower with three petals. The straight, narrow petals come to a point and are partly opened. Sometimes there is a wave or slight twist in each. A close sniff suggests a hint of lemon.

This trillium is found in deciduous woods where leafmold is deep. Though it commonly grows far south of Wisconsin, it has thrived here despite our severe winters.

PERIOD OF BLOOM: May into June. This variety blooms longer than any other trillium, usually for a full month.

SOIL: Neutral to slightly acid, humus-rich soil. I find that when replanted, all trillium rhizomes do best when a bit of sand is placed at their base.

LOCATION AND EXPOSURE: While blooming, this wildflower requires filtered sunlight; at all other times it needs shade. For the best display, plant yellow trillium in groups alongside other wildflowers.

PLANTING TIME: Fall planting is highly recommended to ensure stronger bloom and good foliage development.

ROOT SYSTEM: A large rhizome with many stringy white feeder roots. A strong grower, occasionally sending up two stalks from one node.

PLANTING DEPTH AND SPACING: Plant the tuberlike rhizome 2 to 4 inches deep, depending on the size of the rhizome and the texture of the soil. In heavy soils, plant shallow. All trilliums require a year-round mulch.

PLANTING STOCK AND PROPAGATION: Use nursery-grown stock or freshly dug quality collected stock.

I have never known the seeds to mature, possibly because of the severe climate in my area.

COMMENTS: A most unusual addition to the woodland garden. The fragrant, long-lasting blossoms have a beauty all their own.

Trillium recurvatum • prairie trillium

DESCRIPTION: 10 to 15 inches tall. A solitary maroon flower with three upright petals rests above a whorl of three mottled ovate leaves. The upper part of the petal is often flushed with green.

This trillium is found in moist woods and thickets south of Wisconsin. It has also thrived well in my area, much farther north.

PERIOD OF BLOOM: May.

SOIL: Neutral to slightly acid soil, rich in humus.

LOCATION AND EXPOSURE: Grow in open woods where the plants will be protected from the summer sun. Plant them in colonies or intersperse with other trilliums for contrast.

PLANTING TIME: Fall is best.

ROOT SYSTEM: A medium-sized rhizome with white stringy roots.

PLANTING DEPTH AND SPACING: Set the rhizomes 2 to 4 inches deep. Space several inches apart or in groups.

PLANTING STOCK AND PROPAGATION: Use nursery-grown stock or freshly dug collected stock of good quality.

Seeds must be sown as soon as they are picked or germination will be delayed a year.

COMMENTS: This trillium is grown for its mottled foliage rather than for its flower.

Trillium sessile • toadshade

DESCRIPTION: 6 to 10 inches tall. Mottled green leaves, 1½ to 4 inches long, grow in groups of three or occasionally more; they are almost twice as long as they are wide. The upright flower petals are narrower than those of the yellow trillium; they are fragrant and long-lasting, and come in a distinctive shade of wine maroon.

This trillium is native to the Central States but has proved hardy in northern Wisconsin.

PERIOD OF BLOOM: May into June.

SOIL: Humus-rich soil that is only slightly acid.

LOCATION AND EXPOSURE: Moist woods where the soil is humus-rich. An excellent trillium to grow for contrast among yellow trillium and rose trillium, which finish blooming a little later. Plant toadshade in the foreground of ferns, preferably in high open shade.

PLANTING TIME: Fall is preferable.

ROOT SYSTEM: A stout rhizome with many stringy roots.

PLANTING DEPTH AND SPACING: Plant the rhizomes 2 to 4 inches deep, depending on whether the soil is heavy or sandy. In heavy soil, plant about 3 inches deep.

PLANTING STOCK AND PROPAGATION: Use nursery-grown stock or freshly dug collected stock of good quality.

The toadshade has not set seed in our garden, but new plants will occasionally sprout from the small rhizomes that grow around the parent plant.

COMMENTS: The wine-maroon petals of the toadshade make a handsome display against the background of the mottled green leaves.

Trillium cernuum · nodding trillium

DESCRIPTION: 12 to 18 inches tall. A nodding flower with three wavy petals hides beneath a whorl of three large leaves. The flower is white with deep rose to maroon anthers. Occasionally the blossoms are yellow, pink, or even rose colored, and then the anthers are usually pale yellow or white. A handsome, three-cornered berry forms after the flower blooms, and turns red in July.

The nodding trillium is found in woods where the soil is humus-rich and moist. It also grows along the edge of evergreen swamps.

PERIOD OF BLOOM: May into June.

SOIL: Moderately acid woods soil, moist to wet, but good drainage is important. If the moisture is constant, it will also grow in drier woodlands. The soil in our trillium beds has a pH of 6.

LOCATION AND EXPOSURE: Grow in high open shade with moderately moist, humus-rich soil and plentiful mulch. Planted in

groups of three, this tall trillium provides a bold contrast with smaller varieties. For a natural effect, try growing it in colonies—or in small groups with leatherwood fern or florist fern—among rocks where leafmold is deep.

PLANTING TIME: Fall is preferable for all trilliums because the rhizomes continue to grow throughout late fall and early winter as well as in very early spring, and the new shoots are easily broken in moving.

ROOT SYSTEM: A large rhizome with many stringy feeder roots. Occasionally a single rhizome will send up two stalks during one season and only a single stalk the next season. In my wildflower garden, next to a foundation, a nodding trillium planted ten years ago now sends up six flower stalks.

PLANTING DEPTH AND SPACING: Plant the rhizomes 2 to 4 inches deep in groups of three. Space 6 or more inches apart or plant at random (groups of three together make a better display.)

PLANTING STOCK AND PROPAGATION: Use nursery-grown stock or freshly dug collected stock.

When the seeds are ripe they should be removed from the pulpy hull and immediately planted in flats or in a permanent location. The seedlings may take as many as ten years to bloom.

COMMENTS: This trillium is unusual and outstanding. I especially like its showy red berry, which lasts a long time.

The flowers are sweet-scented.

Trillium erectum • purple trillium

DESCRIPTION: 10 to 15 inches tall. This trillium has a short sturdy stem with a whorl of three ovate leaves at the top. The medium-sized maroon flower in the center of the leaves has an offensive odor (occasionally pale-yellow blossoms come up that have no odor).

Purple trillium grows in moist, rich woods in deep to open shade.

PERIOD OF BLOOM: May.

SOIL: Neutral to slightly acid, humus-rich soil.

LOCATION AND EXPOSURE: Open to deep shade in woodland where leafmold is plentiful. A striking companion for *Trillium grandiflorum*.

PLANTING TIME: Fall is best for all trilliums.

ROOT SYSTEM: Large rhizomes with many stringy roots. Older rhizomes often develop tiny rhizomes which may be detached and planted separately. Plant them only 2 inches deep and they will seek their own level.

PLANTING DEPTH AND SPACING: Plant the rhizomes 2 to 4 inches deep. Space 8 inches or more apart, or plant in groups of three or interspersed with other wildflowers.

PLANTING STOCK AND PROPAGATION: Use nursery-grown stock or freshly dug quality collected stock.

Propagate by removing small rhizomes from the parent plant. Seeds sown as soon as they ripen are slow to germinate and require years to bring to the blooming stage.

COMMENTS: The maroon-red flowers make an excellent contrast for other spring flowers such as the wild blue phlox and other trilliums.

Wake robin is another name for this trillium. It is also called stinking Benjamin because of the foul odor of the blossom. I find that the odor is not noticeable unless one sniffs closely.

Trillium grandiflorum • large white trillium

DESCRIPTION: 12 to 18 inches tall. Three broad, ovate leaves in a whorl top a sturdy stem. (I have found a few plants with four leaves and four petals, but one of the petals was partially curled.) The single pure white flower with yellow anthers is long lasting. The slightly curved, often wavy, petals deepen to a blush pink as they wither. There is also an extremely rare double white form, a gardenialike flower, which is highly prized.

This trillium is found throughout much of the eastern half of the United States and is abundant in Wisconsin. It carpets large areas with green and white, usually growing in colonies in open to deep shade. From year to year it reappears in dry upland woods as well as in wooded gullies. It is rarely found among evergreens.

PERIOD OF BLOOM: May into June.

SOIL: Neutral to slightly acid soil with plenty of humus. In the wild state, the rhizome is often found in sandy soil under the top layer of earth containing the humus.

LOCATION AND EXPOSURE: A woodland spot or a sloping hillside where the sun can filter through leafless trees in spring makes an ideal home for this lovely flower. It can also grow in deep shade. In the wild, *Trillium grandiflorum* always grows in large colonies, but some occasionally stray.

PLANTING TIME: Fall is best.

ROOT SYSTEM: A husky rhizome with many stringy roots.

PLANTING DEPTH AND SPACING: Plant the rhizome 2 to 4 inches deep. Space 8 inches or more apart, or plant in colonies or in groups of three. The plant looks interesting in groups among hepaticas and bloodroots.

PLANTING STOCK AND PROPAGATION: Use nursery-grown stock or freshly dug quality collected stock.

I find that rhizomes planted 2 inches deep and given a good mulch produce a number of rhizomes over a period of years. Be wary of shallow planting in light soil; it invites rodent damage.

Sow seeds as soon as they are ripe, before the caruncle dries. Seedlings require several years to bloom. The double white *Trillium grandiflorum* does not set seed and can only be propagated by detaching the tiny rhizomes from parent stock. This is a slow but rewarding method.

COMMENTS: The *Trillium grandiflorum* is the showiest of the trillium group, often covering hillsides and woodlands with patches of "snow." It is also easily cultivated.

This flower is really two in one, first a splendor of purest white and then a splash of pink turning to rose as it withers.

Trillium undulatum · painted trillium

DESCRIPTION: 8 to 12 inches tall. A white flower with three crimson-streaked petals sits just above a whorl of three leaves. The leaves are medium green and thin textured. In fall, the plant produces a red berry.

This wildflower inhabits cool woods and rarely grows in colonies.

PERIOD OF BLOOM: May into June.

SOIL: Requires a fertile, wet, acid soil, which can be pasty.

LOCATION AND EXPOSURE: A cool, damp, shady nook is ideal. It

is also lovely scattered among occasional clintonias in a moist area carpeted with goldthread.

PLANTING TIME: Fall.

ROOT SYSTEM: A medium-sized rhizome that is slow to multiply.

PLANTING DEPTH AND SPACING: Plant rhizomes 3 to 5 inches deep, 1 to 2 feet apart in a random fashion for a natural effect.

PLANTING STOCK AND PROPAGATION: Nursery-grown stock is best. Also use quality collected stock, freshly dug.

I have never grown this trillium from seed, but I presume sowing the seeds as soon as they are ripe will give the same results as it does with other trilliums.

COMMENTS: The flower is of unusual beauty. Recently a seedling appeared in my garden in the shade of a black cherry tree. When I removed some of the earth carefully to bare the rhizome without disturbing the roots, I found the rhizome top was 3½ inches down in rich humus. The seedling reappeared the following spring.

This trillium will become dormant shortly after blooming unless continued moisture is available.

Trillium ozarkanum • Ozark trillium

DESCRIPTION: 4 to 6 inches tall. This trillium, of the *virginianum* variety, has a dainty white flower which turns rose as the blossom fades, prominent anthers, and an extremely prominent calyx the same size as the blossom. After the flower withers, the calyx almost doubles in size and hides the seed pod. The stem is a striking wine-red color.

The Ozark trillium is found in woodlands south of Wisconsin wherever the soil is moist and somewhat acid.

PERIOD OF BLOOM: In its native home the Ozark trillium blooms in April, but farther north it blooms in May.

SOIL: Neutral to acid soil rich in humus. Constant moisture helps all trilliums retain their foliage throughout the growing season.

LOCATION AND EXPOSURE: A good trillium to plant in front of the taller *Trillium cernuum* in an open woodland spot.

PLANTING TIME: Fall is preferable for all trilliums.

ROOT SYSTEM: A small white rhizome, rarely more than an inch

long. Tiny rhizomes form around the adult rhizome to form a clump.

PLANTING DEPTH AND SPACING: Plant 2 to 4 inches deep. Space 8 to 12 inches apart. Avoid planting in clumps since each rhizome forms a clump with age.

PLANTING STOCK AND PROPAGATION: Use nursery-grown stock or quality collected stock where available.

The Ozark trillium is best propagated by removing small rhizomes from the parent plant in fall only. Do not divide the clumps until 4 or 5 mature stalks appear.

Seeds must be sown as soon as harvested. The following spring only one leaf will appear, and the seedlings usually require three to six years to bloom.

COMMENTS: The Ozark trillium is particularly handsome because of its wine-red stalk.

Trillium stylosum · rose trillium

DESCRIPTION: 10 to 12 inches tall. Slightly nodding flowers, with narrow curved petals, are pink to rose colored with a little white on the undersides. The rather long stems grow out of a whorl of three medium-sized leaves.

The rose trillium naturally inhabits rocky regions of the Appalachian Mountains; it has also proved hardy in northern Wisconsin.

PERIOD OF BLOOM: Early June. It is the last trillium to bloom.

SOIL: Fertile woodland soil that is neutral to slightly acid. Constant moisture is important to all trilliums.

LOCATION AND EXPOSURE: Plant in woodlands among medium-sized feathery ferns.

PLANTING TIME: In fall, only while dormant.

ROOT SYSTEM: A medium-sized rhizome with stringy fibrous feeder roots.

PLANTING DEPTH AND SPACING: Plant 2 to 4 inches deep. Space 6 to 12 inches apart or plant at random.

PLANTING STOCK AND PROPAGATION: Use nursery-grown stock, or quality collected stock where available.

Sow seeds as soon as they are ripe. Several years elapse before the seedlings bloom.

COMMENTS: The rose trillium is the last of the trilliums to bloom in my garden; it just begins to blossom when *Trillium grandiflorum* is fading to pink. It is good company for *Trillium luteum*, which blooms throughout the trillium season.

Trillium nivale • snow trillium

DESCRIPTION: 3 to 4 inches tall. The dainty white blossoms are occasionally streaked with pink. Three bluish green, petiolate leaves grow in a whorl. It is found in rich woodlands and glens.

PERIOD OF BLOOM: In northern Wisconsin it blooms in early April. A tiny node of green appears through the leafmold as soon as the snow melts. Sometimes this trillium blooms during spring snowstorms.

SOIL: Humus-rich soil with a pH of 6 gives fine results.

LOCATION AND EXPOSURE: A dainty little trillium to grow beneath taller shrubs or in colonies in open woodlands.

PLANTING TIME: Fall only.

ROOT SYSTEM: A small rhizome that is slow to multiply.

PLANTING DEPTH AND SPACING: Set the small rhizomes 2 inches deep. They will adjust to their own depth. Plant in groups or colonies.

PLANTING STOCK AND PROPAGATION: Use nursery-grown stock or quality collected stock.

My *Trillium nivale* has never set seed, possibly because there are no bees around to pollinate it when it blooms.

COMMENTS: Drifts of this little trillium are a welcome sight in early spring; they are sometimes covered for a day or so by slushy snows.

AMARYLLIDACEAE [Amaryllis Family]

Hypoxis hirsuta • yellow stargrass

DESCRIPTION: 4 to 6 inches tall. The hairy, upright foliage appears to be folded lengthwise. Bright-yellow starlike flowers,

greenish on the outside, grow midway up the foliage on a single stem.

Usually found in grassy meadows, along roadsides, and often in very open woodlands, this wildflower also grows in prairie regions.

PERIOD OF BLOOM: Late May into July, with scattered blossoms throughout the summer.

SOIL: Many types of fertile, slightly acid to acid soil as well as sandy loam. Constant moisture promotes superior growth and bloom.

LOCATION AND EXPOSURE: Yellow stargrass is native to prairies and open woodland; I find it grows best in full sun where the soil never bakes dry. Excellent for a rock garden amidst blue-eyed grass.

PLANTING TIME: While dormant in spring or fall, but I have moved it in midsummer, cutting back the foliage considerably and letting it grow anew.

ROOT SYSTEM: An almost round, onionlike corm covered with a fibrous papery brown hull.

PLANTING DEPTH AND SPACING: Set the corms a few inches apart in small groups and plant 1½ inches deep. In northern areas, mulch unless grown among grasses.

PLANTING STOCK AND PROPAGATION: Use nursery-grown stock or quality collected stock.

Separate the tiny corms that form around the parent plant. You must inspect the plants every day if you want to collect the elusive black seeds. Sow them in fall and barely cover them with earth.

COMMENTS: The foliage and flowers of yellow stargrass contrast beautifully with those of blue-eyed grass. They are of two different families.

IRIDACEAE [Iris Family]

Iris cristata • crested dwarf iris

DESCRIPTION: 3 to 8 inches tall. Sword-shaped leaves grow in groups up the short flower stem. Often tucked in among the foliage, the dainty flowers are light blue to lavender-blue, with bright yellow crests on each lower petal. The white form is rare.

Crested dwarf iris grows naturally in rich, rocky woods and along streams and lakes. It also grows abundantly in some eastern parts of Wisconsin.

PERIOD OF BLOOM: May.

SOIL: Neutral to slightly acid soil of good fertility.

LOCATION AND EXPOSURE: This iris makes a fine groundcover in high open shade or in sun with constant moisture. Plant it among limestone rocks or in fertile garden soil. It spreads to form mats.

PLANTING TIME: Spring or fall.

ROOT SYSTEM: A small slender rhizome with fibrous roots. Each rhizome sends out new rhizomes in a fan shape to form a clump.

PLANTING DEPTH AND SPACING: Set the rhizomes almost at soil level, leaving the tips partly exposed. Space 6 or more inches apart, depending on the effect wanted. Carefully tuck the fine feeder roots into the soil, and water often. If you are placing the newly transplanted stock in a sunny spot it is wise to provide shade for a week to ten days.

PLANTING STOCK AND PROPAGATION: Use nursery-grown stock or quality collected stock.

Divide plants in very early spring or right after blooming. My crested iris have never set seed.

COMMENTS: The blossoms of this little iris are strikingly different from those of other wild irises. The rhizome has a tendency to creep in a beadlike fashion as it grows, while the feeder roots penetrate deep into the soil.

I find the white form, *Iris cristata alba*, equally easy to grow. It is a prize addition to the wild garden.

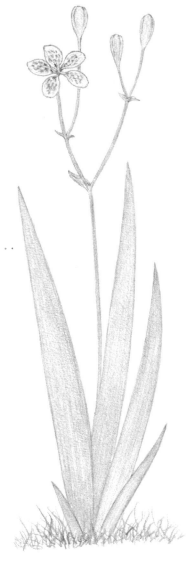

Belamcanda chinensis • blackberry lily

DESCRIPTION: 2 to 3 feet tall. Orange flowers with dark spots grow on a single slender stem. The foliage resembles that of the iris. In fall this lily produces a shiny blackberrylike seed cluster.

The blackberry lily is found in wastelands, along roadsides, and around old homesteads. It was originally a cultivated flower, but now grows wild.

PERIOD OF BLOOM: July into September.

SOIL: Ordinary fertile garden soil. It requires no special care.

LOCATION AND EXPOSURE: Plant the blackberry lily in an airy, sunny spot. If crowded, it sometimes develops leaf spot.

PLANTING TIME: While dormant in spring or fall.

ROOT SYSTEM: An orange-yellow rootstock with a few fibrous roots.

PLANTING DEPTH AND SPACING: Plant the rhizome 1½ inches deep and space 1 foot apart. It forms clumps.

PLANTING STOCK AND PROPAGATION: Use nursery-grown stock or plants collected from old gardens or waysides.

Divide the clumps in early spring or fall. Sow the seeds as soon as they are ripe. Often two years elapse before the seeds germinate, and another two years before the seedlings bloom.

COMMENTS: This flower is often referred to as the leopard lily because of the spots on the flower petals. The dried seed clusters are interesting in floral arrangements.

Sisyrinchium angustifolium • blue-eyed grass

DESCRIPTION: 6 to 10 inches tall. Flat flower stems are studded with clusters of dainty starlike flowers. The flowers are light blue to deep violet-blue, and the slender irislike foliage is blue-green.

Blue-eyed grass is usually found in dry, sunny meadows among grasses. In my area it graces roadsides, growing in gravelly earth.

PERIOD OF BLOOM: May into June.

SOIL: Slightly acid sandy loam to poor sandy soils. Good drainage is important. When cultivated, blue-eyed grass quickly forms large clumps.

LOCATION AND EXPOSURE: Blue-eyed grass blooms profusely in full sun and fertile soil. It is an interesting plant for a sunny rock garden or as edging along a stony walk in full sun.

PLANTING TIME: Spring or fall. Moves easily.

ROOT SYSTEM: Coarse fibrous roots, pale tan-yellow in color.

PLANTING DEPTH AND SPACING: Set the crown about ¼ to ½ inch deep. Space 6 inches apart, or farther apart in fertile soils. It forms clumps.

PLANTING STOCK AND PROPAGATION: Nursery-grown stock has a heavier root system, but you may also use quality collected stock.

Divide clumps in spring or fall. Seeds sown when ripe will

germinate the following spring, and the seedlings will reach a good size the next summer. When grown in barren areas, it readily self-sows.

COMMENTS: Each six-petaled, starlike flower opens for one day and shortly after sets seed. On cloudy days the flower rarely opens. Blue-eyed grass is very interesting in the seed stage. I marvel to see such tiny flowers produce fruit the size of small peas.

Iris versicolor • blue flag

DESCRIPTION: 2 feet tall. The orchidlike flowers are medium-blue with splashes of gold. They resemble cultivated irises although they are smaller. The sword-shaped foliage is long and graceful.

Blue flag grows in wet meadows and marshes, along lakes and brooks, and even in ditches where there is standing water in spring.

PERIOD OF BLOOM: June.

SOIL: Blue flag grows readily in any fertile soil.

LOCATION AND EXPOSURE: For the best bloom, plant blue flag in full sun. If you prefer to emphasize the foliage, plant in a shaded spot next to a rock or at the edge of a pool.

PLANTING TIME: Early spring, or late August into fall.

ROOT SYSTEM: A stout, cream-colored rhizome that creeps in a fanlike manner.

PLANTING DEPTH AND SPACING: Plant the rhizome horizontally, barely below the surface of the soil and with the crown at soil level. Space 1 foot apart. For best bloom, divide and transplant every third year.

PLANTING STOCK AND PROPAGATION: Nursery-grown stock is superior to collected stock.

Division of the rhizomes in August gives good results. Seeds sown as soon as they ripen and kept reasonably moist will produce blooming plants in three years.

COMMENTS: Blue flag deserves a prominent place in a wild garden. Although naturally found in very wet places, seedlings and nursery-grown stock can be grown successfully in ordinary garden soil of good fertility and average moisture.

ORCHIDACEAE [Orchis Family]

Cypripedium Calceolus • large yellow lady's-slipper

DESCRIPTION: 10 to 20 inches tall. Leafy stems bear one or two flowers which resemble pouches or slippers with two twisted frills for ties. The flowers are clear yellow with brown frills.

This large lady's-slipper (the *pubescens* variety) is found in moist deciduous woods that are often somewhat drier in summer. It also grows on hummocks in swamps.

PERIOD OF BLOOM: May into June.

SOIL: Neutral to slightly acid soil, rich in humus and with ample moisture gives best results. Mix some damp peatmoss into the soil. Woods soil is best, as it contains fungi that are beneficial to these plants.

LOCATION AND EXPOSURE: Partial shade in open woods is preferable. Yellow lady's-slippers are especially handsome interspersed with leatherwood and florist ferns. One of the easiest lady's-slippers to establish, it can be grown extensively in wild gardens.

PLANTING TIME: While dormant in spring or fall.

ROOT SYSTEM: A cream-colored, extremely stringy, creeping rootstock that is rather flexible in comparison to that of the pink lady's-slipper. The rhizome of the yellow lady's-slipper works itself down, and in fully established plants the crown may reach 1½ to 2 inches deep.

PLANTING DEPTH AND SPACING: Set the rhizome about 1 to 1½ inches deep with the base of the dormant bud ¾ to 1¼ inches below the soil level. Slant the roots slightly downward so that the tips will be slightly deeper than the base of the bud. Mulch with decaying leaves, weathered straw, or old marsh hay. Mulching helps retain the moisture and also keeps the roots cool in summer. Plants should be spaced 12 to 18 inches apart or planted at random. Multiple-crowned plants should be given ample room. A few rocks in the area lend an air of spaciousness and help protect the roots.

PLANTING STOCK AND PROPAGATION: Nursery-grown collected sods are easiest to move, but you can also use quality collected stock with good roots.

The division of lady's-slipper rhizomes is not always successful, as rot can set in at the crown and destroy both divisions. When the buds are far enough apart, division is less complicated.

As to seeds, there seem to be thousands in each capsule. Although I have never tried growing these plants from seed, I do know people who claim that yellow lady's-slippers appeared in their woods several years after seeds were scattered. It is well worth a trial.

COMMENTS: Give the lady's-slippers a little additional mulch each year unless falling leaves have taken over. The leaves of white birch and soft maple are especially good. The decaying humus will feed the plant and make for better specimens. All lady's-slippers benefit when the soil is kept moist, especially by mulching.

There is a smaller, less common version of the yellow lady's-slipper, the dainty *Cypripedium Calceolus parviflorum*. When established, it too spreads to form a clump. Do not plant it quite as deep as the large yellow lady's-slipper.

Cypripedium reginae • showy lady's-slipper

DESCRIPTION: 1 to 2 feet and taller. The flowers are shaped like large pouches or moccasins; they grow along the stem singly, in pairs, or even in groups of three. Flowers are white, flushed with magenta—pure white flowers are rare. Stems are stout with many broad-pleated leaves. Both stems and leaves are hairy.

The showy lady's-slipper is found in evergreen swamps and moist woods. Throughout our area it is found only off the beaten path.

PERIOD OF BLOOM: June, when other lady's-slippers are fading.

SOIL: Rich soil, neutral to slightly acid, with a generous addition of damp peatmoss mixed in to help retain moisture. Woods soil is essential; the showy lady's-slipper will not grow in cultivated garden soil.

LOCATION AND EXPOSURE: High open woods with shade where the soil does not dry out excessively. Constant moisture is best.

Some fifteen years ago I planted a few showy lady's-slippers in the shade of a large oak tree where the soil was virgin. Here a portion of their roots could creep under a large granite boulder. With a carpet of oak fern and some other small wildflowers planted nearby, the showy lady's-slippers seem to thrive. Each June they put on a regal display, with two to three pouches on each sturdy stem. It takes time to establish showy lady's-slippers, but once established their beauty increases yearly.

PLANTING TIME: While dormant in spring or fall. I prefer fall planting for all lady's-slippers unless they are moved in sods.

ROOT SYSTEM: Fibrous stringy roots extend from the rootstock. The roots are not as coarse as those of the pink lady's-slipper.

This species is a shallow grower. As plants become established, the crowns work up and some new roots will be barely below soil level. Some may even creep at soil level if the humus is well decayed. This is why a rock mulch over a good layer of humus is so beneficial.

PLANTING DEPTH AND SPACING: Set the rhizomes ½ to 1 inch deep, spreading the roots evenly. Cover with woods soil so that the top of the dormant bud is barely at soil level. Taper the tips of the roots slightly downward, a little deeper than the base of the shoot. Showy lady's-slipper plants should be spaced 2 to 3 feet apart. Allow room for future growth and space for the roots to run.

Mulch lightly with old decaying leaves, weathered marsh hay, or old straw. A combination of partly decayed straw, soft maple leaves, and birch leaves is ideal. A little extra mulch may be given the first fall but should be removed in spring.

Large rocks laid around the lady's-slipper plants encourage the roots to run beneath and help to keep the roots cool, which will promote more luxuriant growth. When planting the lady's-slipper, a twig should be put next to each crown so that rocks will not be laid over the buds later on. Winter snow will firm the mulch, and if too much is added, the shoots will not emerge. In this case, the twigs will mark where the plants should come up and some of the mulch can be removed. Once the plants have sprouted, a few inches of mulch can be put back around the stem. The addition of grass clippings as a mulch each time the grass is cut does wonders for this particular plant.

PLANTING STOCK AND PROPAGATION: Stock that has been growing in the nursery for two or more years is by far the best but you can also use sods or quality collected bareroot stock.

I have never tried divisions, as the plants grow much better when left in clumps where each plant helps the other.

Mature, established plants set a quantity of seed, but they do not germinate when sown in a flat. Try scattering seeds in a moist woodland instead.

COMMENTS: Showy lady's-slipper plants develop and improve with age. Established plants should never be moved. At best, it takes several years for a plant to multiply. With time the quality of the bloom improves and the plant becomes more stately. Always keep your showy lady's-slippers reasonably moist, but never soaking wet.

A friend of mine moved her showy lady's-slipper five or six times in as many years. When she built a new home, the "showy" was moved again. With each moving the plant became less vigorous. Now my friend has a permanent home for her clump of showy lady's-slippers on the north side of the house where a large shallow planter is filled with woods soil and damp peatmoss. The planter is bottomless. Following my instructions, she faithfully mulched the clump with fresh grass clippings each time the lawn was mowed. Now, some six years later, the showy lady's-slipper has 23 slippers and has formed a large clump.

Cypripedium acaule · pink lady's-slipper

DESCRIPTION: 6 to 8 inches tall. Each stem bears a single, moccasin-shaped flower and two single, oblong basal leaves. The flowers are rose-pink with reddish veins and wine-colored frills. Pure white ones are rare, indeed, and they have yellow frills.

The pink lady's-slipper grows in dry, open shade in oak woods where moisture and leafmold are ample. Established plants do not seem affected by dryness in the summer in these woodland regions. They are also found under the shade of cedars and balsams, on ridges and hummocks in swampy areas, and at the base of white pine stumps in the shade.

PERIOD OF BLOOM: May into June.

SOIL: Use fertile, acid to slightly acid, humus-rich woods soil

and well decayed leafmold, preferably oak. A generous amount of damp peatmoss should also be mixed in, and the soil should be capable of retaining moisture. It is especially important to keep the roots moist the first few years after transplanting. Mycorhizal fungus must be present in the soil if the plant is to grow successfully.

LOCATION AND EXPOSURE: Partial to deep shade in an open woodland. For a natural effect, plant randomly and intersperse with low groundcovers such as bunchberry, goldthread, and oak fern, or all of these running into each other. Plant a few *Clintonia borealis* and a vine of moneywort for an unusual and beautiful effect. If the soil and location are right, the pink lady's-slipper will grow for years; some will even have multiple crowns.

In one small nook I have some pink lady's-slippers growing under Norway pine with clintonia, bunchberry, and some moneywort. I add a little oak-leaf mulch when it is needed, and nature adds pine needles each fall. This little colony has thrived for over ten years.

PLANTING TIME: Spring or fall, but I prefer fall. One mid-June I rescued a quantity of pink lady's-slippers from an area where a bulldozer was cutting through a road. I removed all the seed pods and flowers from the plants to conserve their strength and vitality. Whenever possible I lifted each plant with some soil adhering, or in a sod, and I planted at the same level under tall evergreens in our yard. A few plants had bare roots. But with care and faithful watering almost every plant survived the move, and most of them bloomed the following year.

ROOT SYSTEM: The rhizomes have coarse, stringy white roots which are very brittle. At no time should the roots of any lady's-slippers be exposed to wind or sun.

The rhizome of this species tends to work upward, and established plants may be only a fraction of an inch under the soil. When the plant is in this condition the buds will be plump in the fall, and most plants will bloom the following spring.

PLANTING DEPTH AND SPACING: Set the rhizome about 1 inch deep with the base of the dormant bud ½ to 1 inch below soil level and the tip of the roots slightly downward, a little deeper than the base of the shoot. Spread the roots carefully when planting and make certain that a liberal amount of damp peatmoss is mixed into the woods soil that covers the roots. A mulch of old straw or decaying oak leaves and some old marsh hay is excellent. When planting, place a twig upright near each plant just in case the mulch was spread too generously and the shoot fails to emerge the following spring. Water all the plants liberally immediately after planting, and never let the soil dry out. (This applies to all lady's-slippers as well as to all transplanted stock.)

In fall my lady's-slipper beds are left to themselves, as leaves scatter across the plot. Never place mulch over freshly fallen leaves; the leaves might heat and smother the plants. If the beds need mulching, do it before the leaves fall in autumn.

PLANTING STOCK AND PROPAGATION: Rhizomes in sods are most desirable, but not easy to obtain. Use stock that has grown in the nursery for a year or more or collected stock with plenty of good roots.

Division of rhizomes is most trying, and I find that it is better to keep them growing in clumps rather than attempting to divide them.

It is extremely difficult to get lady's-slipper seeds to germinate, especially in flats. Ten years ago I scattered seeds in an oak-pine woods and pink lady's-slippers are now blooming there. A nurseryman wrote to me that he had succeeded in getting the seeds to germinate but lost the tender seedlings when he tried to transplant them.

COMMENTS: Growing pink-lady's-slippers can be a challenge. But it is also a great satisfaction. Although these plants are supposedly difficult to grow, I have found that it is quite possible to supply all the necessary conditions.

Cypripedium montanum • mountain lady's-slipper

DESCRIPTION: 12 to 18 inches tall. One or two white moccasin-shaped flowers flushed with purplish-blue and with brown frills grow on leafy stems. The mountain lady's-slipper is a western species, haunting brushlands and meadows where the soil is well drained and slightly acid. It is very rare and becoming more so.

PERIOD OF BLOOM: May and June.

SOIL: We grew a few plants in slightly acid and humus-rich soil, but one spring they failed to appear.

LOCATION AND EXPOSURE: We grew the mountain lady's-slipper in high open shade with yellow lady's slippers and trilliums.

PLANTING TIME: While dormant in spring or fall.

ROOT SYSTEM: Fibrous stringy roots and medium rootstock.

PLANTING DEPTH AND SPACING: Set the rhizome about 1 inch deep with the base of the dormant bud ½ to 1 inch below soil level and the root tips tapering slightly downward somewhat lower than the base of the shoot.

PLANTING STOCK AND PROPAGATION: Use wild stock transplanted to the nursery and grown one or more years, or collected stock if it is available.

I have never tried scattering the seeds.

COMMENTS: The pouches of the mountain lady's-slipper are very similar in shape to those of the yellow lady's slipper and are slightly larger than those of the small white lady's-slipper. In fact, I can see little difference between this species and the small white lady's-slipper except that the mountain lady's-slipper tends to become dormant in August.

Cypripedium candidum • small white lady's-slipper

DESCRIPTION: 6 to 10 inches tall. The flowers are small white pouches (or slippers) with a faint bluish tint. The stems are leafy.

The small white lady's-slipper is very rare. It is supposedly found near lake shores, but I have not been fortunate enough to find a single specimen in the wild. A few years ago a man from southern Wisconsin brought me two plants which he had found in an abandoned pasture where there was ample moisture.

PERIOD OF BLOOM: Early June.

SOIL: My small white lady's-slippers grow in neutral to slightly acid soil (pH around 6), rich in humus. They thrive where yellow and showy lady's-slippers grow.

LOCATION AND EXPOSURE: We grow our few specimens with dainty oak fern in open woodland with high intermittent shade. Each plant has formed a clump, which indicates that this location is satisfactory.

PLANTING TIME: While dormant in spring or fall, preferably fall.

ROOT SYSTEM: Small rhizomes with medium-sized, stringy roots.

This species, like the yellow lady's-slipper, has a tendency to work its way downward. The roots of our plants are 1½ inches deep.

PLANTING DEPTH AND SPACING: Set the rhizomes about 1 inch deep with the base of the dormant bud ¾ to 1 inch below soil level and the root tips slightly downward, a little deeper than the base of the shoot. We use very old decaying oat straw for mulch.

PLANTING STOCK AND PROPAGATION: Nursery-grown stock obtained from divisions is the only kind I have ever seen offered, and even that is seldom available. Collected stock is not available since the plant is very rare.

Our plants have not set seed; the blossoms usually blast right after blooming.

COMMENTS: This lady's-slipper is similar to the yellow in its growth habits but is not as rugged. The small white lady's-slipper should only be planted if you can give it a perfect home.

In the yellow lady's-slipper bed, near but not in the planted row, I found a white lady's-slipper flushed with blue. I have no idea where it came from but I like to think a seed germinated and brought this prize to my wild garden.

ARISTOLOCHIACEAE [Birthwort Family]

Asarum canadense • wild ginger

DESCRIPTION: 4 to 6 inches tall. The handsome leaves are light green and heart-shaped. They hide tiny flowers that resemble little brown stone crocks. The flowers are maroon flushed with soft gray-green on the outside.

Wild ginger inhabits dense, rich woods and partly shaded areas where grass is sparse. It grows in large colonies among rocks in deciduous woods.

PERIOD OF BLOOM: May into June. Blossoms are long-lasting.

SOIL: Woods soil rich in humus is preferable, but I have grown wild ginger with success in fertile garden soil that is neutral to slightly acid.

LOCATION AND EXPOSURE: Wild ginger is an excellent groundcover to plant between taller wildflowers in a woodland region. I have several patches that have formed dense mats on the north side of a stone wall. Under an oak tree another colony is rapidly covering a large area. The plants are near a water pump and often get extra water; the soil is quite dry otherwise.

PLANTING TIME: While dormant in spring or fall.

ROOT SYSTEM: A creeping rootstock forms roots at the nodes and forks as it creeps along. The rhizomes have a spicy, ginger-like fragrance and are pleasant to dig up.

PLANTING DEPTH AND SPACING: Plant the rhizomes horizontally about ½ inch deep, easing the tip to soil level. Make certain to tuck in all the roots along the stolon. Mulch in fall.

PLANTING STOCK AND PROPAGATION: Use nursery-grown or quality collected stock.

Divide the creeping rootstocks, especially where patches have become crowded. Cuttings taken after bloom form roots easily. Seeds are hard to collect, but wild ginger self-sows readily where the earth is constantly moist.

COMMENTS: An old gardener once told me that this plant depends entirely on slugs for pollination. In my garden the chipmunks carry the coarse seeds away and plant them at odd intervals. Wild ginger volunteers in the nursery in the most precarious places. The Indians used the spicy rhizomes for seasoning.

Aristolochia macrophylla · Dutchman's-pipe

DESCRIPTION: A 10 foot vine that entwines itself around nearby plants. The heart-shaped leaves usually grow in pairs along the stem. The brownish purple flower is a 1 inch tube shaped much like an old-time pipe with a flare at the top.

Although it grows naturally in rich, moist woods in regions much farther south, Dutchman's-pipe will grow hardily as far north as Wisconsin, though it may have scant bloom.

PERIOD OF BLOOM: May into June.

SOIL: Woods soil rich in humus, neutral to only slightly acid.

LOCATION AND EXPOSURE: Grow Dutchman's-pipe in open shade. Choose a spot where it can climb on taller flowers or on a support. It will attach itself to anything within reach.

PLANTING TIME: While dormant in fall.

ROOT SYSTEM: Fibrous orange roots and a sturdy rootstock.

PLANTING DEPTH AND SPACING: Space 3 feet or more apart. Set the next year's basal shoot just below soil level.

PLANTING STOCK AND PROPAGATION: Use nursery-grown or quality collected stock.

With age, the Dutchman's-pipe develops a woody stem. It might be possible to grow new plants from soft-wood cuttings, as one can with honeysuckles and bittersweet.

Seeds may be sown as soon as they ripen.

COMMENTS: I grew Dutchman's-pipe only as a novelty and was surprised to find that it had clambered onto a nearby wild cherry.

PORTULACACEAE [Purslane Family]

Claytonia virginica • spring beauty

DESCRIPTION: 4 to 6 inches tall. This plant often grows in a re-clining position. A small cluster of dainty, starlike flowers rests at the end of a fragile stem. The flowers are white or delicate pink, with darker pink to rose-colored veining. The entire plant is succulent.

Spring beauty is found in moist open woods, usually with deep leafmold. As a child I remember picking the flowers along a woodland stream where they literally carpeted the earth with their fragile beauty.

PERIOD OF BLOOM: May.

SOIL: Humus-rich, moist woods soil is best, but I also grow them in drier woodland soil where there is plentiful moisture during their bloom period. The soil may be neutral to only slightly acid, but humus content is more important than pH.

LOCATION AND EXPOSURE: Grow spring beauty in the high open shade of soft maples, aspens, birches, or elms, where the sun filters through leafless trees in spring. Interplant with oak fern, as spring beauty soon disappears after blooming.

PLANTING TIME: As soon as dormant into fall.

ROOT SYSTEM: A tiny, dark-colored tuber shaped much like a potato, with many tiny eyes protruding.

PLANTING DEPTH AND SPACING: Set the tubers 2 to 3 inches deep. Space 4 to 6 inches apart or plant in small colonies.

PLANTING STOCK AND PROPAGATION: Use nursery-grown stock or quality collected stock of good size.

Seeds are difficult to collect. Sow them as soon as they ripen. Spring beauty self-sows readily in the wild.

COMMENTS: This little charmer is excellent in a rock garden among small ferns that will stay green when it becomes dormant.

RANUNCULACEAE [Crowfoot Family]

Thalictrum dioicum • early meadowrue

DESCRIPTION: 1 to 2 feet tall. Greenish yellow to mauve airy panicles are held above compound leaves with many divisions.

In rich dry woodlands early meadowrue grows in colonies, making a lovely display.

PERIOD OF BLOOM: June.

SOIL: Humus-rich woods soil or fertile, slightly acid garden soil.

LOCATION AND EXPOSURE: Plant early meadowrue in open shade or along the edge of a woodland area where it is exposed to the early morning sun. It is an excellent substitute for ferns in regions where the soil is dry or there is a great deal of sun or wind. The foliage is sturdy and makes a fine groundcover when it is scattered in colonies either in semishaded areas or in full sun if moisture is unfluctuating.

PLANTING TIME: While dormant in spring or fall.

ROOT SYSTEM: Fibrous. The parent plant dies and forms two or more new offsets which will become parent plants the following year.

PLANTING DEPTH AND SPACING: Plant with the crown at soil level and mulch if you wish. Space 1 to 2 feet apart. The new shoots are purple when first emerging in springtime.

PLANTING STOCK AND PROPAGATION: Use nursery-grown stock or divisions of offsets collected in fall or early spring, or freshly dug collected stock. Remove all old roots before replanting.

Seeds should be sown as soon as they ripen. Early meadowrue

self-sows readily, especially if there is crumbly humus on the forest floor. Seedlings bloom the third year.

COMMENTS: A good plant to grow for the texture of its foliage and for its airy flowers. I stress the use of early meadowrue as a substitute for ferns where soil is not moist enough for ferns.

The seeds are held in the airy panicles. Male and female flowers grow on separate plants, so that not all plants will set seed. The male meadowrue has greenish yellow blossoms, while the female has an additional tinge of mauve.

Thalictrum polygamum · tall meadowrue

DESCRIPTION: 3 to 4 feet tall. Large plumes of airy white are held above divided, compound foliage on stout, hollow stems. Occasionally a bold lavender plume appears.

Tall meadowrue is found along brooks, in wet meadows, and along roadside ditches where it displays its beauty in full sun. It grows taller in very wet places.

PERIOD OF BLOOM: Late June into August.

SOIL: Use fertile, slightly acid soil, wet or of average moisture. When grown in ordinary garden soil that is not wet, the plant may not be as tall as it is in the wild but the flowers will be just as beautiful.

LOCATION AND EXPOSURE: Tall meadowrue grows best in full sun, but it will grow in partial shade and still flower. In the wild, it is found among Joe-pye and swamp milkweed.

PLANTING TIME: While dormant in spring or fall.

ROOT SYSTEM: Fibrous. Each year after blooming, new offsets form at the base of the parent plant which then dies, leaving the new shoots to produce the next year's flowers.

PLANTING DEPTH AND SPACING: Set plants with the crown at soil level and mulch. Space plants at least 12 to 18 inches apart. Tall meadowrue does not make as dense a clump of foliage as does early meadowrue, but if the flowers and stalks are cut to the ground new growth soon appears.

PLANTING STOCK AND PROPAGATION: Use nursery-grown stock or freshly dug collected stock.

Divide offsets while dormant in spring or fall. Plant seeds as soon as they ripen. Seed germination is much slower than that of the early meadowrue. Often many of the seeds will not germinate until the second year.

COMMENTS: Tall meadowrue is a bold wildflower that commands attention wherever it grows. Plant it next to water where its beauty can be reflected. I grow it beside our pool with *Gentiana Saponaria* and *Lobelia Cardinalis*.

Anemonella thalictroides • rue anemone

DESCRIPTION: 4 to 6 inches tall. In late April, little red stems with folded rose-colored foliage appear through the leafmold. Shortly after some warm spring morning rain, clusters of flowers resembling the hepatica appear. They are held above a lacy spread of foliage resembling meadowrue. The flowers are fragile and come in shades of pink and white; their petals have a quality like fine china.

Rue anemone grows in protected woodlands in high open shade, often among other wildflowers.

PERIOD OF BLOOM: Early May into June. The flowers are long-lasting.

SOIL: Neutral to slightly acid soil, rich in humus.

LOCATION AND EXPOSURE: Open shade with filtered sunlight in a spot protected from strong winds. Plant rue anemone along a partly shaded path, in little colonies among small rocks, or with late wildflowers such as the showy lady's-slipper.

PLANTING TIME: Summer into late fall after the plants go dormant. Rue anemone can be transplanted in spring, even when in flower, but I prefer fall planting.

ROOT SYSTEM: A cluster of tubers resembling those of the dahlia in miniature.

PLANTING DEPTH AND SPACING: Plant tubers about 1 inch deep. Space 4 inches apart or plant closer together in small patches. Mulch with old marsh hay or with small leaves such as birch or willow. Oak leaves are too coarse and tend to smother the plants.

PLANTING STOCK AND PROPAGATION: Use nursery-grown stock.

Propagation may be by division of clusters after bloom, but this is a touchy job, as each tuber must have an eye.

Sow seeds as soon as they ripen; this requires close watching. Seedlings usually do not bloom until the third year.

COMMENTS: The flowering period of this dainty flower is four to six weeks. The plants then set seed and quickly become dormant. I marvel at the capacity of such small tubers to bloom so profusely over such a long period of time.

There is a double pink rue anemone known as Schaaf's double pink. It is lovely, and blossoms last a month.

Hepatica americana • hepatica

DESCRIPTION: 3 to 4 inches tall. In early spring, bouquets of single flowers with individual stems appear from the center of a clump of last year's foliage. The foliage is round-lobed and leathery, wine colored on the underside. The flowers are white or pastel shades of blue and purple. A pink color is the rarest. (I once found a pale yellow hepatica which never grew larger or set seed.) Colors vary with the pH of the soil. As the flowers fade, new furry leaves appear and soon grow to maturity.

In aspen and soft maple woodlands rich in leafmold, colonies of hepaticas suddenly appear in the spring morning sunlight. On cloudy days the flowers do not open. In my area hepaticas are also found on shady slopes, along streams, and in rocky terrain.

PERIOD OF BLOOM: Late April into May.

SOIL: Slightly acid, humus-rich soil is preferable, but I have found it growing nicely in sandy loam and in the black heavy soil of river bottoms.

LOCATION AND EXPOSURE: An excellent flower for open woodlands, or anywhere it is exposed to the morning sun. Hepaticas make a superior groundcover when grown in large colonies or among other wildflowers of equal height.

PLANTING TIME: Early spring or fall.

ROOT SYSTEM: Fibrous. Clumps enlarge with age.

PLANTING DEPTH AND SPACING: Space 8 to 12 inches apart. Plant the crowns at about soil level with the shoots just barely above the earth. Mulch with old straw or small leaves, tucking the mulch around and beneath the foliage. Later in the season (about October), scatter leaves or a little marsh hay to protect the foliage from freezing rain, especially if the bed is in a place where winter sunscald might occur. In spring, pull the mulch away from where the plants have sprouted, but leave some mulch between

the plants. The mulch can be used again later for the self-sowing process which follows.

PLANTING STOCK AND PROPAGATION: Use nursery-grown stock or quality collected stock.

Divide the clumps in fall, but you will find they are slow to increase. When dividing a clump, it is best to leave two or three buds in each division. Clumps can be moved with soil adhering right after blooming and before new leaves have completely developed. This method is the quickest way to establish a showy colony.

Sow the seeds in flats or in the open as soon as they ripen. Cover with a thin layer of old mulch. To promote self-sowing, wait until the plants have stopped blooming and the fruit has reached the stage where they start to bend the stems; new leaves will be little bundles of fuzz. Then cover the entire bed with a light dressing of marsh hay to discourage chipmunks from raiding the seed supply. A good sprinkling of water will settle the hay, and soon new leaves will sprout through the mulch. The seeds will fall into the old mulch, and in a few years the colony of hepaticas will be heavily populated with flowering plants. If thinning is necessary, some plants can be moved in the fall of the second or third year.

COMMENTS: Most hepaticas have eight petals, but occasionally you may find some with twelve to eighteen. I call these semi-doubles. There is a true double form, which is rare.

Hepatica acutiloba is identical with *Hepatica americana* except that the foliage lobes are acute instead of round. I have found the two growing in the same environment, which indicates that their growth requirements are the same.

Anemone canadensis • Canada anemone

DESCRIPTION: 1 to 2 feet tall. Pure white, single flowers with prominent golden centers are held above lanced foliage. The foliage is quite similar to that of the cranesbill geranium.

The Canada anemone is found in moist sunny meadows, along lakes and streams, and beside roadside ditches, often blanketing the whole area in glistening white.

PERIOD OF BLOOM: Late May into July if there is ample moisture.

SOIL: Reasonably fertile soil that is damp or has constant moisture. Otherwise it is adaptable and will spread readily to form colonies.

LOCATION AND EXPOSURE: The Canada anemone is best grown in moist sunny areas where it can spread without restriction. Full sun is preferable, but it will tolerate partial shade.

PLANTING TIME: While dormant in spring or fall. It can also be moved in spring when only a leaf or two has developed.

ROOT SYSTEM: Very slender, almost threadlike, dark rhizomes which often pause to send up several new crowns and then travel on to repeat the process. Rhizomes spread quickly under ideal conditions.

PLANTING DEPTH AND SPACING: Space the rhizomes 6 to 12 inches apart. Plant them not more than ½ inch deep with the eye at soil level. Mulch the area with weathered marsh hay, old straw, or leave bare to weed. Mulch helps to retain moisture in soil.

PLANTING STOCK AND PROPAGATION: Use nursery-grown stock or quality collected stock.

Divide matted clumps in spring or fall.

Each blossom produces a burrlike fruit. As soon as the seeds ripen, sow them in a flat or in a moist open area. Seedlings usually bloom the third year.

COMMENTS: Canada anemone is a vigorous grower and must be restricted in a small garden. Set a few plants in a bottomless gallon can and cut the fruit before the seeds ripen. The pure white blossoms complement the colors of other flowers in the wild garden.

Anemone quinquefolia • wood anemone

DESCRIPTION: 3 to 6 inches tall. The leaves of the wood anemone are thrice-divided and compound. A short stem bears a single flower, white inside, with outside color varying from rose to purple.

Wood anemone congregates in colonies in sheltered, open woods, often making a carpet of color.

PERIOD OF BLOOM: May into June.

SOIL: Slightly acid, rich woods soil. I have also grown it under a grape arbor where the garden soil was moderately fertile.

LOCATION AND EXPOSURE: The wood anemone is an ideal ground-cover mixed with taller flowers in an open shaded woods. This small flower should be grown in masses for best effect.

PLANTING TIME: Potted stock can be planted anytime during the growing season. Sods and bare rootstock should be planted very early in spring or in fall.

ROOT SYSTEM: A very brittle, cinnamon colored rhizome which forks and sends up new shoots.

PLANTING DEPTH AND SPACING: Space potted stock 6 inches apart, setting the pot at soil level. Sods should be planted at the same level and spaced 1 foot apart. Bareroot stock should be planted 1 inch deep and 4 to 6 inches apart. All should be mulched with an airy mulch to a depth of an inch or so.

PLANTING STOCK AND PROPAGATION: Nursery-grown potted stock is best.

Seeds ripen quickly and when sown immediately after ripening will produce flowering plants in three or sometimes four years. The blossoms produce burrlike fruit similar to but smaller than those of the Canada anemone.

COMMENTS: This delicate little plant is very persistent. Where we cleared an area of woodland to add to our lawn, the wood anemone continued to appear despite frequent mowing.

Anemone patens • pasque flower

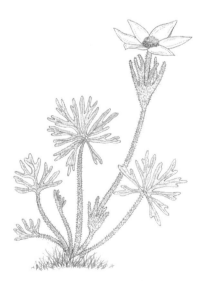

DESCRIPTION: 4 to 6 inches tall. This variety of the pasque flower (*Wolfgangiana*) has a large, single, lavender-blue flower at the top of the foliage. The color may vary; creamy white ones are rare. The foliage is divided, heavily cut, and mostly basal—often there is one small leaf on each stalk. The flowers are soon replaced by a silky plume which bears the seed and quickly disappears.

The pasque flower inhabits dry prairies and sunny slopes where it carpets the earth with color.

PERIOD OF BLOOM: April into May.

SOIL: A neutral or sandy, slightly fertile loam is ideal. Moisture is important at time of bloom, but the plant can stand considerable drought thereafter.

LOCATION AND EXPOSURE: Grow the pasque flower in open areas

where a splash of early spring color is desired. Good drainage is important.

PLANTING TIME: While dormant in very early spring or fall.

ROOT SYSTEM: A vigorous diffused root system in which many of the fibrous roots become fleshy and send out secondary roots in search of food. All pieces of root more than ⅛ inch in diameter left in the ground will produce new plants.

PLANTING DEPTH AND SPACING: Space 1 to 2 feet apart or plant at random among scattered old rocks in a prairie area. Set the plants with the crown 1 inch deep in very cold climates to protect them from alternate thawing and freezing in spring. It is best to mulch for winter.

PLANTING STOCK AND PROPAGATION: Use nursery-grown stock. Quality collected stock also does well, but pasque flower is on the protected list in most areas.

Two-inch root cuttings give quick results for propagation. Insert the cuttings in a rooting medium and keep them slightly moist. Divide large plants in very early spring.

Seeds sown in spring germinate readily. Transplant the seedlings to their permanent location the following spring. The seedlings will bloom the spring after they have been moved and will quickly grow to maturity.

COMMENTS: Prairie smoke is a good companion for the pasque flower, as it will grow under the same conditions. The two contrast well in foliage and flower, and make an interesting display. Goldfinches steal the seeds of both species before they ripen. Cover the silky plumes with wire cages to protect the seed crop.

Anemone pulsatilla • pasque flower

DESCRIPTION: 8 to 10 inches tall. The flower stalks are raised above a carpet of much-divided basal foliage. *Anemone patens* and *Anemone pulsatilla* are often spoken of as the same plant, but there is a considerable difference when they are seen growing side by side. The foliage of the latter is silkier when emerging in spring, the flowers are deeper in color, the bloom period is longer, and the silky plumes are showier and last longer. The flowers of the *Anemone pulsatilla* range from purple-blue to wine-purple and from lavender to creamy white. Flowers and silky plumes appear on the plant at the same time. The white flowers have greenish plumes; the colored flowers have plumes with a hint of purple.

The *Anemone pulsatilla*, like *Anemone patens*, grows in dry prairies and sunny exposed slopes, carpeting the earth with color.

PERIOD OF BLOOM: April into June. When cultivated, the plant occasionally sends up a blossom at any time during the summer.

SOIL: Use either a gritty or a sandy loam soil that is fertile. Good drainage is important. Established plants can stand drought.

LOCATION AND EXPOSURE: This pasque flower is an excellent plant to use for edging along a sunny border. The foliage is good throughout the summer and into fall. Each spring the flowers burst into glorious bloom, and the silky plumes last long into summer.

PLANTING TIME: While dormant in very early spring or fall.

ROOT SYSTEM: A vigorous diffused root system. Many of the fibrous roots become fleshy and send out secondary roots in search of nutrients. All root pieces more than ⅛ inch in diameter left in the ground produce new plants.

PLANTING DEPTH AND SPACING: Space 1 to 2 feet apart, depending on the desired effect. Set the plants with the crowns 1 to 2 inches deep, depending on the size of the plant. This protects the plants from alternate thawing and freezing in spring. I find that no mulch is needed when they are planted in spring.

PLANTING STOCK AND PROPAGATION: Nursery-grown stock of medium size is best and easiest to transplant. Also use quality collected stock when it is available, but this pasque flower is on the protected list.

To propagate, 2 inch root cuttings give quick results. You can divide large plants in spring, but I get better results by planting seedlings.

Seeds sown in spring germinate readily. Transplant the seedlings after one year. They will bloom the second year and rapidly become showy specimens.

COMMENTS: The pasque flower is one of the earliest spring flowers. Every gardener will want this choice plant with its vibrant colors and silky plumes. Goldfinches and other birds are attracted by the ripening plumes.

Caltha palustris • marsh marigold

DESCRIPTION: 12 to 18 inches tall. The marsh marigold has lightly toothed round basal foliage, hollow stems, and single, glistening yellow flowers with showy centers.

Marsh marigold is found growing along brooks, in roadside ditches with standing water, in swamps, and in sunny meadows. In spring it transforms large areas into patches of gold, but by midsummer the plant has almost disappeared.

PERIOD OF BLOOM: May.

SOIL: Use very fertile slightly acid or neutral soil that is wet or has constant moisture. The marsh marigold will grow in drier areas if enough water is supplied during the growing period.

LOCATION AND EXPOSURE: Full sun or high open shade. The marsh marigold is a fine plant for naturalizing along a brook or near a pool. Always grow it with other plants that retain their foliage. Use a mulch if you are growing the plant in an exposed area.

PLANTING TIME: After spring blooms; the plant will remain dormant into fall.

ROOT SYSTEM: An extensive, very coarse and fibrous, stringy root.

PLANTING DEPTH AND SPACING: Space 1 to 2 feet apart. Spread the roots evenly with the crown set at soil level.

PLANTING STOCK AND PROPAGATION: Use nursery-grown or quality collected stock.

Divide clumps after the plants bloom. As soon as seeds ripen, sow them in a wet place or in a container where the soil can be kept moist. Seedlings sometimes bloom the second year.

COMMENTS: Surprisingly, one rarely sees the pretty marsh marigold growing in the wildflower garden. Its color makes an interesting contrast with other spring wildflowers. It is also known as the cowslip, and is often gathered as a pot herb.

Coptis groenlandica • goldthread

DESCRIPTION: 3 to 4 inches tall. The evergreen foliage of the goldthread is toothed, thrice-parted and glossy. It resembles the barren strawberry. The plant has wiry stems holding dainty single white flowers just above the foliage.

97

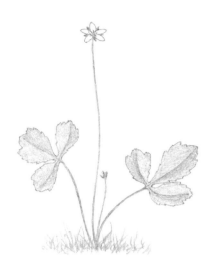

I have seen goldthread literally carpet the floor of evergreen forests. In late autumn the evergreen needles form a light blanket to protect the plants against inclement winter weather. It grows among bunchberry, pink lady's-slipper, wintergreen, and clintonia.

PERIOD OF BLOOM: May into June.

SOIL: Acid to slightly acid humus-rich soil that is wet to slightly damp.

LOCATION AND EXPOSURE: Open or deep shade. Goldthread is an excellent groundcover; it forms a carpet of glossy green.

PLANTING TIME: Spring or fall. Plant potted stock anytime.

ROOT SYSTEM: A dainty, threadlike, creeping rhizome with fine, sparse hair roots. It is bright yellow and forks at frequent intervals. It is easily identified.

PLANTING DEPTH AND SPACING: Set potted stock or collected stock at soil level and mulch lightly, preferably with pine needles. Space in small colonies a few inches apart or plant at random.

PLANTING STOCK AND PROPAGATION: Nursery-grown potted stock is much the best, but you can also use quality collected sods. Bareroot stock dries out too quickly.

Seeds are hard to collect. Sow them in acid to slightly acid soil that can be kept moist.

COMMENTS: Goldthread is a most unusual and admirable groundcover to use with larger plants that grow in acid to slightly acid soils. It can be used as an extensive carpeting under evergreens, where grass cannot grow. Goldthread is an outstanding plant, one of my favorites.

Aquilegia canadensis • wild columbine

DESCRIPTION: 2 to 3 feet tall. Drooping flowers have yellow and scarlet corollas. The coarsely divided compound foliage is mostly basal.

In rough, rocky terrain you will find wild columbine growing at odd angles, sometimes precariously perched among rocks where soil is scarce, but its roots reach deep into the earth. It is also found along the borders of open woods or along roadsides.

PERIOD OF BLOOM: May into June.

soil: Any slightly acid to neutral soil with good drainage. Sandy loam is preferable.

location and exposure: Columbine grows readily at the edge of a woodland or a partly shaded hillside. It is equally at home in the rock garden, or in a sunny border with other flowers. Plant the columbine where you want it to stay, as old roots do not move readily.

planting time: Early spring (before the new growth is 1 inch high), or in fall while dormant.

root system: A fleshy, brittle root, gray to black. Large crowns do not divide readily and have a tendency to be short-lived when divided.

planting depth and spacing: Space 1 to 2 feet apart and set crowns at soil level. In the rock garden, place some rocks over the root area after planting.

planting stock and propagation: Young nursery-grown stock is far superior to collected stock. If you use collected stock, it must be young, as old roots are too gnarled to be moved successfully.

Seeds sown in the garden or in flats produce seedlings that bloom in the second year. Sow the seeds as soon as they are ripe or in fall. Columbine self-sows readily when growing where the earth is bare.

comments: Our native columbine is an easy wildflower to grow, and one of outstanding beauty. When the blossoms sway in a breeze they call to mind a group of skirted elves dancing to the music of rustling leaves. For a charming effect, try growing columbine in a rocky outcropping near a pool where it can be reflected in the water.

Cimicifuga americana • American bugbane

description: 2 to 4 feet tall. American bugbane is similar to its sister plant, black cohosh, but it blooms later. It is a bold perennial with a few compound leaves on a long stalk. Its slender wand of creamy white flowers has a feathery elegance.

Bugbane is found in moist rock woods. Although its natural range is farther south and east, it has proved hardy in Wisconsin despite our bitter cold winters.

PERIOD OF BLOOM: Late August into September and often into October if not injured by frosts.

SOIL: Neutral to slightly acid soil rich in humus and with constant moisture.

LOCATION AND EXPOSURE: Grow bugbane in high shade or along a woods border where it can get only a small amount of morning sunlight. This species can be grown in full sunlight if the soil is rather moist. In areas where frost comes early, it is best planted in a sheltered spot near a foundation.

PLANTING TIME: While dormant in spring or fall.

ROOT SYSTEM: A knotted rootstock with wiry fibrous roots which develop new shoots with age.

PLANTING DEPTH AND SPACING: Space 2 feet or more apart. Spread the roots carefully so that new shoots will be about 1 inch below soil level. Mulch continuously. Bugbane is a good plant for specimen display when planted among rocks where leafmold is deep.

PLANTING STOCK AND PROPAGATION: Nursery-grown stock is much the best, but you can also use quality collected stock where available.

Divide clumps in spring or fall while the plant is dormant. Sow seeds as soon as they ripen. Seeds do not ripen as far north as Wisconsin.

COMMENTS: The white spires are lovely in autumn when few white flowers are blooming. This species blooms about the same time as the cultivated bugbanes offered as perennials under the names of *Cimicifuga simplex* and white pearl. There is a slight difference in foliage.

Cimicifuga racemosa • black cohosh

DESCRIPTION: 3 to 5 feet tall. The black cohosh has ample green foliage with much-divided leaves. Feathery racemes of tiny white flowers grow on tall wands.

Black cohosh is found in deep woodlands and along the borders or woods where the shade is open and the soil is humus-rich. I have also found it growing in river bottoms with *Trillium grandiflorum*, wild ginger, and patches of maidenhair fern. It grows very tall in shaded moist areas where the soil is deep.

PERIOD OF BLOOM: July into August.

SOIL: Fertile, acid to slightly acid humus-rich with an average-to-high moisture content. Good drainage is necessary.

LOCATION AND EXPOSURE: Black cohosh is best suited to a woodland garden in deep shade where branches are high overhead, or to a lightly shaded border. If exposed to sunlight for several hours a day, the white spires will be crooked and grow haphazardly instead of in a stately fashion. Black cohosh is striking when grown with a background of tall ferns among large rocks where humus is plentiful and mulch gathers each fall.

PLANTING TIME: While dormant in spring or fall. Plant black cohosh where you want it to remain, as it resists transplanting and usually does not bloom until the second or third year after being moved.

ROOT SYSTEM: A very knotted rhizome developing many eyes with age. Some of the rhizomes elongate and establish new plants.

PLANTING DEPTH AND SPACING: Space 2 to 4 feet apart. Set the plants with eyes 1 to 1½ inches below soil level. Mulch with leaves or other partly decayed humus. It requires a rich soil.

PLANTING STOCK AND PROPAGATION: Nursery stock is best because the plants have a heavier root system, but you can also use quality collected stock.

Divide the clumps, leaving two or more eyes in each division. Sow seeds in rich woodland soil as they ripen. Germination is slow and uneven. Seedlings usually do not bloom until the fourth year.

COMMENTS: Block cohosh is a bold wildflower, wonderful for the woodland garden or border. Its long-lasting spires are a welcome sight on hot summer days. But do not plant black cohosh where its oversweet odor will be offensive.

The beadlike wands which develop in the seed stage are excellent for dry floral arrangements. In my area black cohosh is known as fairy candles, which I think is a more appropriate name.

Actaea rubra • red baneberry

DESCRIPTION: 1½ to 2 feet tall. The red baneberry has compound toothed foliage and white flower clusters made up of many tiny flowers. A cluster of brilliant red, shiny berries appears in August and September.

101

The baneberry is found in rich woods where leafmold is deep and often where other wildflowers carpet the forest floor.

PERIOD OF BLOOM: Late May into June.

SOIL: Slightly acid, rich woods soil that is humus-rich and does not dry out.

LOCATION AND EXPOSURE: Plant under high branches where shade is open to deep. Baneberry contrasts well with royal, cinnamon, and maidenhair ferns or with white baneberries.

PLANTING TIME: While dormant in spring or fall.

ROOT SYSTEM: Coarse fibrous roots on a rootstock that develops many eyes with age.

PLANTING DEPTH AND SPACING: Plant the rootstock with eyes or new shoots about 1 inch below soil level. Mulch with leaves, old straw, or weathered marsh hay. Space 1½ to 2 feet apart or plant at odd intervals.

PLANTING STOCK AND PROPAGATION: Nursery-grown stock has a superior root system. Quality collected stock should have strong eyes.

If you divide clumps, leave two or more eyes in each division. Sow the seeds as soon as they ripen, as old seeds often remain dormant for over a year before germinating. Fresh seeds planted in fall should germinate the following spring. The seed bed must never dry out. Seedlings often bloom in the third year.

COMMENTS: All baneberry fruits are poisonous. The chipmunks steal the seeds and plant them, but I do not know if they eat any.

Actaea pachypoda • white baneberry

DESCRIPTION: About 2 feet tall. Each stalk bears a single white oblong flower cluster above toothed compound foliage. This flower head is replaced by a cluster of china white berries, each with a conspicuous black eye on a showy red stem, hence the common name "doll's eyes."

Red and white baneberries are often found growing together in rich woods in deep to moderate shade. But when growing alone, the white baneberry is usually found in a drier woodland.

PERIOD OF BLOOM: Flowers, late May into June. Berries, August into September.

SOIL: Slightly acid humus-rich soil. It must not dry out completely or the plant will become dormant that year.

LOCATION AND EXPOSURE: Baneberries must have some shade or their foliage will burn. Light to deep shade under high branches is ideal. Grow baneberries in groups of three or interplant them with ferns. Bloodroot will make nice carpeting in such an area if there is constant moisture.

PLANTING TIME: While dormant in spring or fall.

ROOT SYSTEM: Coarse fibrous roots on a rootstock that develops many new eyes with age. Old rootstocks show scars of previous growth.

PLANTING DEPTH AND SPACING: Space about 2 feet apart. Plant the roots with new shoots or eyes about 1 inch below soil level and mulch. For an outstanding effect, place several plants or a single large one in a shaded opening.

PLANTING STOCK AND PROPAGATION: Nursery-grown stock is best. Choose quality collected stock with prominent eyes.

Divide large clumps, leaving several eyes to each division.

Sow pulp-free seeds as soon as they ripen. The white baneberry seems to be slower to germinate than the red. Seedlings usually bloom the third year.

COMMENTS: The berries of the white baneberry are very attractive and provide a focal point in the wild garden. Occasionally the baneberries form hybrids. I have had several unusual white ones. A white baneberry seedling has pink berries, but the black eyes are missing. Another seedling has the doll's-eyes berries but is set apart from the others by its foliage, which is coarser, not quilted, and has a definite cast of blue-green.

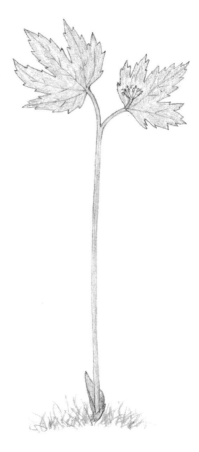

Hydrastis canadensis • golden seal

DESCRIPTION: 6 to 12 inches tall. Golden seal looks something like a maple seedling, but is distinguished by a greenish white globelike flower head, a red-berried seed cluster in fall, and heavily veined leaves which have deeper lobes than those of the maple.

Golden seal is occasionally found in rich maple hardwoods and often in the company of ginseng. The plant is becoming very scarce in the wild.

PERIOD OF BLOOM: May.

SOIL: Humus-rich woods soil that is neutral to only slightly acid.

LOCATION AND EXPOSURE: Light to deep open shade. Golden seal is a good plant for the cool woodland garden where it can be planted in little colonies for a unique display.

PLANTING TIME: Early spring or fall, but with care golden seal can be moved earlier or later.

ROOT SYSTEM: A knotty yellow rhizome with many fibrous roots.

PLANTING DEPTH AND SPACING: Space 6 to 10 inches apart, preferably in little groups. Plant the rhizome ½ to 1 inch deep, depending on the size of the plant.

PLANTING STOCK AND PROPAGATION: Use nursery-grown stock. Quality collected stock is rare because golden seal has been ruthlessly dug up by collectors for its medicinal value.

To propagate by division, divide the rhizomes when the plant is dormant. To grow from seed, pick the berry as soon as it turns scarlet and separate the seeds from the pulp. Sow the seeds in a selected spot where the loose leafmold has been raked to one side. Cover lightly. The seeds will stratify by themselves. Keep the bed moist at all times. Germination can be slow unless conditions are ideal.

To grow by layering, cut the roots into ¼ to ½ inch pieces, leaving the fine hair-roots intact. Put the cuttings in a box in layers with a mixture of sandy loam and sharp sand separating them. Keep them moist but not wet. Put the box in a frost-free place or in the basement over winter. Most pieces will have new plants in about six months. Cuttings put down in November are ready to plant in the open in early spring. Set the new plants barely ½ inch deep and mulch lightly, preferably with leafmold or with old decaying mulch.

My own method is to cut the roots up into pieces of ¼ to ½ inch and layer them in damp sphagnum moss in a plastic bag. I tie the bag and put it in the well pit, which is frost-free. In spring, most of the cuttings are ready to plant. New plants are formed on the cuttings. I get very good results.

COMMENTS: Golden seal derives its name from the golden color of its roots. At one time it was grown commercially in some areas of Wisconsin for its medicinal value as an alterative and tonic.

BERBERIDACEAE [Barberry Family]

Jeffersonia diphylla • twinleaf

DESCRIPTION: 8 to 10 inches tall. A single white hepaticalike flower which is short-lived and produces yellow-green seed capsules with green "lids." The flower rests on a stalk with two leaves rising from the base. Each leaf is like a pair of outstretched bird's wings. After the flower withers both the foliage and the stalk continue to grow, hiding the seed capsule.

Twinleaf is found in open deciduous woods where the soil is humus-rich. It is not found in my immediate area of Wisconsin.

PERIOD OF BLOOM: May into June.

SOIL: Neutral to moderately acid soil with an abundance of humus.

LOCATION AND EXPOSURE: Grow twinleaf in partial to open shade, or plant in colonies like hepaticas. The foliage makes an excellent contrast with other plants.

PLANTING TIME: While dormant in spring or fall.

ROOT SYSTEM: A heavy rootstock with many coarse, fibrous, slightly wavy roots that are light tan.

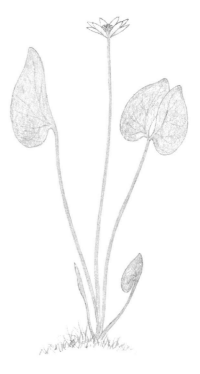

PLANTING DEPTH AND SPACING: Space 6 to 8 inches apart when planted among groundcover or in colonies. Or plant at random to accent the foliage.

PLANTING STOCK AND PROPAGATION: Nursery-grown stock is huskier, but also use quality collected stock.

Divide clumps in fall. Sow seeds as soon as they ripen. Seedlings are slow to reach the flowering stage.

COMMENTS: Twinleaf is grown for its interesting foliage. The leaves resemble a pair of bird's wings poised for flight.

The seeds form in rows in a capsule shaped like a miniature inverted pear. The top of the capsule has a flap like a coin purse horizontally zipped. It is a unique plant.

Caulophyllum thalictroides • blue cohosh

DESCRIPTION: 1 to 3 feet tall. Tiny flowers in drooping clusters grow above coarsely cut blue-green foliage with blunt lobes. The flowers are green to greenish yellow, often with a red tinge. In August, striking, bright blue berries and white blooms vie for attention.

Blue cohosh is found growing in rich, rocky woods and well-drained river bottoms, usually with red baneberry, black cohosh, and *Trillium grandiflorum* under a canopy of soft maples, basswoods or elms.

PERIOD OF BLOOM: May.

SOIL: Neutral to slightly acid fertile soil with a moderate supply of constant moisture. Blue cohosh will also grow in drier woods with a good mulching to retain moisture.

LOCATION AND EXPOSURE: Light to deep high shade. You can alternate blue cohosh with mertensia to fill in the bare spots when mertensia becomes dormant. The foliage contrasts well with tall ferns. When grown with red baneberry, the colors of the berries contrast strikingly.

PLANTING TIME: While dormant in spring or fall; fall is preferable.

ROOT SYSTEM: A sturdy, angled rootstock with coarse, slightly wavy, fibrous roots. It develops many eyes with age.

PLANTING DEPTH AND SPACING: Space 1½ or more feet apart. The plant forms a clump with age, becoming very showy. Spread the roots carefully when planting and have the new shoots about 1 inch below soil level. Keep covered with a mulch of leaves or decaying straw.

PLANTING STOCK AND PROPAGATION: Nursery-grown stock has a better developed root system than collected stock, but also use freshly dug collected stock.

Divide clumps, leaving two to three eyes in each division. Plant the seeds as soon as they ripen in humus-rich woods soil kept constantly moist. Often two to four years pass before the seeds germinate, but the process can be hastened by filing a nick in each seed. Seedlings often commence blooming the third year.

COMMENTS: The blue berries and the handsome foliage of the blue cohosh provide a fine contrast with other plants, and will enhance the beauty and charm of any shaded area in a wildflower garden.

106

Podophyllum peltatum • mayapple

DESCRIPTION: 12 to 18 inches tall. Two umbrella-shaped, round-lobed leaves hide a single creamy-white waxy flower on a solitary stalk. The flower has a lovely fragrance and produces yellow fruit in August, which is edible.

Mayapples carpet large areas under deciduous trees in moist open woods. They also grow in thickets and in dense shade, though not as abundantly.

PERIOD OF BLOOM: Late May into June.

SOIL: Neutral to slightly acid soil very rich in humus or leafmold.

LOCATION AND EXPOSURE: Mayapple blooms more often when planted in open shade, but it will also grow in denser shade where the woods are cool. I find that it is best grown in colonies where it carpets forest floors under a canopy of deciduous trees. Or try planting it randomly in a rocky woodland for a most unusual effect. It grows vigorously and makes an excellent groundcover for large shady areas.

To enjoy mayapple in a small garden it is best to restrict it to a limited area. Plant one or two rhizomes in a bottomless gallon can sunk at soil level; when the plants begin to crowd the container, remove all the rhizomes and start anew.

PLANTING TIME: Fall is preferred.

PLANTING DEPTH AND SPACING: Set the stocky horizontal rhizome about 1 to 1½ inches deep with the tip leading to soil level. Space 1 foot or more apart.

ROOT SYSTEM: The rhizome is coarse, about as thick as a lead pencil, and pale tan in color. It pauses often to fork and send up new growth.

PLANTING STOCK AND PROPAGATION: Nursery-grown stock is best. If you buy collected stock make certain that the rhizome has an eye and is not just a piece.

Sow seeds in autumn. I have had little luck growing it from seed and find that root division in fall is easiest.

COMMENTS: Mayapples are best grown in spacious, shaded woodlands. The fruit was once popular in traditional American cooking; the rootstock is poisonous.

PAPAVERACEAE [Poppy Family]

Sanguinaria canadensis • bloodroot

DESCRIPTION: 6 to 9 inches tall. A starlike, fragile blossom with 8 petals rests on a solitary stem. This short-lived flower is white with a yellow center. There is a rare double form and also a semidouble. The large, deeply lobed leaves are pale green with lighter green underneath.

Bloodroot is found in rich woods or in thickets on river bottoms where the leafmold is deep. It frequently grows in the vicinity of *Trillium grandiflorum*.

PERIOD OF BLOOM: Late April into May, depending on when spring arrives and whether there is enough filtered sunlight to warm the ground.

SOIL: The pH is not important, but good humus content and moisture are necessary.

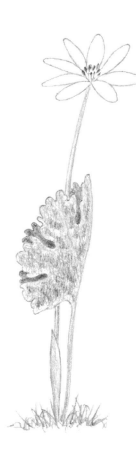

LOCATION AND EXPOSURE: Bloodroot grows best in a sheltered woodland where spring sunshine filters through leafless trees, and where it will later be protected from the strong summer sun. After blooming, the leaves continue to develop and make good groundcover for large areas that do not dry out. In dry woodlands bloodroot becomes dormant in August. Interplant in colonies with clumps of maidenhair fern for continuous groundcover.

PLANTING TIME: Fall planting is preferable, but bloodroot can be moved in spring if growth is not too far advanced.

ROOT SYSTEM: A forking salmon-colored rhizome that oozes red juice when broken, hence the name bloodroot.

PLANTING DEPTH AND SPACING: Space 6 inches or more apart. Plant the rhizome horizontally ½ to 1 inch deep with the budded tip leading to soil level. Mulch continually with decaying leaves or old straw.

PLANTING STOCK AND PROPAGATION: Multiple-crown nursery stock gives the best results, even blooming the first year after transplanting. Also use quality collected stock.

Divide crowded rhizomes. Seeds must be sown as soon as they are harvested, before the caruncle (the little white attached portion) has a chance to dry out. If the caruncle dries out, the seed will stay dormant for a year. This is true of all seeds having caruncles.

Seedlings often bloom the third year.

COMMENTS: The very rare double white form, which does not set seed, was first found in the wilds of lower Michigan and was taken to the Netherlands where it is now grown for export to the United States. Like its single-petaled kin, the double blood-root flower closes each sundown, its petals resembling hands folded in prayer. The white peonylike flowers last about a week and then quickly disappear.

Stylophorum diphyllum • celandine poppy

DESCRIPTION: 10 to 15 inches tall. A showy, deep yellow flower with four petals is supported by a slender, leafy stem. The gray-green oblong foliage is mostly basal and unevenly lobed. The seed pod is oblong, with a rough outer cover and droops on the stem.

Celandine poppy inhabits rich woods where the soil is fertile and damp in spring.

PERIOD OF BLOOM: May into June. The plants produce an occasional flower at any time during the summer if they are grown in a reasonably damp area and do not dry out.

SOIL: Fertile soil, preferably rich in humus, that does not dry out completely. The plant can also be grown in fertile garden soil with constant moisture.

LOCATION AND EXPOSURE: Plant celandine poppy in a woodland garden in very high open shade, or where the sun filters through leaves in early spring. I find that it grows equally well in an open garden with full sun and fertile soil. When grown in the open, the plants should be mulched where winters are severe.

For an outstanding effect, grow celandine poppy in groups of three or more, or intersperse with other woodland plants such as mertensia, trilliums, and medium-sized ferns—especially maidenhair fern for foliage contrast.

PLANTING TIME: While dormant in spring or fall.

ROOT SYSTEM: A pinkish to salmon-colored, brittle rhizome which, like bloodroot, oozes an orange juice.

PLANTING DEPTH AND SPACING: Space the fleshy rhizomes 8 to 12 inches apart or farther if you wish them to develop into showy clumps. Set with the eye 1 inch below soil level and mulch.

PLANTING STOCK AND PROPAGATION: Nursery-grown stock is huskier than collected stock and develops into a showy specimen sooner. Quality collected stock must have strong eyes.

Divide large rhizomes with many eyes, leaving two eyes in each division. Growth may be quite slow. Seeds must be sown as soon as they ripen; they bear a caruncle which must not dry out. Seeds germinate readily the following spring, and seedlings usually bloom the second year. Guard the seeds closely, as chipmunks are very fond of them.

COMMENTS: The gray-green lobed foliage of the celandine poppy makes a unique contrast with other wildflowers.

Dicentra Cucullaria • Dutchman's-breeches

DESCRIPTION: 6 to 10 inches tall. Snow-white to pinkish flowers (occasionally a delicate pink one is found in a colony) hang like pantaloons on arched stems. The foliage is a delicate green and fernlike.

Dutchman's-breeches grows in large colonies, literally carpeting the floor of rich deciduous woods where the leafmold is deep. Usually other vegetation is sparse while these flowers are in full bloom.

PERIOD OF BLOOM: Late April into May.

SOIL: Neutral to slightly acid soil rich in humus. Like all members of the fumitory family, they require rich soil. In fertile woodland soil the plants will bloom profusely.

LOCATION AND EXPOSURE: Grow Dutchman's-breeches in open shade where filtered sunshine can warm the earth in early spring. For a good display, always plant them in groups or in small colonies among other wildflowers like tall white snakeroot or citronella that will bloom much later and grow only slightly in early spring. Maidenhair fern can also be scattered among the colonies to give a lovely effect later in the season when the Dutchman's-breeches become dormant.

PLANTING TIME: Plant anytime after dormancy into late fall.

Spring transplanting is not advisable; the plants begin to sprout as soon as the frost leaves the ground.

ROOT SYSTEM: A small scaly bulb with white fibrous roots. Each bulb is made up of many tiny white or pink kernels. Usually only one or two of the larger bulblets in a cluster contain the internal flower bud which produces the next year's display.

PLANTING DEPTH AND SPACING: Space 4 to 6 inches apart in colonies. Set the bulbs about 1 to 1½ inches deep and mulch with small leaves, old straw, or marsh hay. The bulbs multiply to form clumps.

PLANTING STOCK AND PROPAGATION: Use nursery-grown or quality collected stock with all the kernels intact and forming a compact bulblet (or bulb).

To divide the bulbs, break the tiny kernels from the main bulblet and plant them only about ½ inch deep. Mulch with a light layer of old straw or small leaves. Several years will elapse before these bulblets bloom.

Use the seeds if you catch them in time. Sow them in flats as soon as they ripen, and keep them moderately moist. Mulch the flats lightly. Seedlings may appear slowly, often continuing to emerge throughout the second year. Planting seeds is a slower process than dividing mature bulbs. You can expect some self-sowing.

COMMENTS: Often sizable colonies of Dutchman's-breeches carpet large areas under tall hardwoods where filtered sunlight makes a dappled pattern on their foliage. Here they look like countless pantaloons hung very carefully upside down.

In my woodland garden, where the plants are mulched, I find that I can grow vigorous and beautiful Dutchman's-breeches. Plants do not usually reach their peak until the third year after transplanting.

Dicentra canadensis • squirrel corn

DESCRIPTION: 6 to 10 inches tall. The foliage of the squirrel corn is smooth, blue-gray, and fernlike. The flowers are dainty broad hearts; they are fragrant and pinkish white, sometimes with a pale lavender tint.

Squirrel corn is often found with Dutchman's-breeches in open deciduous woods where leafmold is deep.

PERIOD OF BLOOM: May.

SOIL: Slightly acid humus-rich soil or a neutral soil rich in leaf-mold.

LOCATION AND EXPOSURE: Grow squirrel corn in open woodland where the spring sun filters through leafless trees. Plants become dormant soon after they bloom and should be planted in colonies with later-blooming small plants to keep the woodland floor from looking bare later in the season. Moneywort is an excellent groundcover to use with squirrel corn.

PLANTING TIME: The tiny tubers are best planted after dormancy and into late fall.

ROOT SYSTEM: The tiny tubers look very much like several small yellow peas linked together with a white string. In fall, each tuber sends out tiny white fibrous roots.

PLANTING DEPTH AND SPACING: Plant the tubers 2 inches deep in groups of 3 or more, or in small colonies. Mulch. If you have trouble with rodents stealing the tubers, cover the planted area with ½ inch mesh galvanized wire before mulching; the plants will grow through the wire the next season. Chipmunks love to transplant squirrel corn.

PLANTING STOCK AND PROPAGATION: Use nursery-grown stock or quality collected stock.

The seeds should be sown as soon as they ripen, but it is difficult to catch them before they disperse. They self-sow very readily.

COMMENTS: Mice and chipmunks are adept at carrying away the tubers and planting them elsewhere. Covering the beds with wire mesh before mulching has discouraged further raiding of our beds, and our squirrel corn now grows in lovely colonies each season.

Dicentra eximia • pink bleeding heart

DESCRIPTION: 12 to 20 inches tall. The pink bleeding heart has the familiar cluster of heart-shaped flowers drooping on arched stems. The foliage is green and fernlike. Usually rose-pink, the flowers occasionally have a hint of lavender. The color depends mostly on the amount of sunlight available and soil fertility. Catalogs frequently call this the fern-leafed bleeding heart.

The bleeding heart is usually found in rocky woods with humus-rich soil. Although not a native of Wisconsin, it withstands our severe climate very well.

PERIOD OF BLOOM: Flower buds appear with the first spring foliage, and the plant continues to bloom until the first killing frost. It is one of our longest-blooming wildflowers. If there is heavy rainfall in June and July, this flower often blooms sparsely in August but perks up again in September.

SOIL: Garden or woods soil is suitable.

LOCATION AND EXPOSURE: Pink bleeding heart blooms profusely in high open shade or preferably in full sun. It is also an excellent groundcover under tall, sparsely planted trees where the soil is fertile.

PLANTING TIME: Early spring, late summer, or very early fall.

ROOT SYSTEM: A coarse fibrous rootstock that forms a clump as it grows new eyes for the next year's growth.

PLANTING DEPTH AND SPACING: Space 2 feet apart in fertile soil. Dig a fairly good-sized hole, and plant so that the top pink eyes will be about 1 inch below soil level. Mulch if grown in open shade.

PLANTING STOCK AND PROPAGATION: Use nursery-grown or quality collected stock.

When dividing old rootstocks and old crowns make certain that each plant has at least three strong pink eyes in each division. The old crowns die as they finish blooming and new ones take over each year. To keep the plants growing vigorously, divide them every second or third year, otherwise the dead growth will choke the new eyes as they form. This is very important if you want your bleeding hearts to bloom continuously.

Seeds should be sown as soon as they have been picked, otherwise the caruncle will dry out and the seeds will not germinate until the second spring. Seedlings are very delicate at first and should not be transferred to their permanent home until late July or the following spring.

COMMENTS: Bonemeal and a complete fertilizer (10-10-10) worked into the soil a few inches from the plant in spring and again in midsummer will assure continuous bloom throughout the growing season.

Dicentra formosa • western bleeding heart

DESCRIPTION: 6 to 10 inches tall. Pink heart-shaped flowers flushed with lavender are attached to leafless stems in drooping clusters. The foliage is fernlike. There is a pure white variety known as white sweetheart. Its foliage is fernlike, but paler green in color.

Western bleeding heart is native to western states and southwest Canada. In high cool shade it carpets the ground, displaying its lovely hearts.

PERIOD OF BLOOM: Late May until killing frosts.

SOIL: Slightly acid, humus-rich woods soil that is fertile to a good depth and has constant moisture. Both the pink and the white form need a plentiful supply of organic matter and must be kept mulched with decaying humus.

LOCATION AND EXPOSURE: A cool shady nook protected from the heat of the sun is ideal for bleeding heart. This delightful plant is an excellent groundcover for rich woodlands, where decaying humus and vegetation have made a deep bed of humus-rich soil. In cold climates the western bleeding heart should be heavily mulched with old marsh hay or small leaves during the winter. Remove some of this mulch in spring at about the time when the frost leaves the ground.

PLANTING TIME: Late May when the plants have just begun to grow or when potted stock has shown its first buds.

ROOT SYSTEM: Extensive, very brittle rhizomes that fork and spread to establish colonies. The rootstock spreads at soil level beneath the damp old mulch, sending its feeder roots into the earth. Bleeding heart must have a heavy mulch of decaying old straw, marsh hay, or fine leaves if it is to prosper. The decaying organic matter also helps retain the needed moisture.

PLANTING DEPTH AND SPACING: Bareroot stock should be planted ½ to 1 inch deep with the new shoot leading to soil level. Insert pot-grown nursery stock at soil level. Mulch.

PLANTING STOCK AND PROPAGATION: Pot-grown nursery stock is much the best; collected stock should have a considerable quantity of roots at the rhizome joints.

Rhizomes planted vertically in 2 inch wet peat pots with the eye at soil level will produce small plants that bloom quite well the following year. Potted stock should be kept in an uncovered cold frame over the winter and mulched heavily.

COMMENTS: In cold climates like my own, where the temperature occasionally dips to −35 degrees in winter, it is important to mulch the plants carefully. The pink species seems a little hardier than the white.

Corydalis bulbosa · purple corydalis

DESCRIPTION: 4 to 6 inches tall. Rosy-purple flower clusters are held on a single stem above fernlike, blue-green foliage.

Purple corydalis is a particularly hardy wildflower native to Switzerland; it is not easily damaged by early spring frosts. Many times I have seen my corydalis lying flat on its face after a hard frost only to perk up again when the sun came out.

PERIOD OF BLOOM: Late April into May. Dormant by June.

SOIL: Humus-rich soil that is neutral to only slightly acid.

LOCATION AND EXPOSURE: I find this plant very adaptable. It blooms best when exposed to morning sunlight or to sunlight filtered through leafless branches. Tuck the bulbs among rocks in the garden or plant along the edge of a tulip bed. Corydalis may also be interplanted with very small ferns or later-flowering dwarf groundcovers.

PLANTING TIME: Bulbs are best planted after dormancy in early summer and into late fall. Corydalis blooms too early to be transplanted in spring.

ROOT SYSTEM: A small yellow bulb that looks like an oversized shelled acorn half. White feeder roots develop in late summer. Bulbs usually divide every year or two when conditions are favorable.

PLANTING DEPTH AND SPACING: Space about 6 inches apart. Set the bulbs 2 to 3 inches deep. If the area is ideal, the corydalis will multiply readily.

PLANTING STOCK AND PROPAGATION: Use nursery-grown stock.

You can divide bulbs every two or three years. Seeds are hard to collect, but corydalis occasionally self-sows.

COMMENTS: This little flower is so lovely that all who see it will admire it. *Corydalis solida*, which is very similar to *Corydalis bulbosa*, has not proved hardy in our cold climate.

CRUCIFERAE [Mustard Family]

Dentaria diphylla • two-leaved toothwort

DESCRIPTION: 8 to 10 inches tall. Two toothed leaves grow opposite each other halfway up the stalk. The stalk is topped by
a loose cluster of four-petaled white flowers which turn pinkish
with age. Basal foliage is similar to that on the stalk.

Two-leaved toothwort inhabits moist rich woods. It is also
found in deep woods, growing along streams with hepaticas and
fringed orchis.

PERIOD OF BLOOM: May.

SOIL: Neutral to slightly acid humus-rich soil with constant moisture. I have found that toothwort does well in soil that is damp
in spring and not too dry in summer.

LOCATION AND EXPOSURE: Grow this toothwort in colonies as a
very low groundcover. The foliage stays neat and green all summer.
Select an open spot where the shade is high.

PLANTING TIME: While dormant in spring or fall.

ROOT SYSTEM: A slender white rhizome that is brittle, crinkled,
and easily broken. It often sends up new growth as it creeps
along. The feeder roots are white.

PLANTING DEPTH AND SPACING: Space about 10 inches apart since
the rhizomes will spread. Plant the slender rhizomes 1 inch deep.
Mulch lightly.

PLANTING STOCK AND PROPAGATION: Use nursery-grown or quality
collected stock.

Divide the rhizomes into segments while the plant is dormant.
Pot them in a flat for one year before setting them out in a
permanent location. Each broken portion will produce a new
plant. Seeds sown when ripe will germinate though I have had
little luck collecting them before the chipmunks make off with
the harvest. The plant self-sows.

COMMENTS: This easily grown plant is rarely found in woodland gardens. Because of its crinkled root it is sometimes called
crinkleroot.

Dentaria laciniata • cut-leaved toothwort

DESCRIPTION: 8 to 12 inches tall. Usually two palmate leaves grow midway up the stem. A loose cluster of four-petaled white flowers, occasionally flushed with pink or lavender, grows on top. The foliage is narrower, deeper cut, and more tapered than that of two-leaved toothwort.

This toothwort is found in moist rich woods and along river bottoms in deep shade. I have found it along trout streams that slightly overflow their banks in spring.

PERIOD OF BLOOM: May into June.

SOIL: Humus-rich soil a little on the damp side is best.

LOCATION AND EXPOSURE: Plant in colonies in open-shaded woodland. It can be interspersed with smaller ferns.

PLANTING TIME: Spring or fall when dormant.

ROOT SYSTEM: The tan, jointed rootstock with fibrous roots divides easily. Each portion eventually forms a new plant.

PLANTING DEPTH AND SPACING: Space 10 to 15 inches apart. It will spread. Set the slender rhizomes horizontally 2 to 3 inches deep and mulch.

PLANTING STOCK AND PROPAGATION: Use nursery-grown stock or quality collected stock of good size.

Be careful not to divide dormant rhizomes into sections that are too small.

Sow ripe seeds immediately in rich woods soil.

COMMENTS: This toothwort has a showier blossom than the two-leaved toothwort. Toothworts are also called pepper roots because the rootstock has a piquant taste.

SAXIFRAGACEAE [Saxifrage Family]

Tiarella cordifolia • foamflower

DESCRIPTION: 6 to 8 inches tall. The foamflower has feathery white flower spikes and graceful, maplelike, hairy basal foliage. There is also a rare variety with delicate pink flowers.

In rich cool woods, it carpets large areas. When grown in a protected area, the leaves stay green all winter.

PERIOD OF BLOOM: Late May into June.

SOIL: Humus-rich soil that does not dry out readily. Neutral to slightly acid, rich in leafmold.

LOCATION AND EXPOSURE: Foamflower is a choice plant for a shaded garden. It also makes an excellent groundcover under deciduous trees; it does not fare well under evergreens.

PLANTING TIME: Spring when plants begin to grow or fall while dormant.

ROOT SYSTEM: The parent plant has fibrous roots. In the spring the crown sends out many pinkish runners which develop fine hairy roots at the joints. Each section forms a new plant, which can be severed from the parent plant as soon as the foliage crown develops.

PLANTING DEPTH AND SPACING: Space 6 to 12 inches apart, depending on the desired effect. Set crowns at soil level, spreading the roots carefully. Cover the tiny roots on the runners lightly with damp humus. Mulch with birch, soft maple, or other small leaves. Old straw or weathered marsh hay make good mulches too.

PLANTING STOCK AND PROPAGATION: Use nursery-grown or quality collected stock with good roots.

Divide the rhizomes (rooted runners) of mature plants. Sow seeds on top of rich soil in a flat. Keep them protected the first year, preferably in a cold frame. In Wisconsin our plants rarely set seed.

COMMENTS: The star-shaped flower spikes and the lovely patterned foliage of foamflower lend an airy beauty to the woodland garden. As new leaves appear in spring, old foliage bronzes and disappears, adding a bit of humus to the soil.

Heuchera villosa • hairy alumroot

DESCRIPTION: 6 to 10 inches tall. The white feathery plumes and the foliage are similar to those of the foamflower. Alumroot, however, does not send out rhizomes like the foamflower. Its natural habitat is farther south and east, although it has proved hardy in Wisconsin.

PERIOD OF BLOOM: August into September.

SOIL: Neutral to slightly acid soil that retains some moisture in summer. A moist woodland where leafmold is plentiful is ideal.

LOCATION AND EXPOSURE: Plant hairy alumroot in woodland among rocks in pockets of humus-rich soil. The flower is delightful in late summer when most woodland wildflowers have faded. Alumroot can also grow in fertile garden soil when shade is provided during midday heat.

PLANTING TIME: Spring or fall.

ROOT SYSTEM: A coarse rhizome with many fibrous roots that multiply at the crown.

PLANTING DEPTH AND SPACING: Space 10 to 15 inches apart. The plants will form clumps. Set the crown at soil level, which is usually ½ to 1½ inches deeper than the level at which it previously grew; the plants tend to raise their crowns above the soil as they mature. In rich soil with constant moisture they will form larger clumps if they are set slightly deeper.

PLANTING STOCK AND PROPAGATION: Use nursery-grown stock. Use only the young crowns of quality collected stock.

Divide clumps in spring, and water faithfully. Our plants have never set seed.

COMMENTS: To prolong the beauty of your foamflower bed, interplant it with hairy alumroot. The foliage and flower of the two plants are so similar that only a very close look will reveal the difference. Interplanting gives your foamflower bed a second chance to display its springtime beauty.

Heuchera americana • rock geranium

DESCRIPTION: 1 to 3 feet tall. Several spikes bearing many dainty cream-colored or greenish bells rise up from a rosette of large round scalloped leaves.

Rock geranium is found in moist to dry rocky woods and uplands. I have also found it in rocky crevices where no soil was visible.

PERIOD OF BLOOM: June.

SOIL: Neutral to slightly acid soil. The texture of the soil is not important.

LOCATION AND EXPOSURE: Rock geranium grows in open shade or filtered sunlight. It will also grow in the open if it is protected from strong afternoon sunlight.

PLANTING TIME: Spring or fall, preferably spring.

ROOT SYSTEM: Coarse black rootstock with some fibrous roots. It forms clumps.

PLANTING DEPTH AND SPACING: Space 18 to 24 inches apart. The flowers are most striking when planted singly.

PLANTING STOCK AND PROPAGATION: Young nursery-grown stock transplants more readily than young quality collected stock.

Divide large clumps in spring, discarding the old knotty ones, but this is not always successful. Scatter seeds on a flat as soon as they ripen. Transplant the seedlings when they are half grown.

COMMENTS: The leaves are almost evergreen, especially when there has been ample snow cover. When grown among rocks or when there is some sun, the leaves tend to bronze on the outer edges, the older leaves gradually becoming completely bronze with autumn frosts.

The foliage is similar to that of our house geranium, which explains the common name rock geranium. In my area it is also called crevice alumroot.

Mitella diphylla · bishop's-cap

DESCRIPTION: 8 to 10 inches tall. Two leaves grow opposite each other midway up each flowering stem. The delicate, airy, white flowers are contained in a narrow raceme. The foliage somewhat resembles that of the foamflower but is smaller. Bishop's-cap remains in a neat clump and does not send out runners like the foamflower. After the flowers fade, the plant produces exposed, shiny jet-black seeds which give it new beauty.

Bishop's-cap is found growing with hepaticas, *Trillium grandiflorum*, and bloodroot in moist rich woods and well-shaded woodlands where humus is plentiful.

PERIOD OF BLOOM: May into June.

SOIL: Slightly acid, fertile soil that is damp or only slightly moist. Bishop's-cap is easy to grow.

LOCATION AND EXPOSURE: Bishop's-cap makes excellent groundcover in deep shady woods. It also provides points of interest when grown among rocks where there is deep humus and adequate moisture. Or it can be interspersed with other woodland wildflowers. Its leaves are almost evergreen.

PLANTING TIME: Spring or fall.

ROOT SYSTEM: The rootstock is a rather twisted, pinkish, scaly rhizome that forks but stays close to the parent plant, creating a clumplike effect.

PLANTING DEPTH AND SPACING: When planting in colonies, space 6 inches or more apart. Among rocks, plant at random. Set the crowns of young plants, older plants, and divisions at soil level.

PLANTING STOCK AND PROPAGATION: Use nursery-grown or quality collected stock.

Divide rooted rhizomes. If there are insufficient roots, the plants should be potted and transplanted in the autumn.

Ripe seeds sown at soil level germinate fairly well. A balsam or spruce branch placed over the flat will help retain moisture. Seedlings usually start to bloom in the third year.

COMMENTS: A charming, dainty plant with many uses in a woodland garden. It makes a fine substitute for foamflower in an area that is too small for a plant that spreads so quickly.

Parnassia glauca • grass of Parnassus

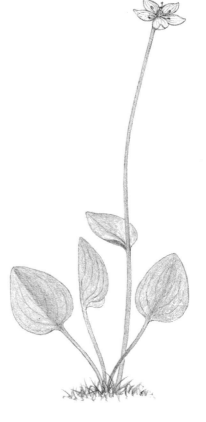

DESCRIPTION: 6 to 10 inches tall. There is a single leaf midway up each flower stalk, and one solitary anemonelike flower at the top. Flowers are waxy white with green veins. The heart-shaped, light-green basal foliage forms a clump.

Grass of Parnassus is found growing in colonies along brooks, grassy lake shores, and in wet marshes. I know a dry hillside where it grows abundantly and blooms in great profusion. I marvel at how this flower manages to survive there. Stock from this dry area has not transplanted successfully.

PERIOD OF BLOOM: August into September.

SOIL: Moist, neutral to slightly acid, fertile soil. Add a sprinkling of lime.

LOCATION AND EXPOSURE: Grow grass of Parnassus among sparse grasses in wet meadows where it might possibly self-sow. I started a colony in an old kitchen sink buried at soil level. I filled the sink with fertile loam and worked in a handful of garden lime. I tucked a mulch of decaying straw around each plant to keep them reasonably moist. The hole in the bottom of the sink provided ample drainage. The first summer I was rewarded with lovely bloom and abundant seeds.

PLANTING TIME: Fall is best.

ROOT SYSTEM: Fibrous roots. The plants form clumps.

PLANTING DEPTH AND SPACING: Space 6 to 12 inches apart. Leave a clump of earth adhering to the roots, and set the plants at the level at which they previously grew. Tuck mulch around the plants and keep moist.

PLANTING STOCK AND PROPAGATION: Nursery-grown stock in a sizable ball of earth is best. Quality collected stock with soil adhering is scarce.

Wild seeds are hard to collect since the slightest breeze will send them scattering as soon as the oval capsule opens. Collect the seeds daily in your garden and plant them immediately. Seeds scattered over a flat containing natural, fertile loam with a sprinkling of lime produce some seedlings that bloom the second year. I cover the flat with ½ inch mesh wire before mulching for the winter; this keeps the rodents from eating the crowns and destroying the young plants. Remove the mulch in spring but keep the wire a bit longer if possible. Germination may be slow and uneven. Seedlings should not be transferred to peat pots until the summer of the second year. When transplanting, remember to leave some of the earth from the flat adhering to the tiny roots. The plants can be moved to their permanent bed in the summer of the third year.

COMMENTS: Grass of Parnassus is not easy to grow, but it is well worth the extra effort.

ROSACEAE [Rose Family]

Gillenia trifoliata • bowman's root

DESCRIPTION: 2 to 3 feet tall. Thrice divided, compound leaves alternate on branching stems. The white to pale pink terminal flowers grow in open clusters.

Bowman's root is found in rich, open woodlands in high shade.

PERIOD OF BLOOM: June into July.

SOIL: Moderately acid soil with good fertility. It should be damp or moderately moist.

LOCATION AND EXPOSURE: Bowman's root is easily grown in wild gardens with high open shade or along borders of deciduous woodland.

PLANTING TIME: Spring is preferable.

ROOT SYSTEM: A coarse root once thought to have medicinal value.

PLANTING DEPTH AND SPACING: Space 1 to 2 feet apart with crowns at soil level. Mulch.

PLANTING STOCK AND PROPAGATION: Use nursery-grown stock or quality collected stock.

Divide crowns in early spring. I have not tried stem cuttings. Seeds sown in fall usually grow to blooming-sized seedlings the second year.

COMMENTS: Bowman's root is best planted in a showy colony or among ferns.

Waldsteinia fragarioides · barren strawberry

DESCRIPTION: 3 to 6 inches tall. Single ½ inch bright yellow flowers grow on bare stems. The shiny green leaves are thrice-parted like those of the strawberry, but lobed like those of the goldthread, which it resembles more closely.

Barren strawberry is found in moist to dry woodlands and cutover lands, especially where aspen and oaks provide shade. It often grows among wintergreen.

PERIOD OF BLOOM: May into June. Long-lasting flowers.

SOIL: Slightly acid, humus-rich woods soil with some moisture and good drainage. In damp areas the barren strawberry sends out many stolons which carpet the forest floor.

LOCATION AND EXPOSURE: Use this plant as a groundcover in the high open shade of woodland, or grow it in small colonies among other wildflowers. It also provides a good groundcover for sunny areas if it has constant moisture. A few single-crown plants set out in full sun in my garden formed neat clumps in one year and proved more vigorous than plants grown in shade.

PLANTING TIME: Early spring or fall.

ROOT SYSTEM: Each plant sends out stolons from the crown, and these form new plants which stay close to the parent. Roots are fibrous and sparse.

PLANTING DEPTH AND SPACING: Space 6 or more inches apart. The

main crown should be at soil level with new leafless shoots and side stolons about ½ inch deep. Mulch the first winter. Keep moist.

PLANTING STOCK AND PROPAGATION: Nursery-grown stock has more fibrous roots, but you can also use quality collected stock.

Divide clumps in early spring or fall. The seeds are always harvested by rodents before I can collect them. They do germinate easily, however.

COMMENTS: I rarely see this plant offered in wildflower catalogs. It makes a neat, conservative groundcover and has a unique beauty.

Fragaria vesca • woodland strawberry

DESCRIPTION: 6 inches tall. Single white ½ inch flowers appear in step fashion above lush, green, upright foliage. The 1 inch long conical fruit bears seeds on the outside, unlike the fruit of *Fragaria virginiana,* which is round with sunken seeds. The fruit of the woodland strawberry is red, occasionally yellow or white.

I have always found the woodland strawberry growing in rather moist cutover lands where the soil is fertile. Its lush green foliage carpets large areas.

PERIOD OF BLOOM: May. Fruit in June and July.

SOIL: Woodland strawberry grows well in fertile garden soil.

LOCATION AND EXPOSURE: Grow the woodland strawberry in full sun in the garden or in high open woodland where there is ample room for it to spread. It is an excellent groundcover and also useful for bordering walks and paths. Some sunshine is essential if the plants are to blossom and bear fruit.

PLANTING TIME: Spring or fall.

ROOT SYSTEM: Each plant has many fibrous roots and forms several crowns.

PLANTING DEPTH AND SPACING: Space 1 foot apart. Set the crowns at soil level.

PLANTING STOCK AND PROPAGATION: Use nursery-grown potted seedlings or quality collected young runners with good fibrous roots.

Seeds sown very early in the greenhouse will produce flowering plants by August and fruit a few weeks later. Seeds are sometimes offered in catalogs under the name "alpine strawberry."

COMMENTS: I recall happy childhood days when I used to gather pailfuls of these luscious strawberries for jams and canning and for eating fresh. The berries are easy to pick, as the calyx remains on the stalk.

Potentilla canadensis • common cinquefoil

DESCRIPTION: 8 to 20 inch prostrate vines develop from a rhizome. The ½ inch five-petaled flowers are bright yellow with yellow centers. The foliage is divided and often referred to as "five-fingers." The stems are reddish.

Common cinquefoil is usually found growing in colonies along the edge of woodlands and in old fields.

PERIOD OF BLOOM: Late May into July.

SOIL: Any dry to average garden or woods soil.

LOCATION AND EXPOSURE: High open shade or full sun is best. Use cinquefoil for groundcover between taller plants that are spaced far apart.

PLANTING TIME: While dormant in spring or fall.

ROOT SYSTEM: A pink-flushed bulblike rhizome with many fibrous roots. Cinquefoil, like strawberries, spreads by runners; the nodes root where they touch damp soil.

PLANTING DEPTH AND SPACING: Space 1 or more feet apart. Set rhizomes about ½ to ¾ inch deep.

PLANTING STOCK AND PROPAGATION: Use quality collected stock.

Cinquefoil self-sows a little, but spreads mostly by rooting runners.

COMMENTS: Some people consider common cinquefoil a weed, but I cannot find it listed in any weed books. A few plants grew up along the path to our pool and have neatly covered an otherwise barren area.

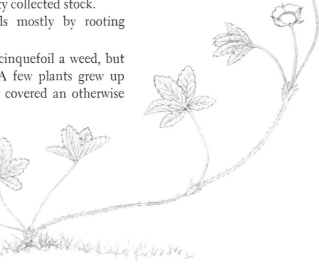

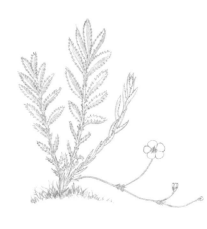

Potentilla anserina • silverweed

DESCRIPTION: 6 to 9 inches tall. Solitary ¾ to 1 inch golden yellow flowers are held on slender stems above pinnate silvery foliage, which shimmers when covered with dew.

In colder climates silverweed is found in damp meadows or around old homesteads, usually carpeting a large area. It is originally from Eurasia.

PERIOD OF BLOOM: June into summer.

SOIL: Silverweed will grow in any but extremely acid soil, but neutral to slightly acid soil is best. Constant moisture is important.

LOCATION AND EXPOSURE: Silverweed thrives in full sun or high open shade. It spreads rapidly and is used where extensive ground-cover is wanted quickly. It does not do well in hot climates, but is extremely hardy in cold ones.

PLANTING TIME: Spring or fall.

ROOT SYSTEM: Silverweed spreads by sending runners from the parent plant in several directions. The stolons root quickly to form new plants.

PLANTING DEPTH AND SPACING: Set the plants as they previously grew with crowns at soil level.

PLANTING STOCK AND PROPAGATION: Use nursery-grown or collected stock where available. Its range is limited to colder climates.

The plant is so easily reproduced by stolons that it is not worth the trouble to grow it from seed.

COMMENTS: Because of the golden yellow flowers and silvery gray foliage, this showy plant is also called silver-and-gold.

Geum triflorum • prairie smoke

DESCRIPTION: 8 to 15 inches tall. Crimson to rose-pink nodding flowers support an upright puff of mauve-pink which is the fruit. The plant is very showy in its budding stage. The basal foliage is oblong, irregularly lobed, and almost evergreen.

Prairie smoke is found in deserted hayfields and prairies where the soil is rocky and often sandy. Each plant forms a horseshoe-shaped clump as it multiplies. Its basal foliage chokes out the grasses as it spreads.

PERIOD OF BLOOM: June into July. In my garden where the soil is a rich sandy loam, it often blooms again later in the summer if there has been enough rain.

126

SOIL: Good drainage is very important. Slightly acid to neutral, sandy soils are best. Garden soil is good too.

LOCATION AND EXPOSURE: An excellent plant to grow along a sunny path or among low rocks in a sunny rock garden. It rarely blooms or multiplies in shade.

PLANTING TIME: Spring or fall. A light temporary mulch is advisable if you plant prairie smoke in fall.

ROOT SYSTEM: A heavy creeping rootstock with many coarse fibrous roots. The newer roots, which are white and lighter than the old ones, are most important for the growth of the plant. Eventually old roots and rootstock die and decay. Be careful not to break off too much of the old rhizome when transplanting, otherwise the plants may not bloom for a year.

PLANTING DEPTH AND SPACING: Space 1 to 2 feet apart, as each plant will multiply in a horseshoe fashion. Set the plants with the crowns at soil level.

PLANTING STOCK AND PROPAGATION: Nursery-grown stock is usually best, especially when it has been divided regularly. Quality collected stock is rare.

Division of rhizomes is the best and easiest method of propagation. As to seeds, I find germination poor.

COMMENTS: I rarely find prairie smoke in wild gardens. It is a striking and unusual plant that is worth growing. Plant it in a sunny garden or in a meadow where patches of grass have been cleared. Prairie smoke is the prettiest of the wild geums. Goldfinches are very fond of the seeds.

Alchemilla pratensis · lady's mantle

DESCRIPTION: 6 to 10 inches tall. Clusters of airy yellow flowers grow above mounds of fluted round leaves with serrated edges.

Originally from Europe, lady's mantle is now native to some eastern states; its range is limited. It is found in dry, gravelly soil.

PERIOD OF BLOOM: Early July to late August.

SOIL: Lady's mantle thrives in a variety of soils as long as there is good drainage. This plant cannot tolerate wet roots. I grow it in sandy loam.

LOCATION AND EXPOSURE: Grow in full sun or very light open shade. Lady's mantle can be used effectively to make a bright, attractive border.

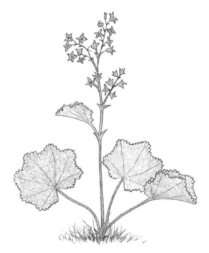

PLANTING TIME: Spring or fall, but I prefer spring.

ROOT SYSTEM: A heavy rootstock with coarse fibrous roots. The rootstock forms a clump which can be divided.

PLANTING DEPTH AND SPACING: Space the plants about 1 foot apart, giving them room to form showy clumps. Set the crown ½ to 1 inch deeper than it previously grew.

PLANTING STOCK AND PROPAGATION: Use nursery-grown stock or quality collected stock if available.

For propagation, divisions of clumps will give the best results. Seeds are slow to germinate.

COMMENTS: Lady's mantle is a particularly beautiful plant. The foliage is silvery gray when beaded with rain or dew and is easily preserved in glycerine for use in dry floral arrangements.

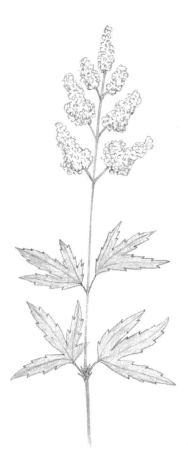

Filipendula rubra · queen of the prairie

DESCRIPTION: 3 to 5 feet tall. Sprays of pink flowers bloom outward from the center of the cluster. The leaves are textured, compound, and very pinnate.

Queen of the prairie is found in moist meadows as well as in soils with average moisture. It grows in full sun.

PERIOD OF BLOOM: Late June into August.

SOIL: Neutral to slightly acid soils or very fertile soils. The moisture content should be high to average.

LOCATION AND EXPOSURE: To bloom well this flower should be planted in full sun. It can be used effectively as a showy border, or naturalized in a meadow. Continuous mulching will promote spreading.

PLANTING TIME: While dormant in spring or fall.

ROOT SYSTEM: A creeping pinkish rhizome, dividing at the nodes to send up new shoots.

PLANTING DEPTH AND SPACING: Set the rhizomes about 1 inch deep with the tip of the plant at soil level. Mulch. Space 1 to 2 feet apart.

PLANTING STOCK AND PROPAGATION: Use nursery-grown stock.

COMMENTS: The airy pink blossoms are elegant, but last only a short while after being cut. The fruit is excellent for use in dried floral arrangements.

LEGUMINOSAE [Pulse Family]

Cassia marilandica • wild senna

DESCRIPTION: 3 to 4 feet tall. The loose racemes of golden yellow flowers with prominent dark-brown anthers remind one of the delphinium "bee." The leafy stalks have pinnate leaves similar to those of the honey locust, and the whole plant becomes quite bushy.

Wild senna naturally inhabits moist open woods and thickets in a region much farther south than Wisconsin. But with a generous mulch of oak leaves, it has proved hardy here.

PERIOD OF BLOOM: July into August.

SOIL: Slightly acid, fertile, sandy loam or any good garden soil with adequate drainage.

LOCATION AND EXPOSURE: I find this plant grows best in full sun. Given enough room, it develops into a handsome deciduous bush. Wild senna is also a good choice for a sunny woodland border.

PLANTING TIME: While dormant in fall or spring. Mulch in winter in cold climates.

ROOT SYSTEM: A coarse and fibrous, fleshy black rootstock that enlarges with age and produces many new eyes.

PLANTING DEPTH AND SPACING: Space 3 feet or more apart. Set the eyes about 1 inch below level with the roots at least an inch deeper. Cultivate or mulch. Mulching is preferable since new shoots come up near the parent stems.

PLANTING STOCK AND PROPAGATION: Use nursery-grown stock or young collected stock where available.

Dividing the clumps in spring gives good results for propagation. New growth is slow to appear. The seeds are hard-shelled and often slow to germinate. Sow them in fall. Seedlings bloom the third year.

COMMENTS: Wild senna is a bold vigorous plant of unusual beauty. This large perennial can be used in place of a shrub. In clusters, the seed pods make good material for dry floral arrangements.

Baptisia australis • false blue indigo

DESCRIPTION: 3 to 4 feet tall. The bushy plants have pealike flowers and foliage of the legume type. The flowers are usually indigo-blue, although there is a white species and a related species (*Baptisia tinctoria*) with smaller, yellow flowers. The latter grows naturally farther south, but a few have survived in my garden. False blue indigo was originally cultivated in the southern states, and now grows wild there in open sandy fields or old gardens.

PERIOD OF BLOOM: Late May into July.

SOIL: False blue indigo prefers a sandy loam, but also grows well in a heavier, more fertile soil if drainage is good.

LOCATION AND EXPOSURE: A showy plant for a border or along the edge of a woodland where there is ample sunshine. I prefer to grow it in full sun.

PLANTING TIME: While dormant in spring or fall, but spring-planted stock grows sooner.

ROOT SYSTEM: A fleshy rootstock that sends out long, stringy, white roots and produces many eyes in a close cluster. Digging up a large plant can be difficult because of its extensive root system, but many roots can be cut without injuring the plant.

PLANTING DEPTH AND SPACING: Set the plants 2 feet apart to allow room for growth. Plant so that the upper eyes are 2 inches below soil level. This encourages the rootstock to send up more new shoots to form a large plant. When transplanting, trim the old roots to 3 inches.

PLANTING STOCK AND PROPAGATION: Nursery-grown stock is best. Quality collected stock may be used if available.

To propagate, divide large plants in spring while they are dormant. Cut each rootstock into pieces, leaving about three eyes in each division and trimming the stringy roots back to 3 or 4 inches. Each of the new eyes will develop a whole new root system.

Sow seeds when they are ripe. Some seedlings will appear the first spring and others may keep appearing throughout the summer and the following spring. Some will bloom in the third year. Often plants do not fully mature until the fifth year.

130

COMMENTS: Seeds are formed in the black, "bloated" enclosures shaped like pea-pods. They rattle when ripe. For dry floral arrangements, cut the stalks with pods when they first show a little black and are not yet fully ripe. Hang them upside down to dry.

Lupinus perennis • wild lupine

DESCRIPTION: 1 to 2 feet tall. Wild lupine usually grows in a semiprostrate position but holds its pealike blossoms erect in terminal racemes. The flowers are clear blue with a hint of purple inside. There are also rare white and pink forms which I have not yet been fortunate enough to find. The blue-green palmate leaves have many divisions.

Wild lupine is found along roadsides, in wastelands and in old hayfields. It blooms profusely in June sunshine, forming a sea of blue. Plants that grow in the shade have few blossoms. The soil in such areas is not fertile but usually sandy, and grasses grow sparsely. In such dry areas the plants quickly go dormant and often do not set seed in drought years.

PERIOD OF BLOOM: June.

SOIL: This lupine prefers a slightly acid, sandy loam soil with good drainage. But it can be grown successfully in a garden where the soil is heavier and drainage is good.

LOCATION AND EXPOSURES: The wild lupine grows best in a well-drained spot with full sun. It goes dormant after setting seed, but after a wet August new foliage appears in early fall. Interplant this lupine with other wildflowers, such as butterfly flower, that will cover bare spots and bloom when the lupines fade. The foliage may mildew if air circulation is poor.

PLANTING TIME: While dormant in spring or fall.

ROOT SYSTEM: A young plant has one tapering rhizome with a few feeder roots. As the rhizome develops, eyes form along its length and send up new growth which forms a clump. You will often find small clumps of nitrogen nodules attached here and there to the distorted branching rhizomes. The roots go deep into the earth in search of minerals.

PLANTING DEPTH AND SPACING: Space the plants 10 to 12 inches apart, setting the eyes of the white shoot about 1 inch below soil

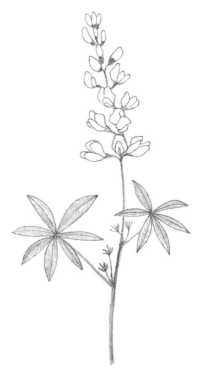

level. If green foliage has formed, then plant with the crown at soil level.

PLANTING STOCK AND PROPAGATION: Use young nursery-grown stock or quality collected young stock. It is a waste of time and effort to try transplanting old plants.

The easiest method of propagation is to sow the seeds in tiny pots and transfer them to a permanent location when the second true leaf appears. To hasten germination, soak the seeds in tepid water 15 minutes before sowing. Seedlings bloom the following summer.

COMMENTS: Wild lupine is a very hardy, long-lived wildflower that grows nicely in a sunny, well-drained garden. It is not difficult to cultivate if young plants are used. Old plants usually die when moved. The foliage is supposedly poisonous to cattle.

GERANIACEAE [Geranium Family]

Geranium maculatum • spotted cranesbill

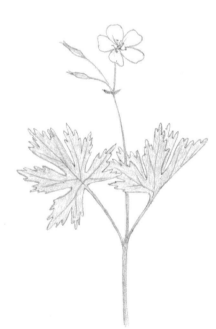

DESCRIPTION: 1 to 2 feet tall. A loose cluster of single magenta-pink flowers are borne on a rigid stem above deeply toothed basal foliage. Two leaves grow midway up the flower stalk. At first glance the foliage is very similar to that of the Canada anemone.

Spotted cranesbill grows in places that are protected from strong winds. It is found in open shade on hillsides and shaded roadsides, where it often grows in the company of false Solomon's seal.

PERIOD OF BLOOM: Late May into June.

SOIL: Average to fertile woodland soils that are neutral to slightly acid. I grow it in garden soil with mulch.

LOCATION AND EXPOSURE: Plant in open shade. If you plant on a hillside, choose a spot protected from strong winds. I also grow spotted cranesbill in the garden in full sun. When planted in a colony, it makes a charming display.

PLANTING TIME: While dormant in fall, or spring when only slightly sprouted.

ROOT SYSTEM: A stout many-branched rhizome that spreads horizontally. When plants become crowded the roots rise above soil level and freeze. The blunt white tips of the rhizomes hold the next year's bud. The smaller white tips will not send shoots above the earth until a year later.

PLANTING DEPTH AND SPACING: Space 10 or more inches apart. Set the rhizome 1 inch deep with the eyes leading to the surface. Mulch. If the nodes on the rhizome are not well developed the plant may stay dormant for a year. If the area is kept moist the plant usually blooms the following year.

PLANTING STOCK AND PROPAGATION: Use nursery-grown stock or quality collected stock.

To propagate, divide clumps in early spring or fall, leaving several plump eyes on each division.

Seeds sown when ripe usually mature enough to bloom in the second or third year. Cranesbill self-sows readily where leafmold is bare.

COMMENTS: The beaklike seed capsule is most unusual and interesting when the seed has been dispersed. The seeds themselves are difficult to collect because the pods open suddenly—changing from green to almost black overnight, they almost burst open and scatter the seeds far and wide.

POLYGALACEAE [Milkwort Family]

Polygala paucifolia • fringed polygala

DESCRIPTION: 3 to 5 inches tall. Dainty, orchidlike flowers, ranging in color from rose-purple to magenta, grow in the axils of oval-shaped leaves. Rarely, the flowers are white. The leaves form on the upper part of the purple stems; they take on a bronze cast in autumn.

Fringed polygala usually grows in rich dry woods and on hillsides under deciduous trees where the forest floor is quite free of grasses. Shinleaf and merrybells are often found nearby.

PERIOD OF BLOOM: May into July.

SOIL: Acid to slightly acid woods soil rich in humus and not too dry in summer.

LOCATION AND EXPOSURE: Fringed polygala is a choice plant for a woodland garden where sunlight filters through the trees in spring. It is a very neat groundcover to grow between taller wildflowers that bloom later. Or grow it in small neat colonies. Its foliage lasts late into fall and often remains through the winter.

PLANTING TIME: Sods are best moved in fall. Potted stock can be planted either in spring or fall.

ROOT SYSTEM: The extensive white stringlike rhizomes wander far from the parent plant to form new plants. Like some violets, it bears, in addition to its larger blossoms, cleistogamous (closed, self-pollinated) flowers, and subterranean fruit. This double system of propagation ensures rapid spreading.

PLANTING DEPTH AND SPACING: Space sods 1 foot apart and potted stock 6 inches apart. Plant both at soil level. Mulch with birch or other small thin leaves.

PLANTING STOCK AND PROPAGATION: Nursery-grown potted stock is superior, but is not always available.

Large sods with soil adhering give good results. Sods are best selected from an area where the plants grow close together.

Stem cuttings taken in early summer and put in a propagating frame give fair results.

COMMENTS: The plant is also called gay wings. It is not easy to establish, but once established it spreads readily.

Polygala Senega • Seneca snakeroot

DESCRIPTION: 8 to 15 inches tall. Upright stems with narrow, willowlike leaves bear spikes of white to greenish white flowers in dense racemes. The racemes are also interesting in the seed stage.

Seneca snakeroot grows in dry meadows where the grass is short, along gravelly roadsides, and at sunny edges of woodland.

PERIOD OF BLOOM: May into June.

SOIL: Sandy loam or garden soil that is only slightly acid and has good drainage.

LOCATION AND EXPOSURE: Naturalize Seneca snakeroot among other wildflowers or sparse grasses. It needs full sun or very light open shade. It is not easy to establish.

PLANTING TIME: While dormant in spring or fall.

ROOT SYSTEM: A stout, wiry, cream-tan rhizome with few feeder roots.

PLANTING DEPTH AND SPACING: Space 10 to 15 inches apart to allow room for it to form a clump. Set the plants with eyes about ½ inch below soil level, making certain that the taproot is planted straight down since it seeks deep levels.

PLANTING STOCK AND PROPAGATION: Use young nursery-grown stock or quality collected young stock.

Take cuttings in July or as soon as the stalk seems firm and mature. Cuttings should have at least three or four nodes in the soil and 2 inches of leafy stalk above the soil. Remove the flowering portion of the stalk or tip if the flowers have not yet developed. Pot individually and put in a propagating frame.

Sow seeds when ripe and keep moist. Seedlings usually send up one flowering stalk the second or third year.

COMMENTS: Seneca snakeroot is not a strikingly beautiful plant, but its tiny flowers and beadlike seeds lend it an air of loftiness. Plant it where you want it to remain as it resists transplanting.

There is a dainty pink species, *Polygala polygama*, which occasionally appears in my garden. It tends to die out, however, and does not transplant readily although it has a compact root system and produces subterranean seeds like the fringed polygala. None of the polygalas are easy to establish.

EUPHORBIACEAE [Spurge Family]

Euphorbia Cyparissias • Cypress spurge

DESCRIPTION: 4 to 6 inches tall. The showy, leaflike yellow flowers of the Cypress spurge turn reddish as they fade. The foliage is very fine and feathery on very upright stems; it, too, turns yellow and often reddish in fall.

Cypress spurge is found along roadsides, in dry sandy fields, and around old homesteads. Originally from the Old World, this plant has found its way to North America and has readily established itself here.

PERIOD OF BLOOM: June into July.

135

SOIL: Any sandy, gritty, or poor soil with good drainage. The pH is not important.

LOCATION AND EXPOSURE: Plant the Cypress spurge in full sun and very poor soil for the best display and compact beauty. In shade it grows rampantly, sometimes becoming a nuisance, and for this reason is not suited for a garden. But it is perfect for hot, sunny, sandy, gravelly areas where little else grows and groundcover is needed to keep the earth from blowing or washing away. Cypress spurge can be easily cultivated in such areas and serves its purpose well. If you do want to grow Cypress spurge in your wild garden, plant it in the sun in a bottomless gallon can to restrict its growth.

PLANTING TIME: While dormant in spring or fall.

ROOT SYSTEM: A creeping rhizome that often sends up new shoots and forms dense clumps. The rootstock is scaly and white with pink eyes which will produce next year's growth.

PLANTING DEPTH AND SPACING: Set the plants ½ to 1 inch deep. Space only 6 inches apart for quick groundcover. Clumps may be spaced even farther apart.

PLANTING STOCK AND PROPAGATION: Pot-grown stock is easiest to plant. To propagate, divide rhizomes.

COMMENTS: Cypress spurge is a good, neat groundcover for those dry, sandy areas where little else survives. I also find it very ornamental; the foliage remains long into fall and is strikingly colorful. But it can become a pest if not planted with care.

MALVACEAE [Mallow Family]

Malva moschata • musk mallow

DESCRIPTION: 1 to 2 feet tall. The single flowers with notched petals ranging from rose-pink to purest white resemble those of the wild rose. The deeply cut, leafy foliage grows on rigid stems.

Musk mallow is found along roadside fences, in old fields, and around abandoned homesteads. Originally grown only in cultivation, it has taken readily to the wild.

PERIOD OF BLOOM: June into late August and often into September.

SOIL: Any neutral to slightly acid garden soil with average moisture content.

LOCATION AND EXPOSURE: Musk mallow blooms best in full sun but will tolerate light open shade. It is a good plant for a border. When musk mallow is naturalized in meadows it should be planted in patches where the grass is sparse or the grass will choke out the plants. A little mulch helps keep the grass down.

PLANTING TIME: While dormant in spring or fall.

ROOT SYSTEM: A wiry, coarse, fibrous, white rootstock that does not transplant well when mature.

PLANTING DEPTH AND SPACING: Space 1 foot apart. When given enough room the plants develop into nice bushes. Set the crowns at soil level and spread the roots evenly. Mulch if you wish.

PLANTING STOCK AND PROPAGATION: Use young nursery-grown stock or quality collected young stock.

I have not been successful in propagating by division of clumps. Cuttings may be taken in July, but they, too, give poor results. Seeds sown in fall or spring will produce blooming-sized plants the second year.

COMMENTS: The outstanding leafy foliage of the musk mallow provides an excellent contrast to plants with linear foliage. Musk mallow derives its name from its musky odor.

Callirhoe involucrata • wine cups

DESCRIPTION: 1 to 2 foot trailer with forking vines. Wine cups have beautiful rose-shaped flowers and blunt-tipped, deeply lanced foliage. The color of the flowers ranges from a luscious wine-red to the color of an American beauty rose. The seed pods are little circles, resembling those of hollyhocks.

Wine cups are native to the southern and southwestern prairies of the Dakotas.

PERIOD OF BLOOM: June until hard-killing frosts.

SOIL: Neutral to slightly acid soil, either sandy or fertile. Good drainage is very important.

LOCATION AND EXPOSURE: The wine cups requires full sun throughout the day for best bloom. It is an excellent plant for a dry sunny spot where it can spread or for a rock garden on a sunny bank. If grown in the open, mulch in winter.

ROOT SYSTEM: The rootstock is white and resembles a small slender parsnip.

PLANTING TIME: Early spring or fall. Spring is preferred.

PLANTING DEPTH AND SPACING: Set root at crown level and space two feet apart, as they will run.

PLANTING STOCK AND PROPAGATION: Use young nursery-grown stock or, where available, young collected stock.

Seeds sown when ripe or in very early spring will produce blooming sized seedlings the second year. Transplant the seedlings to a permanent location before they mature.

COMMENTS: For continuous bloom it is best not to let the plant set seed and to water it during periods of extreme drought.

Wine cups are charming as they spread their vivid colorful flowers over bare areas. The plant is also known as buffalo rose and poppy mallow.

VIOLACEAE [Violet Family]

Viola pedata • birdfoot violet

DESCRIPTION: 3 to 5 inches tall. The pansylike flowers with outstanding yellow eyes are usually shades of lavender-blue. The color varies from plant to plant depending on soil fertility, acidity, and location. There is also a bicolored variety with two upper petals of rich royal purple. On rare occasions a white flower with dark veins appears among the blues. The foliage is deeply toothed and resembles an outstretched bird's foot.

As early woodland flowers fade, birdfoot violets blanket sunny fields and roadsides with sandy banks. When the prairie grasses grow tall this showy violet becomes partly dormant until August rains revive it.

PERIOD OF BLOOM: May into June. I find that when the birdfoot violet is cultivated it blooms again in August and does not go dormant after blooming in early summer. Blossoms continue to appear until the plant is killed by frost.

SOIL: Acid to slightly acid sandy soil with good drainage. Birdfoot violets will also flourish in average garden soils. In its native habitat, it tends to grow in poor sandy soils or in areas with little humus. When cultivated, it thrives in good but not too fertile soil with good drainage. Cultivated plants are showier and do not go dormant in midsummer. They need mulch over the winter or they may winter-kill. The wild birdfoot violets are protected by grasses.

LOCATION AND EXPOSURE: The birdfoot violet must have full sun to grow and bloom vigorously, otherwise it gradually weakens and dies. In a sunny spot each plant will form a showy clump. This is an excellent wildflower for planting in a rock garden, on a slope, or along a walk where the sun shines all day.

PLANTING TIME: Early spring or fall for nursery-grown stock. Collect wild plants just after they finish blooming and before they go dormant. Or move plants in late August when the rains encourage new growth.

ROOT SYSTEM: The rootstock is very different from that of other violets. It is bulblike and looks much like a miniature celeriac root with coarse feeder roots.

PLANTING DEPTH AND SPACING: Space 6 to 12 inches apart, depending on the fertility of the soil. Set the rhizome about ½ to 1 inch deep and spread the roots evenly.

PLANTING STOCK AND PROPAGATION: Nursery-grown stock is superior to quality collected stock.

Divide the clumps in late summer, fall, or early spring. Plant "bulbs" about 1 inch deep in sandy loam soil that retains moisture. Remove some of the upper feeder roots from the rootstock. Many small bulblike rootstocks will form; these can be transplanted and usually bloom in the second year.

The seeds are difficult to find, especially when they are dispersed among grasses. In sandy areas the birdfoot violet self-sows readily. The bi-colored and white forms rarely retain their distinctive coloring when planted from seed.

Birdfoot violets seem to fare better and make a much prettier display when they are permitted to take over an entire area. Find a sunny nook where they can grow among sparse prairie grasses, and they will propagate themselves.

COMMENTS: The birdfoot violet is our choicest native violet, growing profusely in dry, sunny areas. Reforestation has killed huge patches of these violets; it is painful indeed to see young trees grow taller while the birdfoot beneath them grows scarcer and more precious each year. Do not pick the birdfoot violet since it does not have self-fertile hidden seed pods, as do most of the other violets without leafy stems, and requires the flower to produce seed.

139

Viola papilionacea • common blue violet

DESCRIPTION: 4 to 5 inches tall. The common blue violet blooms profusely. The flowers are rich purple-blue with a white throat and dark veining on the inside of the lower petal toward the base. The *albiflora* form is white with dark veining and a touch of blue or chartreuse on the inside of the lower petal towards the base. The white flowers make a pretty contrast with the purple-blue ones. The deep green foliage is long-lasting in either sun or shade if the soil is not too dry.

Blue violets are often found around old homesteads, in sunny open meadows, and along roadsides.

PERIOD OF BLOOM: May into June.

SOIL: This violet grows vigorously in any ordinary garden soil with average moisture.

LOCATION AND EXPOSURE: The common blue violet grows equally well in sunlight or open shade. It makes a quick groundcover for a slope, spreading rapidly by self-sowing. It spreads too profusely for the small garden and is best when naturalized among tall plants of equal vigor.

PLANTING TIME: Spring or fall. Moves easily with care at other times as well.

ROOT SYSTEM: A knotty rootstock with many fibrous feeder roots.

PLANTING DEPTH AND SPACING: Space 10 inches or more apart, depending on the effect wanted. Set the crown ½ to 1 inch deep. I have tilled the rootstock of this plant into the earth to a depth of several inches—they not only persisted but grew even more vigorously, forming large clumps.

PLANTING STOCK AND PROPAGATION: Use nursery-grown stock or quality collected stock.

Divide the clumps in spring, fall, or right after blooming. Keep the plants well watered until they are established. This violet self-sows freely. It has many hidden seed pods which disperse the seeds widely and establish new colonies.

COMMENTS: The lovely purple-blue flowers are intriguing despite the plant's tendency to overrun small gardens. For slopes and large areas it is unexcelled as a quick low groundcover. I find that the white variety is not quite so aggressive.

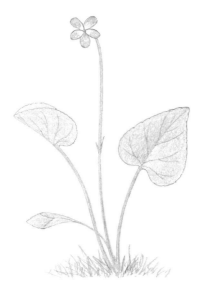

Viola Priceana • Confederate violet

DESCRIPTION: 4 to 6 inches tall. The white flowers are flushed with gray-blue or lavender. Although the Confederate violet is considered a variation of *Viola papilionacea,* its foliage is a little lighter green and possibly a little broader. It is not as aggressive unless grown in very fertile soil.

The Confederate violet is usually found in old gardens and around deserted homesteads where it was probably once cultivated.

PERIOD OF BLOOM: May into June.

SOIL: Slightly acid to neutral soils. This violet grows readily in most soils.

LOCATION AND EXPOSURE: Grow the Confederate violet in woodlands, along a border of deciduous woods, or in a shaded area at the base of a stone wall. In cold areas it should be mulched, as it does not seem to be as hardy as *Viola papilionacea,* nor does it do as well when cultivated in the hot sun.

PLANTING TIME: Spring or fall.

ROOT SYSTEM: A coarse knotty rhizome with many fibrous feeder roots.

PLANTING DEPTH AND SPACING: Space rhizomes 6 to 10 inches apart. The crown should be ½ to 1 inch below the surface of the soil. Mulch lightly. The Confederate violet has a tendency to grow itself out of the soil. In cold climates this will winter-kill it unless some extra mulch is added in late fall.

PLANTING STOCK AND PROPAGATION: Use nursery-grown or quality collected stock.

Divide the rootstocks in spring or fall. Also grow from seed. This violet self-sows to some extent.

COMMENTS: The Confederate violet is one of the showy spring violets that is especially lovely when planted in a colony. It produces self-fertile hidden seed pods near the surface of the soil. When these pods ripen they burst open and scatter seeds far and wide.

Viola (a sport) • Jessie's red violet

DESCRIPTION: 3 to 4 inches tall. The dainty, orchid-red flowers have wine-colored veins extending into their pale chartreuse throats.

141

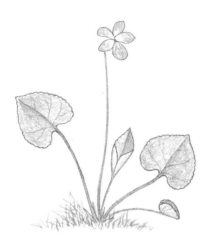

The leaves are medium green and heart-shaped. The white form is known as Jessie's white violet and has a clear chartreuse throat veined with purple. It is not as robust as *Viola papilionacea albiflora*. Examination leads me to believe Jessie's red violet is a smaller offspring of *Viola papilionacea albiflora*, the major difference being that Jessie's red violet is smaller.

My plants came from a grower in New York who had had them so long he could not recall their source.

PERIOD OF BLOOM: May into June. If there is sufficient rainfall in August, Jessie's red violet will often bloom again in September.

SOIL: Neutral to slightly acid garden soil. I grow it in sandy garden loam.

LOCATION AND EXPOSURE: Jessie's red violet is very adaptable. In our nursery it grows in colonies in open shade, full sun, and in one spot with an eastern exposure, where it has morning sunlight.

PLANTING TIME: Spring, fall, or after blooming.

ROOT SYSTEM: The medium-sized rootstock is knotty and has many fibrous feeder roots.

PLANTING DEPTH AND SPACING: Space 4 to 8 inches apart, as the violets form small clumps. Set the rootstock ½ to 1 inch deep.

PLANTING STOCK AND PROPAGATION: Use nursery-grown stock.

Clumps can be divided in spring or fall.

Jessie's red violet self-sows. Do not transplant until the seedlings are large enough to bloom.

COMMENTS: A most unusual violet. The orchid-red flower provides a welcome color contrast with other wild violets or small spring wildflowers.

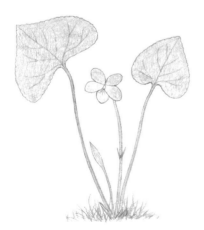

Viola latiuscula • broad-leaved wood violet

DESCRIPTION: 4 to 6 inches tall. The medium-blue flowers of this violet are dark-veined and have a white throat. The leaves are broad and continue to develop after the plant has ceased to bloom.

The broad-leaved wood violet is found in meadows where it grows in the shade of other plants and in open woodlands where leafmold is plentiful.

PERIOD OF BLOOM: May into June.

SOIL: Ordinary garden soil or slightly acid woods soil. This violet is very easy to grow.

LOCATION AND EXPOSURE: Select an open woodland or a partly shaded area.

PLANTING TIME: Spring or fall.

ROOT SYSTEM: A knotty rhizome with fibrous feeder roots.

PLANTING DEPTH AND SPACING: Space 6 to 12 inches apart. Set the crowns ½ to 1 inch deep and mulch. Each crown will form a showy clump. This wood violet does not grow as aggressively as the common blue violet.

PLANTING STOCK AND PROPAGATION: Use nursery-grown stock or quality collected stock.

Divide the clumps in spring or fall. This violet is easily grown from seeds. It self-sows readily—many hidden self-fertile seed pods just below the soil surface rise and disperse the seeds as they ripen.

COMMENTS: You will know this species by its seed pods which are flushed with purple or frequently completely purple flushed with green. This is a neat violet that will not crowd out other woodland plants.

Viola palmata • early blue violet

DESCRIPTION: 5 to 8 inches tall. The dark blue flowers have light cream-colored throats. The lower petals are veined with purple. There is little variation in color within this species. The coarsely cut foliage is deeply toothed, somewhat resembling that of the birdfoot but not as airy.

Early blue violets are found in rich deciduous woods in light to partial shade, growing in large colonies.

PERIOD OF BLOOM: May into June.

SOIL: Average to dry fertile soils that are neutral to slightly acid.

LOCATION AND EXPOSURE: Early blue violets grow vigorously in high open shade. They are suitable for colonizing in shaded woodlands under the branches of tall trees. Or use them as groundcover between taller wildflowers that bloom later.

PLANTING TIME: Spring or fall.

ROOT SYSTEM: The coarse rhizome has many fibrous feeder roots. It becomes knotty with age.

PLANTING DEPTH AND SPACING: Space 6 to 12 inches apart, as each plant forms a neat clump. Set the rootstocks ½ to 1 inch

deep and mulch. When crowded, these violets have a tendency to grow out of the soil. They must be mulched in winter in cold climates.

PLANTING STOCK AND PROPAGATION: Use nursery-grown stock or quality collected stock where available.

Divide the clumps in spring or fall. This violet self-sows readily in open woodland soil.

COMMENTS: When seedlings first emerge, the first leaves are plain and not palmate. Usually the third to fifth leaf produced by a seedling starts to show the toothing of the parent plant.

Early blue violets look lovely when planted in large groups.

Viola blanda · sweet white violet

DESCRIPTION: 2 to 3 inches tall. This violet has light green, heart-shaped foliage and tiny flowers. The fragrant blossoms are white with purple veins extending toward the throat. The stems are flushed with a red that is especially bright on plants that grow in dry sunny areas.

Sweet white violet is very adaptable. It can be found in damp cool swamps, moist meadows, and partly shaded areas in deciduous woods where it makes a neat groundcover. It even grows in woodland soil that becomes very dry during the summer.

PERIOD OF BLOOM: May, sometimes into June.

SOIL: Neutral to slightly acid fertile soil with average to very high moisture content. Sweet white violet will also grow in drier woodlands where leafmold is plentiful.

LOCATION AND EXPOSURE: The sweet white violet is equally at home in a partly shaded dry woodland and in a sunny, moist spot. Plant it among taller wildflowers in shady woods or use it as groundcover under mulched shrubs. It is a very neat groundcover and spreads quickly when given a light fall mulching of partly decayed leaves or old marsh hay.

PLANTING TIME: While dormant in spring or fall. Potted stock may be planted anytime.

ROOT SYSTEM: A dainty fibrous rhizome that forks and sends out white filiform stolons which grow tiny feeder roots and eventually become mature plants. The sweet white violet spreads prolifically when planted where leafmold is plentiful. When planted in the

open in ordinary garden soil without mulch, it stays in a neat clump and does not set new rhizomes as freely.

PLANTING DEPTH AND SPACING: Space 6 to 10 inches apart. This violet spreads to make neat mats. Set the crown of the **main** plant at soil level, making certain to cover all the smaller rhizomes and tiny rootlets. Mulch lightly with old humus or preferably with partially decayed small leaves.

PLANTING STOCK AND PROPAGATION: Nursery-grown potted stock is the easiest to transplant. You can also use wild quality collected stock.

The rhizomes can be divided when an area becomes **too** crowded. The tiny, plump, red-flushed seed pods burst and scatter the seeds widely, thus populating more distant areas.

COMMENTS: The sweet white violet is an excellent small low groundcover to use between taller wildflowers such as baneberries, black cohosh, and even lady's-slippers.

Viola pubescens • downy yellow violet

DESCRIPTION: 9 to 12 inches tall. Bright yellow flowers, veined with purple toward the throat, grow on leafy stems above sturdy green foliage.

The downy yellow violet is found in rich, dry, deciduous woods where the sunlight filters through leafless branches in spring. It is rarely found growing in large patches.

PERIOD OF BLOOM: May into June.

SOIL: Average to dry fertile soils that are neutral to only slightly acid. I have grown this violet in full sun in sandy garden loam; the foliage remained green and the plant set an abundance of seed.

LOCATION AND EXPOSURE: The downy yellow violet is an excellent flower to grow in a deciduous woods or along a border exposed to brief morning sunlight. Plant at least three or more together or they will not be very noticeable. This plant, unlike so many violets without leafy stalks, does not form clumps.

PLANTING TIME: While dormant in spring or fall.

ROOT SYSTEM: A medium-sized rhizome with fibrous feeder roots.

PLANTING DEPTH AND SPACING: Space about 6 inches apart. Set the plants so that the crown is barely ½ inch below soil level. Mulch.

PLANTING STOCK AND PROPAGATION: Use nursery-grown stock or, when available, quality collected stock.

If you propagate by planting seeds in flats, do not transplant the seedlings until the second year. The plant self-sows under ideal conditions where there is an abundance of leafmold.

COMMENTS: This violet never becomes weedy. In my garden the chipmunks steal the downy seed pods just before they ripen, thus cheating me of my seed supply. To outfox them, I set wire cages over several plants.

Watch the seed pods closely. Pick them when they are ready to pop open, just as they are about to turn tan, and drop them into a glass jar with a piece of tissue to keep them from molding. Do not use a shallow container; the seeds may disperse when the pods pop open.

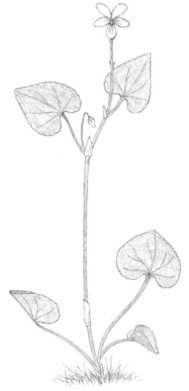

Viola pensylvanica • smooth yellow violet

DESCRIPTION: This small violet (Var. *eriocarpa*) has small flowers that are clear yellow with black veins deep in their throats. The stems are leafy, and there is some basal foliage. The smooth yellow violet resembles the downy yellow but is smaller, has lighter green foliage, and lacks the downiness on the leaves and seed pods.

It is found in moist woodlands, often with *Trillium grandiflorum* and bloodroot.

PERIOD OF BLOOM: May into June.

SOIL: Humus-rich soil that is neutral to only slightly acid. The soil can be moist or have the average moisture content of garden soils.

LOCATION AND EXPOSURE: The smooth yellow violet is an excellent plant to grow in small colonies in the woodland among rocks or tall spring wildflowers. When planted in dry woodland it will become dormant in periods of drought. It can be grown in full sunlight.

PLANTING TIME: Spring or fall, while at least partially dormant.

ROOT SYSTEM: A compact rootstock with stringy fibrous roots which form a large clump. A vigorous grower, it forms large colonies quickly.

This violet self-sows readily wherever the ground is open. Collecting seeds is a problem, as the seed capsules burst open unexpectedly.

PLANTING DEPTH AND SPACING: Space 4 to 6 inches or more apart. Spread the roots evenly and barely cover the crowns. Mulch lightly.

PLANTING STOCK AND PROPAGATION: Use nursery-grown stock or, when available, quality collected stock.

If you propagate by planting seeds in flats, do not transplant the seedlings until the second year. The plant self-sows under ideal conditions where there is an abundance of leafmold.

COMMENTS: Smooth yellow violet is best suited for planting among taller, more robust woodland wildflowers. It provides a neat groundcover for moist areas.

Viola canadensis • Canada violet

DESCRIPTION: 10 to 15 inches tall. The pointed heart-shaped leaves of the Canada violet grow on leafy stems. The flowers are predominantly white; the plant may simultaneously bear white, magenta-flushed, and lavender-flushed flowers. They have dark purple veins inside, from the lower part of the petals to the base, and yellow centers.

The Canada violet grows in cool shady woods, usually in rocky terrain and often with Dutchman's breeches and wild blue phlox. It favors cold climates.

PERIOD OF BLOOM: May through June, often into midsummer.

SOIL: Neutral to slightly acid soil that is rich in humus and reasonably moist. Once established, the plants can withstand drought as well as severe cold without mulch.

LOCATION AND EXPOSURE: Cool shaded woodland where the soil is rich in humus and rather rocky; such a spot is often found near a brook. Grow the Canada violet in colonies to promote longer periods of bloom.

PLANTING TIME: While dormant in spring or fall. This violet should not be moved bareroot once it has begun to grow.

ROOT SYSTEM: A knotty rhizome with many fibrous roots. It forms a compact clump that is difficult to divide.

PLANTING DEPTH AND SPACING: Space 1 inch apart or more. Set the rootstock with the crown just barely below soil level.

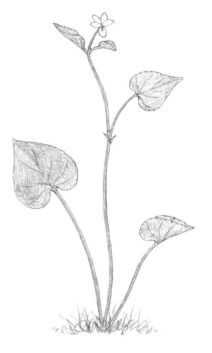

PLANTING STOCK AND PROPAGATION: Use nursery-grown stock or quality collected stock.

Seeds are scarce, but sowing is the best method of propagation. This violet self-sows to some extent, but spreads very slowly and never becomes weedy.

COMMENTS: The peculiarity of having white and partly colored flowers on the same plant at the same time makes the Canada violet an interesting specimen. The blossoms are long-lasting.

Viola conspersa • American dog violet

DESCRIPTION: 2 to 6 inches tall. The dainty flowers are light to medium blue, with dark veining extending into the white throat. The stems are slender, with a number of rounded leaves. Each plant usually has two to four flowering stalks.

The American dog violet grows in dry, open woodland with sparse grasses or in damp, rocky woods. When we cleared land to make our lawn, the dog violet volunteered abundantly and still persists in some shady spots.

PERIOD OF BLOOM: May into June.

SOIL: Neutral to slightly acid soil of average fertility.

LOCATION AND EXPOSURE: Partial to high open shade or places exposed to the morning sun. Plant this violet in colonies among other small wildflowers, or tuck it into shady, humus-filled niches of a rock garden.

PLANTING TIME: While dormant in early spring or fall. This variety does not transplant easily once it has begun to grow.

ROOT SYSTEM: A small rootstock with fibrous roots.

PLANTING DEPTH AND SPACING: Set the plants about 4 inches apart and as deep as the level at which they previously grew. Always move the plants with a little dirt adhering to the roots.

PLANTING STOCK AND PROPAGATION: Use nursery-grown stock or collected stock with soil adhering.

Seeds are hard to collect. This violet self-sows to some extent.

COMMENTS: Along with the sweet white, the American dog violet is our daintiest violet. Unlike the former, it does not spread by rhizomes; it multiplies slowly and never gets weedy. To make the dog violet more noticeable, plant in groups of three to six.

Viola (a sport?) • an unidentified violet

A short while ago I found in my wild garden a strange new violet growing where *Viola papilionacea*, the common blue violet, had previously grown. The flower is a delicate sky-blue and the lower petal is flushed with a deeper blue and veined with dark purple. The two lateral petals are downy toward the throat, which is a delicate chartreuse. The foliage is light green and similar in shape to that of Jessie's red violet. It does well in either full sun or light shade.

The intruder has been separated from the other plants and I am now waiting to see what the seedlings will be like. Will their flowers be purple-blue like the common blue violet's, or remain, like their parents', a lovely sky blue?

LYTHRACEAE [**Loosestrife Family**]

Lythrum Salicaria • purple loosestrife

DESCRIPTION: 2 to 4 feet tall. The showy flower spikes have tiny flowers ranging from rose-purple to magenta. The leafy square stems have lanced foliage on either side.

Purple loosestrife is found in damp ditches, sunny wet meadows, and marshes. It grows very tall and stately in wet places. I first came upon it growing in a wet ditch, where it has continued to grow for years.

PERIOD OF BLOOM: June through September, reaching its peak in July and August.

SOIL: Slightly acid to neutral, fertile soils with constant moisture, though not necessarily wet. Purple loosestrife does reasonably well in ordinary garden soil that does not bake dry.

LOCATION AND EXPOSURE: To best display their beauty, set the plants singly or in groups of three. Plant all members of the loose-strife family where you want them to remain, since they develop heavy roots with age. A single plant sends up many spikes as it

149

matures. Purple loosestrife is excellent for naturalizing in a wet meadow or as a specimen plant at the back of a border.

PLANTING TIME: While dormant in spring or fall.

ROOT SYSTEM: A very unyielding, woody rootstock with fine fibrous roots. When moving old plants, prune the roots considerably to encourage new growth.

PLANTING DEPTH AND SPACING: Space 1 to 3 feet apart. Set young or medium-sized plants with the pink eye about 1 inch below soil level. Trim off ragged old roots, leaving only the fine fibrous ones.

PLANTING STOCK AND PROPAGATION: Use young to medium-sized nursery-grown stock or quality collected young stock. Use old plants only as a last resort.

Cuttings taken from the center length of the stem in July give very good results and is the best method of propagation. Purple loosestrife self-sows in some areas.

COMMENTS: Purple loosestrife is a bold plant that lends color and beauty to the landscape. Originally found only in cultivation, it has taken to the wild and prospered remarkably well.

ARALIACEAE [Ginseng Family]

Aralia racemosa • spikenard

DESCRIPTION: 2 to 5 feet tall. The large, tapered flower clusters, made up of many tiny flowers, are white with a tint of yellow or green. They grow upright above large compound foliage on heavy, leafy stems. The stems are a wine-flushed green. Purple-red to wine-colored berries ripen in the fall and are very showy. Spikenard is a robust grower, and seems almost tropical. You will know this bold plant whenever you meet it, which will usually be quite unexpectedly.

Spikenard is rarely found in large patches. It seeks high open shade in deciduous woods where leafmold is deep but where the terrain is rocky and bare of other vegetation.

PERIOD OF BLOOM: Late June into July.

SOIL: Slightly acid to neutral rich woods soil with constant moisture is best. But I have also grown spikenard in partial shade and in full sun in a fertile sandy loam with no more than average moisture.

LOCATION AND EXPOSURE: For a bold effect, plant spikenard alone in full display, with a shady border as background, or along the border of open woodlands. It is equally effective when planted in high open shade where only leafmold or small wildflowers and ferns carpet the forest floor. A few plants here and there are sure to draw favorable comments.

PLANTING TIME: While dormant in spring or fall.

ROOT SYSTEM: A large knotty and scarred rhizome grayish in color and forked several times. Each year's growth leaves a scar on the rootstock. The roots have a very pleasing aroma. It is next to impossible to dig up large rootstocks without breaking them, but this does not hinder future growth. The top growth is deciduous.

PLANTING DEPTH AND SPACING: Cut the heavy portion of rootstocks into 4 to 5 inch lengths and plant horizontally 1 to 2 inches deep in sandy loam in partial shade. Keep the soil reasonably moist.

PLANTING STOCK AND PROPAGATION: Nursery-grown transplants between one and two years old are best. Or use quality collected stock that is not too large. Young plants that have not yet bloomed are easiest to move.

Divide old rootstocks. During the fall the plants go dormant. A good number of the divisions will grow into plants worth transplanting. Some may bloom the following year.

I have had considerable success with cuttings by packing them in plastic bags with damp sphagnum moss and keeping them in the well pit over the winter. I set the cuttings out in mid-June, mulch them, and keep them moist. Over 85 percent grew.

COMMENTS: The large compound leaves and colorful fall fruit of the spikenard make it an unusual plant of great beauty. Planted alone in full display, it is a bold specimen. The plants are slow to bloom after being disturbed, but they are not demanding; once established they last for many years.

Aralia nudicaulis • wild sarsaparilla

DESCRIPTION: 8 to 12 inches tall. A solitary stem bears three compound leaves, which usually grow horizontally. Each flowering plant has only one bare stalk topped with one to three round flower heads. The flower heads are made up of many tiny greenish florets. Green berries turn black in fall.

Wild sarsaparilla is found growing in conservative little colonies in dry deciduous woods and thickets.

PERIOD OF BLOOM: May into June.

SOIL: Acid to slightly acid woods soil or garden soil. The plant is easily cultivated.

LOCATION AND EXPOSURE: Wild sarsaparilla makes a good open groundcover in high shade where the forest floor is covered with leafmold and other vegetation is sparse. If you grow it along the edge of the woodland it will usually work its way inward.

PLANTING TIME: While dormant in spring or fall.

ROOT SYSTEM: The knotty rootstock, bearing scars of each previous year's growth, forms rhizomes that send up new plants at frequent intervals.

PLANTING DEPTH AND SPACING: Space 12 to 18 inches apart. Set plants with dormant shoots at soil level and mulch. Any attached rhizomes should be planted horizontally.

PLANTING STOCK AND PROPAGATION: Use nursery-grown stock or quality collected stock.

Divide rootstocks when they are dormant. Sarsaparilla can be grown from seeds sown when ripe, but it propagates so easily from rootstock divisions that I hardly ever bother with seeds. Seedlings mature slowly.

COMMENTS: The foliage of the wild sarsaparilla makes a striking contrast interspersed with other woodland plants. Do not plant it among very small woodland plants or it may block out too much light. My plants send up new shoots at intervals of 6 to 10 inches, but this might vary according to soil fertility.

The wild sarsaparilla is not of the sarsaparilla family but derives its name from the similar flavor of its roots, which are often used as a substitute for making syrup and medicinal extracts.

Panax quinquefolium   •   ginseng

DESCRIPTION: 8 to 15 inches tall. Each plant sends up a solitary stalk with three compound leaves and one round, white to yellowish flower cluster. In early autumn the crimson berries appear. The rootstock is yellowish brown.

Ginseng is found in northeastern and north central hardwood forests, in cool shade where leafmold is plentiful. It is rare.

PERIOD OF BLOOM: July.

SOIL: Ginseng will grow only in a humus-rich woodland soil. The soil should be preferably from hardwood areas—never from the high-acid evergreen areas.

LOCATION AND EXPOSURE: This plant must have shade. Cool shade in an open woods is ideal. In the wild garden, ginseng is grown mainly for the contrast of its foliage and the bright color of its berry rather than for its flower. Because of its history, ginseng is certain to be a conversation piece in any wild garden.

PLANTING TIME: While dormant in spring or fall.

ROOT SYSTEM: A cylindrical, fleshy rootstock of a yellowish brown color that forks as it matures. It is aromatic.

PLANTING DEPTH AND SPACING: Space 8 or more inches apart. Or plant a few at random. Set the eyes of the rootstock 2 to 3 inches deep, making certain that the tapering rootstock is not bent over. Mulch lightly, preferably with old leafmold.

PLANTING STOCK AND PROPAGATION: Nursery-grown stock, one to two years old, is best. Or use quality collected stock if you are fortunate enough to find it. Ginseng is becoming increasingly rare in the wild.

Ginseng seeds take eighteen months to germinate; they should never be allowed to dry out. Fresh seeds should be layered immediately in damp earth and kept until the following August or September, then planted in beds in the open. Space them several inches apart. Or try sowing the seeds in the open and letting them fend for themselves. This method has given me the best results. Seedlings may appear the second spring. They require about two years to bloom, and five years to mature.

COMMENTS: Ginseng once grew abundantly in our hardwood forests. Unfortunately, so many plants were dug up for export to China, where they were prized for the medicinal value of their roots, that it is now rarely found growing wild.

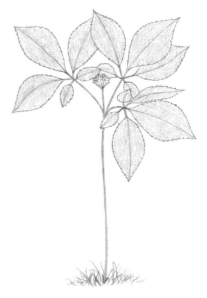

Panax trifolium • dwarf ginseng

DESCRIPTION: 3 to 5 inches tall. This neat little plant has a small ball of tiny white florets above a whorl of three small, compound palmate leaves. Yellow berries appear in the fall.

Dwarf ginseng is found in moist rich woods, usually where there is a mixture of evergreen and deciduous trees. It may be found on moist hummocks in high open shade. It is quite rare.

PERIOD OF BLOOM: May into June.

SOIL: Acid to slightly acid humus-rich woods soil that retains moisture. Add some damp peatmoss to the soil.

LOCATION AND EXPOSURE: Plant dwarf ginseng in damp, moist woodland or at the edge of a shady bog that is free from grass and covered with low sphagnum moss.

PLANTING TIME: Fall is best. The plant must be dormant.

ROOT SYSTEM: A tiny, globe-shaped, blackish tuber.

PLANTING DEPTH AND SPACING: Space only about 4 inches apart in a small colony. Set the tubers 2 inches deep; in the wild they are even deeper.

PLANTING STOCK AND PROPAGATION: Nursery-grown stock is rarely offered. Use quality collected stock dug in fall. Never transplant dwarf ginseng until it goes dormant. Mark the area where you find it growing and return to collect it in fall.

Sow the seeds when they are ripe. The seeds are scarce.

COMMENTS: Dwarf ginseng is a dainty, much prized plant for the wildflower garden. Always set out three or more tubers in a colony —otherwise they will be obscured by the surrounding plants. A small colony perched on a hummock makes a delightful picture.

CORNACEAE [Dogwood Family]

Cornus canadensis • bunchberry

DESCRIPTION: 3 to 5 inches tall. Four white dogwood-like bracts with yellow centers give the effect of a full-bodied flower. The flower grows on a single short, rigid stem above a whorl of four to six almost ovate leaves. Heavy clusters of bright orange-red berries appear in fall.

Bunchberry is found in deep, cool woodlands. It creeps over old decaying logs and sends rhizomes through rotted pine logs. I have even found it growing at the top and along the sides of decaying white pine stumps where chipmunks evidently hid some seeds.

Bunchberry has a way of taking over old logging roads that had the soil scraped bare. When the road is in the shade, bunchberry grows luxuriantly, blooms abundantly, and sets out a heavy seed crop. In sunnier, moister areas the plant is smaller.

PERIOD OF BLOOM: Late May into July.

SOIL: Very acid to slightly acid humus-rich soil with high to average moisture content. However, I once found bunchberry growing along an old logging road in a bank of pure red sand with barely a sprinkling of humus. Since it was on a shady hillside the moisture was constant, and a nice colony of blooming plants was firmly established despite the poor soil.

One little colony which has persisted and bloomed freely along a concrete walk grows in soil with a pH of only 6. I am therefore inclined to believe that shade, constant moisture with good drainage, humus-rich soil or damp sand, are much more important than an acid soil.

LOCATION AND EXPOSURE: Bunchberry is an excellent groundcover under evergreens or deciduous trees where there is ample humus and where falling needles and leaves furnish a continuous mulch and make the soil sufficiently acidic and fertile. Bunchberry is a good companion plant for the pink lady's slipper or bluebeard lily. All three need shade but tolerate filtered spring sunlight or shifting shade in summer.

PLANTING TIME: Plant bareroot stock while dormant in spring or fall. Potted stock can be planted almost anytime.

ROOT SYSTEM: A slender rhizome, forking and spreading in many directions to send up new plants. New rhizomes are white or pinkish with rose-colored buds. They become woody as they mature and therefore more troublesome to establish. When several plants are confined to a small container (2¼ inch rose pot) of woods soil and kept moist, they develop a great many roots in one growing season under ideal conditions. When the plants are removed from the container intact and planted in a permanent home, they soon form a neat colony.

PLANTING DEPTH AND SPACING: Space bareroot stock 6 inches apart

and potted stock 1 foot apart. Set the eye of bareroot stock about ¼ inch deep and mulch lightly. Keep moist. Potted stock should be planted at soil level and also mulched and kept moist. A light mulch of evergreen needles or partly decayed leaves is excellent.

PLANTING STOCK AND PROPAGATION: Nursery-grown potted stock is far superior. You can also use quality collected sods taken from an area where the plants grow close together. Replant the sods at the same soil level. Bareroot stock can be difficult to establish. It must be freshly dug for fair results. I do not recommend it.

Pulp-free seeds planted in peat pots and kept moist sometimes give excellent results. Plant 6 to 8 seeds in each pot. They may not germinate until the second or third year.

COMMENTS: Bunchberry is one of our choicest groundcovers but often difficult to grow successfully. Once established, however, it will continue to spread, densely carpeting the forest floor. Bunchberries do not seem to thrive in isolation; it is best to plant them in groups of three or more.

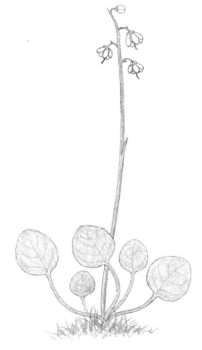

PYROLACEAE [Wintergreen Family]

Pyrola virens • shinleaf

DESCRIPTION: 6 to 8 inches tall. A solitary stem bears a raceme of waxy-white fragrant flowers above roundish basal foliage. The flowers are reminiscent of widely opened lily of the valley.

Shinleaf is found in dry to moist deciduous woods. It grows among fringed polygala and large merrybells on slopes where tall birches, soft maples, aspens, and a few oaks furnish shade. It blooms best where the shade is not too deep.

PERIOD OF BLOOM: June into July.

SOIL: Slightly acid to acid, humus-rich woods soil with some moisture available while the plants are blooming.

LOCATION AND EXPOSURE: High open woodlands where the sun filters through leafless trees in spring. Grow shinleaf in colonies or among other small woodland plants that also thrive in humus-rich soil.

PLANTING TIME: While dormant in spring or fall.

156

ROOT SYSTEM: The running, threadlike white rhizome is very extensive, making it difficult to collect sods with enough rhizomes in each clump.

PLANTING DEPTH AND SPACING: Space about 1 foot apart. Set potted stock or sods at soil level and mulch lightly wth small leaves, preferably birch or willow.

PLANTING STOCK AND PROPAGATION: Nursery-grown potted stock is best, but not often available. Plant quality collected sods, at least 8 inches square, in fall.

You can plant the seeds if they are available, though germination is poor.

COMMENTS: Pyrolas are choice plants with lovely delicate flowers. They make excellent groundcovers but are very difficult plants to establish unless all their requirements are met.

ERICACEAE [Heath Family]

Epigaea repens • trailing arbutus

DESCRIPTION: A 6 to 10 inch creeper. The stems of this vinelike plant are woody and have oval, hairy but somewhat leathery leaves. The clusters of delicate, tubular flowers are white to pale pink and fragrant.

By scuffling the fallen leaves in an oak-pine wood, you may discover trailing arbutus growing in lovely mats. It usually grows in the vicinity of bunchberry, wintergreen, starflower, clintonia, and goldthread.

PERIOD OF BLOOM: May.

SOIL: An acid to moderately acid sandy loam soil, rich in humus to a shallow depth, and with a sandy soil below providing good drainage. I use a soil with a pH of 6.

LOCATION AND EXPOSURE: Trailing arbutus grows well in a cool open woods where it is protected from the hot summer sun but where early spring sunshine filters through leafless branches. Choose a spot where the forest floor is covered with decaying leaves or evergreen needles. Also, woodland soil contains the mycorhizal fungi that are beneficial to the plant.

PLANTING TIME: Plant sods in spring or fall. Potted stock can be planted almost anytime.

ROOT SYSTEM: Except for the taproot, the plant feeds on the first few inches of soil. Feeder roots develop where the vines are covered with damp humus.

PLANTING DEPTH AND SPACING: Set sods or potted stock at soil level and mulch by scattering a mixture of evergreen needles, birch leaves, and soft maple leaves. Keep the plants moist until they are well established.

PLANTING STOCK AND PROPAGATION: Nursery-grown potted stock is superior to quality collected sods.

Cuttings taken in early fall should be put in a sand–peat mixture and placed in a cold frame over the winter. A hormone rooting compound is beneficial. Mulch the cuttings lightly for the winter. There will usually be good stock at the end of the second year (though not always). Diligent care and patience is important.

Seeds sown in a humus-rich acid soil produce a sparse scattering of seedlings. Germination is poor.

COMMENTS: Trailing arbutus is on the protected list in Wisconsin and should never be dug or picked without the permission of the landowner. It is best not to pick arbutus at any time, but rather to enjoy its beauty in the wild. Some of these plants must be preserved for future generations to see.

Gaultheria procumbens • wintergreen

DESCRIPTION: 2 to 4 inches tall. The tiny white bell-shaped flowers, often tinged with pink, are hidden by three thick aromatic leaves. The red berries that appear in fall last a long while, sometimes until spring. These edible berries are known for their flavor.

Wintergreen is often found carpeting large areas of woodland, whether damp or dry, deciduous or evergreen.

PERIOD OF BLOOM: Late June into August.

SOIL: Acid to only slightly acid humus-rich soil with some sandy base beneath to ensure good drainage. Sometimes wintergreen is found growing in peaty soil, usually on hummocks.

LOCATION AND EXPOSURE: Wintergreen grows well under the open shade of oaks and pines. It makes a sturdy groundcover for large woodland areas free from underbrush. It can also be grown in the shade of sparsely planted tall wildflowers or ferns.

PLANTING TIME: Spring or fall. Plant potted stock anytime.

ROOT SYSTEM: A creeping rootstock 1 to 2 inches beneath the soil forks to send out new rhizomes which form new plants. These rhizomes are white to deep pink, and pinkest at the end where the new bud is to form.

PLANTING DEPTH AND SPACING: Space about 1 inch apart exactly at soil level. Mulch lightly with small decaying leaves, pine needles, or preferably a mixture of both.

PLANTING STOCK AND PROPAGATION: Potted nursery-grown stock is best but is rarely offered. Use quality collected sods from areas where the plants grow close together.

You can take cuttings of new plants or rhizomes in July, but I do not get very good results. Seeds are very slow to germinate and give very poor results.

COMMENTS: The mealy red berries have a mild and pleasant minty flavor; they stay on the plants unless plucked by birds or rodents. The leaves also have the wintergreen flavor and can be dried and used as a tea.

Gaultheria hispidula • creeping snowberry

DESCRIPTION: 3 to 6 inch dainty trailing vine. Tiny round evergreen leaves, which taste like wintergreen, are opposite each other on a brown woody stem. The tiny white flowers are bell-shaped. The small aromatic berry that appears later is also white.

I searched for a bed of creeping snowberry for a long time until my husband showed me a patch he had found in a white-spruce swamp while hunting. This patch made a showy carpet. It grew protected from hot sun on hummocklike spots overgrown by dense hugging mosses, on old logs decayed almost to humus, and it reached out into sphagnum-moss beds where an occasional pitcher plant stood out boldly.

PERIOD OF BLOOM: May into June.

SOIL: I found the snowberry growing in a medium that could hardly be called soil; it was composed of moss-covered decaying wood covered with layers of old needles, tiny mosses, and decaying

vegetation. I constructed a similar medium by the following process, which proved successful. Select a cool dampy site and dig a hole. Make a rim around the top of the hole with a ring of metal at least 6 inches wide. Fill the hole to the top with equal portions of sharp sand, coarsely sifted rotted pine wood, shredded damp sphagnum moss, and damp peatmoss, all mixed together thoroughly. Moisten and firm the mixture as you fill the hole.

If you can find a well rotted white pine log in your woodland just let the snowberry ramble over it, and skip the above procedure.

LOCATION AND EXPOSURE: Creeping snowberry requires deep cool shade and a constant supply of moisture. Moisture is *very* important. Plant the creeping snowberry in a carefully prepared bed or near a rotted log where it can ramble to form a dense colony.

PLANTING TIME: Plant sods in spring or fall. Potted stock can be planted anytime.

ROOT SYSTEM: Fine hairy roots form on the underside of the woody stems wherever the plant lies on damp moss or decaying humus. These tiny roots do not continue growing when planted directly into ordinary woods soil.

PLANTING DEPTH AND SPACING: Space 1 foot apart. Set potted stock or sod at soil level, tucking in any tiny rootlets that may have formed along the stems. When you grow snowberry in a prepared bed try to find a piece of rotted, moss-covered wood to put nearby to create a natural effect. If the wood is kept moist, some of the stems will root and gradually spread over the entire surface.

PLANTING STOCK AND PROPAGATION: Nursery-grown potted stock is by far the best, but rarely offered. With proper care, quality collected stock will give good results in an ideal location.

Seeds are very scarce and very slow to germinate.

Six-inch cuttings taken in early May give good results. My method of propagation: Place a plastic sheet about 6 by 24 inches on a table. Cover half of it lengthwise with damp shredded sphagnum moss. Over this, lay the 6 inch cuttings on their sides so that the lower 2 inches (trimmed of tiny leaves) rest on the moss and the upper 4 inches extend 1 inch beyond the other side of the 6 inch plastic width. Sprinkle another ½ inch layer of damp sphagnum moss over the stems on the mossy side of the plastic. Now fold the clear side of the plastic over the mossy side; roll up the entire length of the sheet carefully and tie it. This should give you a roll with the 1 inch of leafy stems covering one end. Place the roll with the leafy side up in a tin can punched with holes, and loosely invert a plastic bag over both. Put the whole thing in the propagating frame or cold frame. In the propagating frame the cuttings may be ready for potting in late August; in the cold frame they will take another year. Always keep the moss moist.

Pot the cuttings in the mixture described above in the soil section. Hold the potted cuttings in a cold frame for a year or two before moving them to their permanent bed.

When transplanting to pots, let any moss adhering to the fragile roots remain. Particular care must be taken at this time not to injure the fine roots. This method will produce stock that should grow into showy specimens.

COMMENTS: Cultivating creeping snowberry is a challenging pursuit needing special care and patience; you may well be proud once you have succeeded in establishing it.

Arctostaphylos Uva-ursi • bearberry

DESCRIPTION: 8 to 20 inch trailing vines. The small, white to pinkish flowers resemble those of blueberry and wintergreen. The small, ovate, alternate leaves on a woody vine form a dense carpet of glossy green. The stems of vines over two years old are often tinted with red. Long-lasting red berries appear in August.

Bearberry grows along sandy roadsides, in open oak and pine woods, and in places where there is barely an inch of top soil and plenty of red sand. On sunny sandy banks in reforested areas, where fire lanes interlace the countryside, bearberry is often found crawling along and rooting as it travels. Bearberry is beautiful in such areas, always lush and green.

PERIOD OF BLOOM: Late May.

SOIL: Acid to moderately acid, gritty soil. It should be moist enough to allow for good growth, but must always have good drainage. A generous amount of sharp sand and damp peatmoss should be added to average soils.

LOCATION AND EXPOSURE: Bearberry is an unexcelled groundcover for sandy soil on a gently sloped bank or in wide patches of open sand. It blooms best in sunny areas. It is also a good groundcover

161

to plant in intermittent sunlight under high-branched evergreens.

PLANTING TIME: Plant potted stock or sods in early spring or fall.

ROOT SYSTEM: Fine hairy roots develop wherever the tender young vines rest on the damp earth as they creep along. When the vines become woody the hairy roots break away, and the plant dies from lack of nourishment.

PLANTING DEPTH AND SPACING: Set potted stock at soil level or slightly deeper. Cover any bare branches with soil. New roots will develop on two-year-old stems. Space potted stock or sods about 1 foot apart. Time and patience are required to establish this plant successfully, but once established it grows luxuriantly.

PLANTING STOCK AND PROPAGATION: Nursery-grown potted stock is best though expensive. Sods are difficult to dig up and not always reliable. Planting bareroot stock is a waste of time and money.

Cuttings taken in July give poor results, but cuttings taken in early September when the wood has hardened a little give better results. You may use the same procedure that I described for propagating from creeping snowberry cuttings. Or dip the cuttings in a hormone rooting compound, pot them in a sand-peat mixture, and put them in a propagating frame. It may take one or two years before the plants can be placed in their permanent home.

Seeds sown as soon as they ripen may take two years to germinate and another two or three years for the seedlings to mature enough to bloom.

COMMENTS: Bearberry is not an easy plant to grow, but once established it quickly carpets large areas with glossy green.

In autumn, when the foliage takes on a bronze tinge, the partridges come searching for bearberries to eat.

DIAPENSIACEAE [Diapensia Family]

Galax aphylla • galax

DESCRIPTION: 8 to 15 inches tall. Racemes of dainty white flowers grow on leafless stalks. The round basal foliage is a lustrous shiny green, often with a reddish tint. The leaves are slightly toothed and have a leathery texture.

Galax grows naturally in rocky mountainous woods with heavy soils in the southern part of the country.

PERIOD OF BLOOM: May into June.

SOIL: In the wild, galax grows in heavy clay soil. In my wild garden I grow it in an acid to slightly acid woods soil with a generous layer of decaying oak leafmold. It needs constant moisture.

LOCATION AND EXPOSURE: Galax is an excellent groundcover to grow in the deep shade of high open oak and evergreen woods where there is humus to hold in the moisture. It is best displayed when grown in its own exclusive colony.

PLANTING TIME: Spring or fall.

ROOT SYSTEM: A knotty, twisted, pinkish-red rhizome that forks to send up new shoots. It has fibrous feeder roots.

PLANTING DEPTH AND SPACING: Space 6 to 12 inches apart. Set bare roots horizontally about 1 inch deep with the red tip leading to soil level. Set potted stock or sods at the same level at which they previously grew. Give extra mulch in winter in very cold climates.

PLANTING STOCK AND PROPAGATION: Nursery-grown potted stock is best, but you can also use quality collected sods.

When dividing large clumps, leave soil adhering. I have never grown galax from seeds, as the plant does not set seed this far north.

COMMENTS: Galax, which is also known as beetleweed or wand-flower, is a plant of high quality, but difficult to grow. It is much sought after by florists for its long-lasting, leathery leaves.

I had almost given up hope of growing galax this far north; despite frequent waterings, my plants did not flourish. Then, after a good soaking, I decided to smother them with decaying oak leaves (no white oak). I set the galax in an out-of-the-way place and completely neglected them. Late in August I went back to the site and was surprised to find that all the plants had sent up healthy new leaves. They had taken hold despite neglect and severe drought, and I can only attribute this growth to the 6 to 8 inch layer of oak leaves I had spread over the area.

I will take some root cuttings from this acclimated stock in early spring before new growth appears.

PRIMULACEAE [Primrose Family]

Dodecatheon Meadia • shooting star

DESCRIPTION: 10 to 15 inches tall. Clusters of starlike flowers with curved petals are borne on sturdy hollow stems above a rosette of round-lobed oblong foliage. The stars vary in color from white to pink or lavender. (The white variety is supposedly rare, but most of my plants are white.) The centers of the flowers are yellow with blackish circles. The interesting cuplike seed pods have little toothed edges.

Shooting star is found in open woods, fertile prairies, meadows, and old cemeteries.

PERIOD OF BLOOM: May into June.

SOIL: Fertile sandy loam, heavier soils, or humus-rich woodland soil that is neutral to slightly acid. The plants must have moisture when they are blooming.

LOCATION AND EXPOSURE: Plant shooting stars along a path, among rocks in shade, or in the open woodland where they will have sun during the spring. Shooting stars can also be planted in full sun among other plants that will take over when it goes dormant. Established plants can endure extreme drought if they are well mulched. I keep the nursery beds under continuous mulch, adding some each year after the plants go dormant.

PLANTING TIME: Fall is preferable.

ROOT SYSTEM: A coarse rootstock with white fibrous roots and many feeder rootlets. As the plant grows older, it sends up several crowns. Mature plants form little eyes near the crown, and these develop into new plants. The rootstock is very fragrant.

PLANTING DEPTH AND SPACING: Space 10 to 15 inches apart. Set the eye of the dormant stock about ½ inch deep, making sure to spread the roots evenly. Mulch.

PLANTING STOCK AND PROPAGATION: Use nursery-grown or quality collected stock, the latter will not usually bloom the first year.

The easiest method of propagation is to divide the crowns in late summer or fall. To divide the rootstock, break away from the mother plant each segment that bears an eye. Remove part of

164

the lower portion so that the new segment is about 3 inches long. Set in a flat or in a pot. Usually two years elapse before new plants will bloom.

Seeds are plentiful but very slow to germinate. Seedlings are very fragile for the first two years and may die in transplanting.

COMMENTS: There is a much showier species, *Dodecatheon amethystinum*, with blossoms in shades of glowing amethyst and magenta. They require more moisture, however, and are not as easily grown as the more common *Dodecatheon Meadia*. Shooting star is sometimes known as American cowslip.

Lysimachia terrestris • swamp candles

DESCRIPTION: 10 to 15 inches tall. The upright stalks have willow-like leaves and are topped with a wand of clear yellow, starlike flowers with reddish purple markings. The flowers bloom over a long period if there is ample moisture. Bulbils form in the axils of the leaves.

Swamp candles are found in lowlands and roadside ditches. Once plentiful in my area, they are now found only along lesser country roads because of weed spraying along the highways.

PERIOD OF BLOOM: June through August, and sometimes into September.

SOIL: Moist to wet soils of moderate acidity and fertility. When swamp candles are grown in average garden soil that is constantly moist, the blossoms will be smaller and will not last as long.

LOCATION AND EXPOSURE: Swamp candles are best planted in colonies in a dampish place where they can spread to form a large mass. Mulch or plant among sparse grasses. Full sun is necessary for good bloom.

PLANTING TIME: Spring or fall, but I have moved swamp candles with soil adhering while they were blooming. I watered them carefully and they continued to bloom.

ROOT SYSTEM: Creeping rhizomes with a pinkish tint often send up new shoots which eventually develop into plants large enough to bloom.

PLANTING DEPTH AND SPACING: Space the plants at least 1 or more feet apart since they spread. Plant the rhizomes horizontally 1 inch deep and mulch. It is best to weed the beds by hand when the plants are growing in cultivated soil, as young plants continuously appear beside parent plants.

PLANTING STOCK AND PROPAGATION: Use nursery-grown stock or quality collected stock.

Divide crowded clumps. Bulbils planted as soon as they ripen produce plants which are often mature enough to bloom in the second year.

COMMENTS: I had searched long and hard to find this plant when I came upon it quite by accident in a swamp not far from home.

Lysimachia Nummularia • moneywort

DESCRIPTION: 6 to 15 inch vines. Moneywort forks as it creeps along and has round leaves opposite each other on the vine. Single, bright yellow flowers are found in the axils of the leaves.

Moneywort is found in damp areas, dry open fields, and in old gardens. It was orginally grown only in cultivation.

PERIOD OF BLOOM: Late June into August.

SOIL: Poor sandy soil to soil of good fertility that is slightly acid. Damp soil and soil which never becomes extremely dry is satisfactory.

LOCATION AND EXPOSURE: Moneywort will grow in sun or light shade, but it blooms more profusely when grown in full sun and fertile damp soils. This neat groundcover hugs the earth closely and is excellent used with wildflowers such as lady's-slippers, trilliums, or baneberries. It is also useful as a hanging vine in window boxes.

PLANTING TIME: Spring or fall.

ROOT SYSTEM: Tiny white roots form along the vines wherever the nodes touch the damp earth or where a little mulch falls over the vines. At these intervals, where the new roots form, clusters of pink eyes soon appear, giving rise to a new plant.

PLANTING DEPTH AND SPACING: Space 1 foot or more apart to allow for spreading. Set the crowns at soil level, but any pink eyes at

the base of the crown should be planted ¼ inch below soil level.

PLANTING STOCK AND PROPAGATION: Use nursery-grown or quality collected stock. Potted or bareroot stock should have several leaders. To propagate, divide well-rooted vines that have formed a colony of new plants, or take stem cuttings in June or July. I have not tried growing moneywort from seed, since it is too easily propagated by other means.

COMMENTS: Moneywort is a good plant to use where there is too much shade or the soil is not fertile enough for grass to grow. Moneywort makes dense mats and stays green all summer. It is not damaged by mowing, and its spreading is easily restricted since its roots are very shallow.

Trientalis borealis • starflower

DESCRIPTION: 4 to 8 inches tall. A single wiry stem supports a whorl of six or more leaves. Above this on a short stem appear one or two showy white stars. These are replaced later by a tiny white seed-ball containing several seeds.

Starflower is found in the damp, deep shade of hardwoods as well as in somewhat drier woods of oak, aspens, soft maple, and occasional balsams. Leafmold is always deep and humus abundant.

PERIOD OF BLOOM: May into June.

SOIL: Acid to moderately acid soil, rich in leafmold and humus, with constant moisture.

LOCATION AND EXPOSURE: Starflower must have some shade. If the soil is too dry the plant goes dormant shortly after blooming. Starflower is an excellent groundcover. I have planted a few in the shade of a birch tree among rocks and mulched them with an inch-deep layer of sphagnum moss. Over this I placed a thin sod of dainty growing mosses. Each spring the starflowers emerge through the mosses and put on a lovely show of their own, always adding new plants to their growing colony.

PLANTING TIME: Fall planting is best; the plant is too easily broken in spring when growth has started.

ROOT SYSTEM: A tiny, irregular-shaped tuber with many white threadlike roots. The tubers are connected by threadlike stolons, which pause at intervals to produce new tubers.

PLANTING DEPTH AND SPACING: Always plant in colonies, spacing

6 to 9 inches apart. Plant bareroot stock 1 inch deep in moist, humus-rich soil and plant potted stock at soil level. Starflowers spread gradually by slender rhizomes.

PLANTING STOCK AND PROPAGATION: Nursery-grown potted stock is best: the root system will not have to be disturbed during transplanting and the tubers have usually multiplied. If you collect stock, gather a bit of the immediately surrounding leafmold to add around the roots when transplanting.

Sow seeds in flats ½ inch deep as soon as they ripen—the soil in the flat should contain a lot of leafmold. Place an evergreen bough over the flat to shelter it in winter. When the seeds germinate, give them light shade. A slow process, but fun to try.

COMMENTS: The delicate starflower will naturalize and spread once it is established. When transplanted, it may stay dormant for a year before showing any growth.

GENTIANACEAE [Gentian Family]

Gentiana Andrewsii • bottle gentian

DESCRIPTION: 1 to 2 feet tall. Clusters of bottle-shaped flowers are a gorgeous copen blue of great intensity. White flowers are rare. These clusters are located in the axils of the upper leaves. Pointed and lanceolate leaves on opposing sides of the stem are often tipped with bronze late in summer.

The bottle gentian grows in damp sunny meadows and among the sparse grasses along shady brooks and lake shores.

PERIOD OF BLOOM: August into September.

SOIL: Neutral to slightly acid fertile but sandy soil as well as heavier black soils. I grow bottle gentian in sandy loam of average fertility with moderate to ample moisture. The soil need not be as wet as in its native habitat.

LOCATION AND EXPOSURE: When grown in open, damp sunny meadows with Cardinal flowers bottle gentians are outstanding. Or grow in light shade beside a brook or next to a pool. The bottle gentians adapt readily when transplanted if you do not disturb the soil around their roots. Mulch for best results or plant at a shallow depth.

168

PLANTING TIME: Fall transplanting is best. Stock transplanted in spring requires watering to establish. Never transplant gentians after they are a few inches tall.

ROOT SYSTEM: A coarse rootstock with many fleshy white roots extending away from the crown. In nursery-grown stock with trimmed roots, many new fibrous roots develop.

PLANTING DEPTH AND SPACING: Space 8 to 12 inches apart. In the wild, I find that the roots are near the surface, but in cultivation I get better results by setting the crown at least 1 inch deep, especially for large plants. Always trim all the roots back to 3 to 4 inches before transplanting. This encourages new fibrous roots to grow, and the plants will be more vigorous.

PLANTING STOCK AND PROPAGATION: Nursery-grown stock is best. You can also use freshly dug collected stock with roots trimmed to 3 to 4 inches so that new fibrous ones may develop from the cut ends.

Scatter seeds on a flat when ripe and cover with a ½ inch mesh to protect them from rodents and wind. Cover with an evergreen bough or light mulch until spring. Seedlings should be left in the flats until the end of the second growing season or early the following spring. Then trim the roots and transplant to their permanent home.

COMMENTS: A colony of blue-flowered bottle gentian makes a memorable sight. Gentians are choice long-lived wildflowers. They need little care other than keeping them free of weeds.

Gentiana Saponaria • soapwort gentian

DESCRIPTION: 18 to 30 inches tall. Bottle-shaped flowers are a slightly lighter blue than bottle gentian and fade to lavender with age. White flowers are rare. The blossoms are long-lived and bloom well. The pointed lanceolate foliage, with opposing leaves, is narrower than that of the bottle gentian.

Soapwort is found in roadside ditches, along wet lake shores and brooks, at the edge of marshes, and in damp meadows. It often grows in large colonies, especially to the west of us along the Wisconsin River.

PERIOD OF BLOOM: Late July into August. It is the first gentian to bloom.

SOIL: Neutral to slightly acid soil of good fertility. In the nursery we grow it in fertile sandy loam, sometimes in very light shade, but mostly in full sun.

LOCATION AND EXPOSURE: Interplant soapwort gentian with other gentians to extend the blooming period of the area. Near our pool, where the soil is sandy and barren and overrun by a groundcover of wine cups, a lone gentian seedling volunteered. In a few years it grew into a large flowering clump despite the poor, dry soil. It is growing next to a stone, which may account for its ability to thrive without watering and endure periods of drought.

PLANTING TIME: While dormant in spring or (preferably) fall.

ROOT SYSTEM: A coarse rootstock with many white stringy roots that are fleshy and tapering. Unpruned roots of seedlings that are left to develop without transplanting may reach up to 2 feet for moisture and nutrients.

PLANTING DEPTH AND SPACING: Space about 10 inches or more apart. Trim the roots to 3 to 4 inches before planting. Set the crowns 1 to 1½ inches deep. Because the roots are trimmed and set deeper than wildlings, with age, the plants develop extra flower stalks and form larger clumps.

PLANTING STOCK AND PROPAGATION: Nursery-grown stock has a better, more compact, heavier root system than collected stock. Quality collected stock should have all roots trimmed back to 3 to 4 inches before transplanting.

Gentians rarely self-sow. For seedlings follow the directions for bottle gentian.

COMMENTS: This gentian is the most robust of those mentioned in this book. I prefer it for its long-lasting flowers.

Along the Wisconsin River at a friend's home, I came upon the white form of soapwort gentian. These plants have been moved to the far end of the nursery, away from the blue kind, so that hopefully the seeds may produce white seedlings.

Gentiana decora • Allegheny Mountain gentian

DESCRIPTION: 1 to 2 feet tall. The flowers of this gentian are smaller than those of the bottle or soapwort gentians, and the color is as intensely blue as the bottle gentian. The foliage is narrower and more refined.

The Allegheny Mountain gentian is native to the Allegheny Mountain country and nearby areas of Tennessee. It has also proved hardy in the very severe winters of Wisconsin.

PERIOD OF BLOOM: Late September into November. This gentian blooms somewhat late; its bottles remain blue for a long while, even after frost has faded the foliage.

SOIL: Neutral to slightly acid soil with damp to average moisture. Constant moisture is important for all gentians.

LOCATION AND EXPOSURE: Plant in sun or very light shade. In the north it should be planted in a sheltered area to keep the frost from harming its blossoms.

PLANTING TIME: While dormant in spring or fall; fall is preferable. I find mulching is easier when a bit of old growth is left on the plant.

ROOT SYSTEM: A small crown with fine white stringy roots.

PLANTING DEPTH AND SPACING: Space 8 to 10 inches apart to form neat clumps. Set the crown 1 to 1½ inches deep and spread the trimmed roots evenly. Mulch for winter and keep reasonably moist, but not necessarily wet.

PLANTING STOCK AND PROPAGATION: Nursery-grown stock is best. Or use quality collected stock if available.

In the north, the plant matures too late to set seeds. If seeds are available, follow the directions for sowing other gentians. It is important to plant fresh seeds as soon as they ripen.

COMMENTS: Often some of the bottles of Allegheny Mountain gentian open slightly. This makes it easier for the bees and insects to pollinate this species.

A lovely plant.

APOCYNACEAE [Dogbane Family]

Amsonia Tabernaemontana • amsonia

DESCRIPTION: 2 to 3 feet tall. The willowlike medium-green leaves alternate along the entire length of the stem. At the top of the stem are panicles of pale blue, starlike flowers with narrow petals. Soon after these fade, white clusters of slender cylindrical seed

pods develop. The leafy stalk continues to grow a few more inches and almost hides the seed pods until they begin to ripen. The pods deepen from pinkish to tan. The seeds are cinnamon brown; they are shaped like ¼ inch long pieces of round toothpicks.

Amsonia is native to southern Illinois and spreads both east and west. It has also proved hardy in northern Wisconsin. Some of my plants, now bushy, have lasted more than ten years.

PERIOD OF BLOOM: May into June.

SOIL: Although amsonia grows in standing water or very damp soil in its native habitat, it adapts to ordinary garden soil with only constant moisture and also to neutral and slightly acid woods soil. In the nursery, soil is a sandy fertile loam that retains moisture reasonably well.

LOCATION AND EXPOSURE: Full sun or partial shade. With age the plant sends up many stalks and becomes large and bushy, capable of taking over a large area left by earlier-blooming spring flowers or bulbs.

PLANTING TIME: While dormant in spring or fall.

ROOT SYSTEM: A fine cream-colored taproot on young plants; as plants mature, the root system becomes coarse and fibrous.

PLANTING DEPTH AND SPACING: Space 2 feet apart to allow for growth. Set the taproot with the eyes about 1 inch below soil level. In very cold areas mulch in winter, or all year if you wish.

PLANTING STOCK AND PROPAGATION: Young to medium-sized nursery-grown stock transplants more easily. You can also use quality collected stock of medium size.

Propagation by division of the roots has proved successful. Seeds are more reliable; as soon as they are ripe sow them in flats or in the open. Transplant seedlings to a permanent location in late summer or the following spring. Plants may bloom the third year.

COMMENTS: Although the amsonia normally grows in wet soils, it will thrive in drier soils; once established the roots seek moisture and nutrients at deeper levels. The foliage remains green until hard-killing frosts.

ASCLEPIADACEAE [Milkweed Family]

Asclepias tuberosa • butterfly flower

DESCRIPTION: 1 to 2 feet tall. Each hairy-velvet stem bears many alternating willowlike leaves. The stems are topped with a cluster of showy flowers that attract many butterflies—as well as hummingbirds and bumblebees. Most flowers are orange, ranging from pale orange to deep red-orange or, occasionally, deep yellow.

Butterfly flower grows in sunny areas along roadsides, deserted fields, and grassy lands. It is also found among shorter grasses along fence lines.

PERIOD OF BLOOM: Late June into August. Transplanted plants often bloom again in September.

After plants have become established for several years, they can be cut back completely after the first blooming to induce a second. Only well-established plants can be selected for cutting back, and it should not be done to the same plant year after year.

SOIL: A sandy loam that is acid to almost neutral is preferable, but butterfly flower also grows in gritty or gravelly soils or even heavier soils. Good drainage is essential—it is much more decisive to the plant's life than pH.

LOCATION AND EXPOSURE: Full sun and good drainage are the first considerations. Set in permanent locations immediately, since established roots grow very deep into the soil for food and moisture.

Butterfly flower is an excellent companion plant for other prairie wildflowers such as harebell, prairie phlox, hoary puccoon, and blazing star.

PLANTING TIME: While dormant in spring or fall. The plants do not move readily when foliage is mature.

ROOT SYSTEM: A cream-colored, fleshy tuberous root that is long, very brittle, and delightfully fragrant.

PLANTING DEPTH AND SPACING: Set the fleshy roots with the eyes 2 inches deep. This depth is important! In nature the eyes grow at soil level, so one assumes that in transplanting the same procedure should be followed—this plant is an exception.

Space 1½ to 3 feet apart. Mature plants growing in full sun and good sandy loam will reach the size of a bushel basket in a few seasons.

When transplanting large seedlings from the nursery, cut off all roots at the lower end, making them a uniform length of about 4 inches. New feeder roots grow from the bottom of the severed roots. The result is a more compact, sturdy rootstock. In very cold climates where snow is scarce, the plant should be well mulched in winter.

PLANTING STOCK AND PROPAGATION: Nursery-grown transplanted stock is superior to collected stock. Do not be dismayed if you do not get the entire root when digging in the wild. Trim all jagged ends. Fall is the best time for collecting.

Root cuttings can be made in spring. Insert 2 inch sections of roots upright into a mixture of sharp sand and some peatmoss or shredded sphagnum moss. To make sure the root remains upright, as you work cut the top of the root straight across and the lower end at an angle. Keep reasonably moist but not wet.

At times I have had poor seed germination, with best results from seeds sown in May. Mulch seedlings the first winter and transplant them the following spring to a permanent location.

COMMENTS: The butterfly flower was once widely used as a tonic and expectorant, and was commonly prescribed for pleurisy, hence it is also called pleurisy root. Most botanical books list this lovely flower by the name butterfly weed, but in nursery catalogs you will find it listed as butterfly flower, a name it rightly deserves.

Asclepias incarnata · swamp milkweed

DESCRIPTION: 3 to 4 feet tall. An unusually showy plant with clusters of flat-topped, wine-rose-colored flowers on top of a well-branched stem. White flowers are rare. The heavy stalk is hollow and flushed with wine color. It bears only a few willowlike, lanceolate leaves. The swamp milkweed inhabits wet meadows, brooksides, lake shores and marshes, growing among boneset and Joe-pye.

PERIOD OF BLOOM: July into August.

SOIL: Neutral to slightly acid soil, wetlands to average garden moisture.

LOCATION AND EXPOSURE: Should be grown in full sun, though it tolerates very light shade for part of the day. An excellent plant for open meadows with tall meadowrue, Joe-pye, and goldenrod.

I have grown swamp milkweed in the perennial border where it did well in slightly dry soil.

PLANTING TIME: While dormant in spring or fall.

ROOT SYSTEM: Numerous white threadlike roots, 6 to 8 inches and longer, extend from a sturdy crown with many buds.

PLANTING DEPTH AND SPACING: Space 2 feet apart. Trim the extensive roots back to 3 inches and spread evenly, setting the new shoot at the crown just barely below soil level. The roots should taper slightly downward.

PLANTING STOCK AND PROPAGATION: Use nursery-grown stock of medium size, or quality collected young stock.

Propagate by division of the crowns of the young plants in spring, or sow seed.

My seeds were slow to germinate and gave poor results at times. The plant did, however, volunteer here and there in my garden among the evergreens where the soil is not cultivated and grasses are sparse.

COMMENTS: Every one of my swamp milkweed plants has its own group of butterflies hovering over it.

Asclepias syriaca • common milkweed

DESCRIPTION: 3 to 5 feet tall. A large stout stalk, with blunt-tipped opposite oval leaves, bears large clusters of almost ball-shaped flowers in the axils of the upper leaves. The flowers are mauve-lavender, globe-shaped, and very fragrant.

Found in wastelands, along fence rows and roadsides. Quite common.

PERIOD OF BLOOM: July into August.

SOIL: Easily grown in most soils.

LOCATION AND EXPOSURE: Open sunny areas are best. A dozen plants in a colony make a handsome display. After the plant has bloomed, pull up the stalks; if enough of the root is left in the ground to produce a new plant, it will grow enough to bloom again the following season. If any plants are unwanted, pull up the stalks as they appear and the plant will eventually die.

PLANTING TIME: While dormant in spring or fall.

ROOT SYSTEM: A heavy white rootstock creeps underground and

sends up new shoots at frequent intervals. Rhizomes from the plants by our doorstep have crawled under a 3 foot width of sidewalk to appear in the nearby rock garden.

PLANTING DEPTH AND SPACING: Space 1 foot apart. Set the eyes 1 to 2 inches below soil level. If only one colony is wanted, grow them in a bottomless gallon can buried at soil level.

PLANTING STOCK AND PROPAGATION: Use quality collected stock. The plant self-sows readily.

COMMENTS: The sweet fragrance of the common milkweed permeates the air for a considerable distance from the plant.

POLEMONIACEAE [Polemonium Family]

Polemonium reptans • Greek valerian

DESCRIPTION: 8 to 12 inches tall. The compound leaves resemble those of the Christmas fern but are shorter and a little broader. Leafy stems display china-blue, bell-shaped flowers.

Greek valerian is found in rich deciduous woodlands. It is much improved by cultivation.

PERIOD OF BLOOM: May into June.

SOIL: Ordinary garden soil or rich woods soil, or any soil that is fertile and neutral to only slightly acid.

LOCATION AND EXPOSURE: Grow plants in full sun or shade. Excellent interplanted with mertensia which goes dormant after blooming while the Greek valerian retains its green foliage until hard-killing frosts. This flower goes well with yellow merrybells when grown in shade.

PLANTING TIME: Spring or fall.

ROOT SYSTEM: A tightly crowded clump of fibrous roots.

PLANTING DEPTH AND SPACING: Space 1 to 1½ feet apart since each plant will form a large clump. It should be divided every third year.

PLANTING STOCK AND PROPAGATION: Nursery-grown stock has a more extensive root system, but quality collected stock does well too.

To propagate by division, cut into several clumps in early

spring or mid-August. Sow seeds as soon as they ripen or in very early spring. On bare, uncultivated soil it will self-sow.

COMMENTS: An excellent plant to grow for foliage contrast with plants that have a coarser leaf. Its bright blue flowers vie with the blue of a sunny June day.

Phlox divaricata • wild blue phlox

DESCRIPTION: 8 to 12 inches tall. Opposite lanceolate leaves on wiry stems that support a loose, terminal cluster of single-petaled flowers. The petals often show variation in notching. The flowers are lavender-blue to purple-blue. Occasionally one finds patches of clear blue. Wild blue phlox is often found on shady roadsides, in open woods, and in moist, deciduous rocky woods. Where shade is high it is often found in colonies (especially in Menominee County, Wisconsin).

PERIOD OF BLOOM: Late May into June.

SOIL: Neutral to slightly acid fertile soils. Humus-rich woodland soil is ideal. In the nursery, we grow it in rich garden loam in partial shade.

LOCATION AND EXPOSURE: Filtered sunlight or open shade is preferable. When wild blue phlox is grown with foamflower it offers a lovely blend of blues to accent with white. Cut back the flowering stalks as soon as seeds have dispersed, or sooner if no seed is wanted. In the mulched woodland it does not self-sow readily.

PLANTING TIME: Spring or fall. Also August.

ROOT SYSTEM: A tough, fibrous, stringy root system. New roots will form at the nodes on stems that come into contact with moist earth or even damp mulch.

PLANTING DEPTH AND SPACING: Space about 1 foot apart or scatter in the woodland garden. When transplanting, set the nodes about 1 inch deeper than the level at which the plant previously grew. This will give you a stronger plant because the nodes covered with soil will root and send up extra flower stalks.

PLANTING STOCK AND PROPAGATION: Nursery-grown stock has a more compact and abundant root system. Select quality collected stock with good roots.

Divide clumps in spring (preferably) or in August. Always set plants an inch deeper.

Take cuttings in June from new shoots that appear after flowering stems have been cut back, or take cuttings from the tops of new growth in spring.

The cutting propagation procedures for all varieties of *Phlox divaricata* are the same: Nip out the terminal leaf growth and set cuttings so that two nodes with leaves are above soil level and two nodes without leaves are below soil level. Dip in rooting compound. Pot individually. Put pots in a propagating frame or cover with plastic bags and apply bottom heat. If bottom heat is not available, sink the plastic-covered pots halfway into a "working" compost heap. Enough heat will be present to encourage root growth.

Seeds are not easily collected, but should you get some, sow as soon as they ripen. Seedlings appear the following spring and bloom the following year. Transplant seedlings a few inches high with one node set deeper.

COMMENTS: This is a versatile wildflower that can have many uses —in the rock garden, along a woodland trail, among tulips, or grown along other flower beds in patches for contrast in spring.

Phlox divaricata • phlox

DESCRIPTION: 8 to 12 inches tall. The phlox (var. *Laphamii*) has medium-green foliage on opposing sides of the stem. It holds its color better than other *Phlox divaricata*, rarely having reddish tints in the sky-blue flower. Close observation will show that it is distinctly different. The erect stems are topped by loose terminal clusters of five-petaled flowers. The petals are broader and do not have notches. The bloom is superior, too, but they all make lovely companions in the woodland garden.

Found in rich woodlands in high open shade with other spring wildflowers.

PERIOD OF BLOOM: May into June.

SOIL: Neutral to slightly acid, fertile soil. In humus-rich moist soil the plants form large clumps.

LOCATION AND EXPOSURE: Filtered sunlight is preferred, but it will grow in sun where moisture is constant. Interplant with spring bulbs or other woodland wildflowers. Cut back foliage after blooming. New growth soon appears and remains green late into fall.

PLANTING TIME: Spring or fall.

ROOT SYSTEM: A vigorous but tough fibrous root system, with each node that touches damp earth sending out new roots and later new shoots. Under ideal conditions this plant spreads steadfastly.

PLANTING DEPTH AND SPACING: Space 1 foot or more apart. When transplanting phlox set it deeper so that one or two nodes previously above ground are now covered with soil. These covered nodes will develop new shoots and roots, which will provide heavier bloom the next season. In the woodlands surround the plants with a generous mulching to conserve moisture.

PLANTING STOCK AND PROPAGATION: Cuttings from one-year-old plants are best. Also use quality collected stock when available.

Divide clumps in spring or August, and set plants one or two nodes deeper than previously grown. Take cuttings from new shoots in June before the plant blooms or from the new growth that appears after bloom. Collecting seeds is difficult. Use the cutting propagation procedures described for the wild blue phlox.

COMMENTS: When *Phlox divaricata* varieties are grown together you will readily notice differences among them that are hard to describe. Yet even within this *Laphamii* variety, a bed of these plants grown from cuttings makes an exciting display.

Phlox divaricata • white phlox

DESCRIPTION: 6 to 10 inches tall. White phlox (var. *albiflora*) has wiry stems with light-green lanced leaves and a terminal cluster of five-petaled white blossoms.

The wild white phlox is found in rocky woods east and south of Wisconsin. My original stock came from Kansas and proved as hardy here as native phloxes.

PERIOD OF BLOOM: May into June.

SOIL: Neutral to slightly acid soil with constant moisture. Fertile garden or woodland soil.

LOCATION AND EXPOSURE: Light open shade is preferable. Grow plants in masses for a show of cool white, or plant with colored phloxes for contrast.

PLANTING TIME: Spring or fall.

ROOT SYSTEM: A compact, tough fibrous root system. New roots form where the nodes touch damp earth.

PLANTING DEPTH AND SPACING: Space 6 to 10 inches apart or plant at random among small woodland wildflowers. Always set the plants one or two nodes deeper than their previous level to encourage bushier plants and greater bloom. This is very important!

PLANTING STOCK AND PROPAGATION: Nursery-grown stock is best. Also use quality collected stock where available.

Divide large plants in spring or in August. Take cuttings before or after blooming when new growth appears. Use the cutting propagation procedures described for the wild blue phlox. The white phlox does not take kindly to propagation by cuttings, but rooting hormones will hasten root development. Do not expect the same results with this form as with the colored varieties.

The white phlox is grown more easily from seeds than the colored ones. When the white phlox parent plants are grown unmixed with other phloxes, seedlings usually come 100 percent pure white. If there are a few strays you can distinguish them by their darker green foliage. If white plants are grown next to colored varieties, some colored seedlings will result.

Seedlings may be transplanted when 2 inches tall to pots or to a sheltered place in the open. Always remember to plant one or two nodes deeper than the previous level. This is the secret of getting wild phloxes to form bushy plants that bloom abundantly.

COMMENTS: You will find that this wild phlox requires a little more care, but with fertile soil, light shade, and ample moisture, it will form lovely masses of cool white.

Phlox pilosa • prairie phlox

DESCRIPTION: 1 foot tall. In cultivation, this plant reclines and each rootstock sends up several flower stalks instead of just one. The stalk is slender with opposite linear leaves and bears a loose cluster of flowers, their color varying from pink to violet-lavender. Completely white ones and white ones with red eyes are rare. Occasionally the petals are flared.

Prairie phlox is found in dry prairies, meadows, and along roadsides. In my area of Wisconsin it grows in large colonies along roadsides where the grasses are not too aggressive, making a splash of color.

PERIOD OF BLOOM: June. Cultivated seedlings often bloom again in August and make very bushy plants. Well-established plants

180

may be cut back after blooming, and they, too, often bloom again.

SOIL: Slightly acid sandy loam is best. In the nursery we use fertile but sandy loam. Good drainage is important.

LOCATION AND EXPOSURE: In cultivation, prairie phlox is best planted among sparse prairie grasses or in full sun. If planted in shade, the plants become straggly and die. An open meadow or a rock garden with sun is ideal. In the wild state, the foliage dies after the plant blooms and sets seed but reappears in August. In cultivation, the leaves usually stay green. This is an interesting plant to grow with hoary puccoon.

PLANTING TIME: Spring or fall when new growth is only an inch or so high.

ROOT SYSTEM: Fibrous roots become wiry with age. Old plants do not transplant as readily as young plants. In cultivation each plant develops several buds at the crown, but it cannot be divided and to do so is certain to kill the plant.

PLANTING DEPTH AND SPACING: Set the crowns at soil level and spread the roots evenly outward and slightly downward. Space about 1 foot apart.

PLANTING STOCK AND PROPAGATION: Use nursery-grown stock or young quality collected stock.

Prairie phlox is easily grown from seeds, but they are difficult to collect because the seed pods open immediately after ripening. It self-sows. Seedlings often bloom the first year, but surely the second year.

COMMENTS: Prairie phlox is an excellent plant for dry, open, sunny areas. It must never be moved while blooming or the plants will perish. Should you find an unusual color variation in the wild it is wise to mark the spot and transplant when new growth appears in August.

Phlox ovata • mountain phlox

DESCRIPTION: 4 to 6 inches tall. Mountain phlox has clear pink to rose-colored single flowers on upright stems. White ones are rare. It is almost an evergreen creeper with reclining branches.

Native much farther south and east, mountain phlox has proved very hardy in northern Wisconsin. It is found in thickets and moist open woods where it makes a lovely green carpet with its contrast of pink flowers in spring.

PERIOD OF BLOOM: May into early June.

SOIL: Slightly acid to moderately acid humus-rich soil, somewhat moist, especially while plant is blooming. I grow it under oak trees where the leafmold nourishes the plants.

LOCATION AND EXPOSURE: A fine groundcover for a moist shady area or one that does not become too dry. Given a good location it will soon carpet the forest floor with green. Mountain phlox is a good groundcover to grow with lady's-slippers. It likes to creep among leaf mulch.

PLANTING TIME: Spring or fall. Potted stock anytime.

ROOT SYSTEM: Fibrous. Roots form whenever nodes of the lower branches touch the damp earth. Thus new plants form and new reclining branches appear after blooming.

PLANTING DEPTH AND SPACING: Space 6 inches or more apart. Set the crowns at soil level and tuck any rooted runners gently into the soil surface and mulch. Plant potted stock at soil level. Mulch lightly with small leaves or shredded larger leaves. Let some of the green peek through.

PLANTING STOCK AND PROPAGATION: Potted stock is preferable, either quality nursery-grown or collected bareroot stock.

Divide plants that have formed mats, after blooming or in very early spring. Seeds are very fine and almost impossible to collect. I have had the most success with stem cuttings when I take them in June.

COMMENTS: Mountain phlox is a permanent groundcover that improves in beauty with the years. Ideal.

There is a blue-flowered variety of *Phlox ovata* with similar growing habits.

BORAGINACEAE [Borage Family]

Lithospermum canescens • hoary puccoon

DESCRIPTION: 8 to 10 inches tall. A cluster of golden yellow flowers, shaped like forget-me-nots but larger, are held above gray-green foliage. The foliage tends to be willowlike, blunt-tipped, and downy.

Hoary puccoon graces dry sunny fields and roadsides among

grasses. It is also found growing in gravelly areas, often with prairie phlox.

PERIOD OF BLOOM: June.

SOIL: Poor sandy soils or slightly acid fertile loam. Good drainage is very important. When grown where soil is heavy with clay, a liberal amount of sand should be incorporated into the existing soil.

LOCATION AND EXPOSURE: Place hoary puccoon in a sunny, well-drained spot and each plant will become a clump with age.

PLANTING TIME: While dormant in early spring or fall, but fall is best.

ROOT SYSTEM: The gray-to-black-coated rootstock is very irregular, with few feeder roots. The color depends on root size and age. New roots are usually a light tan, turning grayer as they age and becoming black in about three years. The inside of the fleshy root is pure white.

PLANTING DEPTH AND SPACING: Space 10 to 15 inches apart, depending on the size of the plants and the effect wanted. Planting depth is important. In the wild you will find that the eyes of the plant are just below soil level—a little deeper where it is very sandy; when transplanting, the eyes should be set 2 inches deep. This will give strong plants that will improve with age.

PLANTING STOCK AND PROPAGATION: Two-year-old nursery-grown stock has the best root system for transplanting. Also use quality collected stock, freshly dug, in fall.

For cuttings, use roots about the size of a wood lead pencil. Cut into 2 inch pieces. Cut the top portion of the root straight across and the bottom portion at an angle. This is a signal to yourself to keep the root pieces right side up. Set cuttings in sand or sandy loam about 1 inch deep and keep slightly moist. These cuttings usually root in one year, and some may even bloom the second year.

If roots break off, while digging, new shoots will develop and another plant will grow from the portion left in the soil. Often several eyes are formed on the stub and a plant with a multiple crown is born.

COMMENTS: Hoary puccoon is very effective when grown among tufts of grass in a prairie type of garden.

Try this: Pour about a gallon of sharp sand over a well-

established plant that has at least six stems. Spread the sand about 2 inches deep and leave permanently. The tops of the stems should be upright above the sand. The buried portion of the stems will develop new eyes, which in time will send up new multiple shoots. The sand does wonders for this plant.

Myosotis scorpioides • forget-me-not

DESCRIPTION: 6 to 15 inches tall. Angled prostrate stems with light-green, lanced foliage. Short leafy stems grow mostly from each joint and have small, delicate sky-blue flowers with yellow eyes.

The forget-me-not grows in damp areas in sun or very light shade. I first came upon this plant in Menominee County, Wisconsin, where a large colony of forget-me-nots was growing in the wilderness. The plants grew at the edge of a clear, slow-moving shallow brook, their roots firmly anchored in the fine gravel of the creek bed. It was early spring and only here and there a flower had opened, but there were many budded spikes, promising an expanse of gorgeous blue very soon.

PERIOD OF BLOOM: May into August, and even later if faded flowers are picked or if the location is moderately moist. Where moisture is abundant, bloom period is extended into autumn.

SOIL: Slightly acid to neutral soils with constant moisture. Make sure the soil never gets extremely dry. Wet gravel beds at the edge of a creek are choice spots.

LOCATION AND EXPOSURE: Full sun or partial shade. The forget-me-not is adaptable to a wide range of growing conditions. If soil is too dry the plants may become shaggy and tend to go dormant, but with rains or watering they will grow anew. Plant in a rock garden over a protruding rock in light shade. Or plant potted stock in gravelly beds of slow-moving streams that remain rather quiet and clear. Put the plants near shore.

PLANTING TIME: Potted stock anytime. Bareroot stock in spring or fall, but spring is preferred.

ROOT SYSTEM: Fibrous roots. New roots form where stems or branches recline on damp earth.

PLANTING DEPTH AND SPACING: Space 2 feet apart or farther if you wish to keep the effect of individual clumps. Set plants at same level at which they grew previously or slightly deeper.

PLANTING STOCK AND PROPAGATION: Potted nursery stock is best. Clumps from nurseries are also good, as is quality collected stock.

Divide large plants in spring. Cuttings taken in summer root readily. Seeds are difficult to collect.

COMMENTS: Although forget-me-not is at home in the average garden that does not get too dry, it is also ideal for areas that are too damp for most plants. Use it as a groundcover in wet places.

The forget-me-not is an escapee from early gardens.

Mertensia virginica · Virginia bluebell

DESCRIPTION: 1 to 2 feet tall. Drooping clusters of pink buds become beautiful porcelain blue flowers. When new growth first emerges above the mulch in spring, it is somewhat purplish tinted with green. This disappears as the leafy stems develop. The oval leaves are mostly on the lower half of the stem. There is also a white form.

Mertensia is found in woodland rich in leafmold as well as in moist rocky woods and along streams, where it often grows in colonies.

PERIOD OF BLOOM: May into June.

SOIL: Slightly acid to neutral soil of good fertility. Moisture in spring is very important, even if the earth becomes very dry in summer after dormancy.

LOCATION AND EXPOSURE: This wildflower is equally at home in full sun or in a shaded nook. When it is in full sun, bumblebees are attracted in droves. Grow it with other wildflowers that have good foliage and will take over when the Virginia bluebell becomes dormant in early summer. In open shade grow it with wild ginger or with other groundcovers.

PLANTING TIME: As soon as roots become dormant and into late fall.

ROOT SYSTEM: A fleshy but very brittle black-coated tuberous rootstock that takes on many odd shapes. Old, gnarled rootstocks do not produce well and are best discarded. Young roots grown in very sandy soil are cinnamon-brown in color. All roots are white inside.

PLANTING DEPTH AND SPACING: Space 1½ feet apart or farther

when interplanted with other wildflowers. Set tubers with the white eyes 1 inch below soil level and mulch generously.

PLANTING STOCK AND PROPAGATION: Nursery-grown stock of medium size is best. Quality collected stock, preferably young roots, is good.

Seed sown as soon as ripe will produce some seedlings large enough to bloom the third year. The plant self-sows readily, especially where the soil is rich in leafmold and somewhat damp.

COMMENTS: A very popular, charming spring wildflower. Beautiful with large golden merrybells, which bloom at the same time and have good foliage.

I call Virginia bluebell the chameleon of my garden because the purplish thumbs that first emerge above the earth turn to green leaves and the pink buds become beautiful blue flowers.

Mertensia albiflora · white mertensia

DESCRIPTION: 10 to 15 inches tall. This is a smaller version of Virginia bluebell (*Mertensia virginica*). Clusters of greenish white buds open to pure white. The foliage is light green, oval, and smaller.

My stock has been grown from a specimen of the white mertensia found in the wild in Iowa. Because of its smaller overall growth I believe it is a white version of the midwestern bluebell known as *Mertensia lanceolata*.

PERIOD OF BLOOM: May into June.

SOIL: Fertile slightly acid woods soil that is moist during the blooming period.

LOCATION AND EXPOSURE: I planted my seeds in open woodland in a cleared area. The soil is rich in leafmold and quite damp in spring. Plants are removed only as needed, but otherwise have remained in their original bed to self-sow. For color contrast, grow the white and blue mertensias together.

PLANTING TIME: After plants become dormant, in early summer into fall.

ROOT SYSTEM: A fleshy, black-coated tuberous rootstock that grows in many fantastic patterns. One root tends to grow directly downward. Rootstocks are very brittle and easily broken while being dug up.

186

PLANTING DEPTH AND SPACING: Space about 1 foot apart or plant at random among other wildflowers that retain their foliage throughout the season. Set the rootstock with the white eyes 1 to 2 inches deep. In my original bed I find that some of the seedling rootstocks are 5 inches deep. Evidently the plants have sought their own depths.

PLANTING STOCK AND PROPAGATION: To be certain of color, use nursery-grown stock that has already bloomed. Collected stock is very rare.

Seeds sown as soon as they ripen or left to self-sow where leafmold is moist give good results. If your nursery-grown stock was grown with the Virginia bluebells, you may find some blue seedlings appearing in your new bed. Remove them promptly as soon as foliage fades. Also remove all blue buds as they appear to avoid cross-pollination, and mark the plants.

COMMENTS: The unusual beauty of the pure white mertensia is certain to be an added attraction to your wild garden.

VERBENACEAE [Vervain Family]

Verbena canadensis • rose verbena

DESCRIPTION: 2 to 3 feet long. A trailing-vine type of plant, spreading to make a circle. Clusters of rose-colored flowers are held above deeply toothed, ovate, medium-green leaves that are hairy. Where the soil is moist, the reclining branches root at the nodes as they spread.

This verbena is found in sunny, rocky prairies where the soil is lean and sandy. It is native in more southern and western parts of Wisconsin than mine, but I have found it hardy with a cover of mulch in winter.

PERIOD OF BLOOM: Late May until heavy frosts. Pick the spent flowers to encourage bloom.

SOIL: Poor, sandy soils or a fertile, sandy loam with good drainage. Add sand to very fertile, heavy soil. This plant does best on a lean diet.

LOCATION AND EXPOSURE: Verbena must be planted in full sun for abundant bloom. It is best suited for the prairie, a sunny garden, or groundcover on a sunny bank.

PLANTING TIME: In areas where the temperatures dip far below zero it is best to plant in spring. In warmer climates, fall planting is practical.

ROOT SYSTEM: Very coarse, fibrous roots becoming wiry with age. The nodes along the trailing branches aboveground send down new roots wherever they touch the damp soil.

PLANTING DEPTH AND SPACING: Space 3 feet apart. For a dense groundcover, space only 2 feet apart. Set the crowns at soil level. Mulch in cold areas during the winter months.

When plants become too crowded, remove some of the older ones. Merely clip the branch and dig up the unwanted plants.

PLANTING STOCK AND PROPAGATION: Pot-grown nursery stock or stock grown in the field for one season have vigorous young root systems.

Select only the younger plants for division. Stem cuttings in July are the easiest method of propagation. Seeds are often slow to germinate, and seedlings bloom the second year. The plant self-sows.

COMMENTS: *Verbena canadensis* makes a fine groundcover for a rocky, sandy area that seems to grow little except weeds.

LABIATAE [Mint Family]

Ajuga reptans • bugleflower

DESCRIPTION: 5 to 8 inches tall. Dainty, semihooded flowers rest on short spikes above oval, lightly scalloped leaves. The spikes are clear blue and occasionally purple. At times a pure white will volunteer among a long-established bed of blues. It is possibly a seedling.

Bugleflower is found on roadsides and hillsides, and in open sunny fields. It usually grows in large colonies.

PERIOD OF BLOOM: May into July.

SOIL: Bugleflower is not particular about soil texture or pH, but it does need good drainage. In fertile soils it grows lavishly.

LOCATION AND EXPOSURE: An excellent groundcover for a sunny spot, a steep hillside to hold the soil in place, or under high shrubs where sunlight is ample. When grown as groundcover, the neat rosettes of basal foliage make an interesting pattern among widely spaced taller flowers in full sun or very light shade.

PLANTING TIME: It moves easily almost anytime except while blooming. Water faithfully when first transplanted and it will soon spread.

ROOT SYSTEM: Some fibrous roots on well-established plants. White cordlike rhizomes creep along just a little below soil level, pausing at intervals to send up new growth.

PLANTING DEPTH AND SPACING: Space about 6 inches apart. Plant crowns at soil level or slightly deeper in well-drained soil. Where climates are severe, mulch in winter if snowfall is scant.

PLANTING STOCK AND PROPAGATION: Nursery-grown stock has a better root system. When collecting stock, select only the stronger plants with good root systems.

Divide offsets when clumps become crowded. Seeds are hard to collect, but the plant self-sows readily.

COMMENTS: Bugleflower is a charming groundcover, useful for replacing grass on steep banks where mowing is difficult. Although this plant is rugged, it does need some moisture to thrive.

Bugleweed is another common name for bugleflower.

Scutellaria ovata · early blue skullcap

DESCRIPTION: 1½ to 2 feet tall. Hooded flowers, violet to clear blue, are held upright on squarish stems with multiple branches. Leaves are ovate and serrated. Seed pods have interesting shapes, usually oval. They resemble miniature old-fashioned bed-warmers.

This skullcap is found in moist, rocky woods in areas that have very little shade, in full sun along river banks, and in the drier parts of meadows.

PERIOD OF BLOOM: Late June into August.

SOIL: Neutral to slightly acid sandy loam or a fertile, heavier soil with good drainage. Constant moisture, though not soaking. Not demanding otherwise.

189

LOCATION AND EXPOSURE: Full sun or very light shade; direct sunlight produces plants with sturdier stalks. Excellent grown in colonies.

PLANTING TIME: While dormant in spring or fall. Spring only in extremely cold climates.

ROOT SYSTEM: A fibrous root system, purplish in color, with both the eyes for next year's bloom and the side rhizomes sending up new growth.

PLANTING DEPTH AND SPACING: Space 1 foot apart. Set the eyes of the plant 2 inches deep, spreading any attached rhizomes horizontally. In cold climates, mulch over winter (or permanently) with 6 inches of loose straw or marsh hay. Remove some in spring. The roots and eyes cannot tolerate alternate thawing and freezing.

PLANTING STOCK AND PROPAGATION: Nursery-grown stock is far superior to quality collected stock, but the latter is scarce.

To propagate, divide large clumps, preferably in spring, or sow seeds when they ripen. A few seedlings may bloom the first year, but three years are required to form a clump.

Cuttings taken in July and treated with rooting hormones give poor results. Those cuttings that do root should be left in propagation beds until the following June.

COMMENTS: Skullcaps are very seldom seen in wild gardens although they are easily cultivated and have lovely, long-lasting flowers. They are versatile and make a wonderful addition to a garden nook or an open meadow.

Set markers next to all plants since they are slow to sprout in spring. Easier still, leave a few inches of the old stubble if you are not a meticulous gardener.

Scutellaria serrata • showy skullcap

DESCRIPTION: 1 to 2 feet tall. Ovate leaves are located opposite each other on square stems. Usually two or more blue flowers are found on top. The plants form neat clumps.

Showy skullcap inhabits rich woods and glens farther east of and south of Wisconsin. But they have proved hardy in my severe climate when I mulch them for the winter.

PERIOD OF BLOOM: May into June.

SOIL: Slightly acid, humus-rich soil. Also will grow in fertile

190

garden soil (as will all skullcaps). Constant, moderate moisture; do not let the soil get too wet.

LOCATION AND EXPOSURE: Use showy skullcap for naturalizing in an open area in full sun or very high open shade.

PLANTING TIME: While dormant in spring or fall.

ROOT SYSTEM: Fibrous.

PLANTING DEPTH AND SPACING: Space 1 foot apart. Set the rootstock with the eyes 2 inches below soil level. Mulch in winter and remove some in spring.

PLANTING STOCK AND PROPAGATION: Nursery-grown stock, or quality collected stock where available.

To propagate, divide clumps, preferably in spring, or sow seeds when ripe. Some seedlings will bloom the second year. I have never tried growing this one from cuttings.

COMMENTS: The skullcaps should be better known and enjoyed more. Their blue color adds a touch of beauty to the wild garden.

Scutellaria incana • downy skullcap

DESCRIPTION: 1 to 2 feet tall. Medium-blue hooded flowers with serrated, oval foliage on forking square stems. It forms clumps.

Downy skullcap is found in open lightly shaded areas of moist woods, and along river banks, and in drier woods and thickets.

PERIOD OF BLOOM: July into August.

SOIL: Average garden soil that does not get too dry, or a moist, humus-rich soil that is slightly acid.

LOCATION AND EXPOSURE: Although this skullcap is usually found in shade, it does best in full sun. Plant the blue downy along a woodland border with brilliant red Oswego tea for contrast. The addition of early-blooming white snakeroot will give you a red, white, and blue color scheme. Mulch.

PLANTING TIME: While dormant in spring or fall.

ROOT SYSTEM: Fibrous roots are dark gray-black with a purple tint, and the rhizomes are pink tipped. An extensive root system.

PLANTING DEPTH AND SPACING: Space 1 to 1½ feet apart. Set the crowns, with rhizomes attached, about 2 inches deep. Mulch during the winter. Plants are slow to appear in spring. All plants should be marked clearly.

PLANTING STOCK AND PROPAGATION: Nursery-grown stock is best. Also use quality collected stock where available.

Divide clumps in spring, and keep the area moist; the plants are slow to grow. Seeds sown when ripe give some bloom the first year. Stem cuttings I took in July gave fair results. Plants from cuttings must be kept in propagation frames until the following June.

COMMENTS: Skullcaps are beautiful flowers that have many uses in the perennial garden as well as in the wild garden. They are easily cultivated and bloom abundantly over a long period. I cannot praise them too highly.

Scutellaria integrifolia • pink skullcap

DESCRIPTION: 1½ to 2 feet tall. The hooded flowers of the pink skullcap range from a rose-pink to a pale lavender-pink. This plant is a highly prized form of *S. integrifolia*, which is commonly purplish blue with a white throat, the blue of an even deeper hue than that of downy skullcap (*S. incana*). The stems are rigid and square with many serrated, oval leaves.

Pink skullcap is native to open meadows, thickets, and along woodland borders. My original stock came from southern Indiana, but it has proved hardy here with winter mulching.

PERIOD OF BLOOM: July into September.

SOIL: Regular garden soil of good fertility that does not become extremely dry. Constant moisture is best. Neutral to slightly acid soil produces good flowering plants.

LOCATION AND EXPOSURE: Full sun or very light partial shade. Provides a fine contrast among blue skullcaps. Interplant with other wildflowers or grow in a colony on the sunny side of a woodland border.

PLANTING TIME: Fall or spring, preferably spring.

ROOT SYSTEM: A fibrous, purplish root system with eyes for the next year's growth. Rhizomes stay nearby and bloom the following year.

PLANTING DEPTH AND SPACING: Space 1 foot apart. Set the eyes 2 inches deep and spread roots and attached rhizomes horizontally. Mulch with 6 inches of straw or marsh hay in cold climates. Mark planted areas..

PLANTING STOCK AND PROPAGATION: Use nursery-grown stock; collected stock is rare.

Divide larger plants, preferably in spring. Seeds sown when ripe produce plants of blooming size the second year. Some blue seedlings may appear, since the plant does not come 100 percent true from seed.

COMMENTS: The pink skullcap is a rare prize.

Scutellaria lateriflora • mad-dog skullcap

DESCRIPTION: 1 to 2 feet tall. This skullcap has many branches. In the upper axils of the ovate leaves, which are opposite each other, the flower sprays form a grand display. The flowers are blue and sometimes have a hint of purple. White ones are rare. This variety of skullcap is readily identifiable because the flowers favor one side of the stem.

Mad-dog skullcap is found along thickets near stream beds, in open damp shady woods, and also in moist meadows. It is very much at home in regular garden soil with only moderate moisture.

PERIOD OF BLOOM: July into September.

SOIL: Fertile, slightly acid soil with constant moisture, though it need not be wet. The soil in our nursery that does not dry out has proved satisfactory.

LOCATION AND EXPOSURE: Skullcaps grow best in full sun or very light partial shade with constant moisture. Reasonably good flowers can be grown under more trying conditions. Mulch helps to protect plants in winter and to retain moisture in summer.

PLANTING TIME: Spring or fall, spring preferred.

ROOT SYSTEM: A fibrous rootstock with eyes and extensive thread-like roots, plus long, slender, creeping rhizomes that send up new plants around the parent plant.

PLANTING DEPTH AND SPACING: Space 1 foot or more apart to leave room for the plant to form neat clumps. Set the eyes 2 inches deep and mulch for winter protection in cold climates. Mark the area.

PLANTING STOCK AND PROPAGATION: Use nursery-grown stock. Collected stock is rare.

Division of parent plants should be done in spring. Seeds sown when ripe give some bloom the second year, and plants mature in three years.

COMMENTS: The skullcaps awaken slowly in spring so it is important that all plants be staked.

Scutellaria baicalensis • skullcap blue heaven

DESCRIPTION: 15 to 18 inches tall. The bushy skullcap has terminal clusters of intense medium-blue flowers, which are about 1 inch, tubelike in shape, and hooded. The plant has numerous stems bearing abundant clusters, which give it a tall, moundlike effect. The leaves are opposite to each other and are willowlike. They are not very noticeable during the blooming period. This rare wildflower is a foreigner from Lake Baikal, Siberia. It does well in our cold climate.

PERIOD OF BLOOM: July into August and often September.

SOIL: This skullcap grows well in fertile, slightly acid, sandy loam soil. It can stand some extreme conditions. Constant moisture with good drainage is best.

LOCATION AND EXPOSURE: Give this plant plenty of elbow room when grown in the border or wildflower garden. Full sun is a must for healthy specimens with abundant flowers.

PLANTING TIME: Spring or fall when dormant.

ROOT SYSTEM: The roots are very different from those of all the other species. Its rootstock is a coarse yellowish rhizome with few feeder roots, often forked. It breaks easily and should be handled carefully. Over a period of years additional eyes form at the crown of the plant, and the rhizome becomes very coarse and almost impossible to transplant, often parts of it rotting away for new rhizomes to form (in the same way as the rhubarb).

PLANTING DEPTH AND SPACING: Space at least 1½ feet apart. Set the plants with eyes 1½ to 2 inches deep and dig deep holes to accommodate the tapelike root, which is often forked.

PLANTING STOCK AND PROPAGATION: Young or medium-sized nursery stock is best.

The propagation of skullcap blue heaven is best limited to seeds (which always come up true to the parent plant). Seeds sown as soon as they ripen or in very early spring give small to medium-sized blooming plants the second year.

Root cuttings and stem cuttings produced no satisfactory results.

COMMENTS: Skullcap blue heaven is the prettiest of all the skullcaps. Catalogs and books list it only by its botanical name. I am responsible for giving it the name listed here. When growing in a drift, they remind me of a patch of deep blue sky.

Glechoma hederacea • gill-over-the-ground

DESCRIPTION: A fast-growing vine. Blue-lipped flowers form in the axils of the round, scalloped, opposite leaves.

This wildflower frequents shady damp areas and old homesteads as well as sunny places. Originally it grew only in cultivation.

PERIOD OF BLOOM: May into June, even earlier in warm climates.

SOIL: Use soil of any kind. This is the most versatile plant I know and will adapt itself to a variety of growing conditions.

LOCATION AND EXPOSURE: Fairly deep shade to full sun. Not the least bit particular. Gill-over-the-ground is an excellent vine for problem areas. Use it with grasses to hold the soil on a slope; it hugs the earth closely.

PLANTING TIME: Almost anytime, but during the growing season it must be carefully watered to establish.

ROOT SYSTEM: The main rootstock is a fibrous clump. Tiny roots form where running vines touch the damp earth at the nodes, and soon new plants are born. Each rooted portion may be separated and planted separately.

PLANTING DEPTH AND SPACING: Space ½ to 1 foot apart, depending on the size of the plant. Set the plants with the tiny crowns at soil level. Tuck in carefully.

PLANTING STOCK AND PROPAGATION: Use nursery-grown stock or quality collected stock.

Root propagation is done by cutting rooted vines into pieces between the joints and planting each portion separately. Cuttings taken in July for potting give good results. Seeds are difficult to collect, and the plant self-sows.

COMMENTS: I highly recommend this little plant. When grown in its proper place, it is unsurpassed. But do not plant it where it can run into the lawn or it will become a pest!

I say, "Give me an ash pile, a clinker heap, or a pile of sand, gravel, or earth—and I will soon turn it into a spot of beauty by covering it with gill-over-the-ground."

Physostegia virginiana • false dragonhead

DESCRIPTION: 1 to 3 feet tall. Terminal clusters of lipped flowers on spikes. Rose-lavender is the most common form. There is also a white form, which is rare in the wild but frequently grown in cultivation. A deep vibrant rose variety, *Physostegia vivid,* is offered as a perennial. The stem of the false dragonhead is square with toothed, willowlike leaves growing opposite each other.

False dragonhead grows in colonies in moist meadows, along streams, and around deserted homestead gardens.

PERIOD OF BLOOM: June into September. The rose-lavender variety grows rampantly, while the white grows more conservatively. The *Physostegia vivid* blooms later and is very showy.

SOIL: Ordinary garden soil with constant moisture is quite satisfactory. In damp to wet soils, it grows tall and abundant; in semidry areas, its growth is more restrained.

LOCATION AND EXPOSURE: The rose-lavender species is best grown in an open meadow or where it can spread. The pure white and vivid rose varieties are ideal as a border or near a pool or stream where their beauty can be reflected in the water.

PLANTING TIME: Spring or fall.

ROOT SYSTEM: New shoots form near the parent plant, which dies after blooming. The fibrous roots are coarse, white, and threadlike.

PLANTING DEPTH AND SPACING: Space 1 foot apart. Plants form clumps which should be divided every three years. Only the strong new outside shoots should be used. Set new plants with green growth at the crown just at soil level. Dormant stock should be planted about ½ inch deep. Fall plantings should be mulched.

PLANTING STOCK AND PROPAGATION: Nursery-grown stock is best, or use quality collected stock.

Divide clumps in spring or fall, and select only the husky outer shoots for transplanting.

Seeds sown in fall give mature plants the second year. All three species grow from seed.

COMMENTS: Both the white and vivid rose dragonheads are excellent for cut flower arrangements since they are long lasting. This plant is also called by the name obedient.

Salvia azurea • blue salvia

DESCRIPTION: 1½ to 2 feet tall. The broad lanceolated basal leaves are heavily quilted and prominently veined in pale green against dark green bodies. Numerous erect flower stalks have lateral branches, which form dense spikes in racemes. The large, lipped flowers are intense blue, suggestive of delphinium and monkshood.

Originally grown only in cultivation, blue salvia is now found in dry plains, prairies, and around old homesteads.

PERIOD OF BLOOM: June into July.

SOIL: Easily grown in ordinary garden soil with moderate fertility.

LOCATION AND EXPOSURE: Ideal in a sunny garden where its interesting green foliage will persist until killing frosts. Also, an excellent, showy plant along the border.

PLANTING TIME: Spring or fall.

ROOT SYSTEM: A robust rootstock with coarse fibrous roots.

PLANTING DEPTH AND SPACING: Space the plants 1 foot apart and set the crowns slightly deeper than the level at which they grew previously.

PLANTING STOCK AND PROPAGATION: Use nursery-grown stock, or quality collected stock where available.

Division of clumps is the easiest method of propagation.

Blue salvia is easily grown from cuttings taken after the plant has hardened, usually in mid-July. If cuttings are potted and kept in a propagating frame until rooted, they can be planted in the open in August.

Sow seeds as soon as they ripen or in early spring. Seedlings often bloom the second year.

COMMENTS: Blue salvia is a charming plant grown with earlier wildflowers that go dormant after blooming. Its basal rosette of foliage covers bare spots.

Monarda fistulosa • wild bergamot

DESCRIPTION: 2 to 3 feet tall. Clear lavender flowers are most common; occasionally, a few have hints of lavender-pink. White is very rare (I found a white-flowered plant that propagated well). The flowers end in terminal whorls, with each floret lipped. Stems are square with light gray-green foliage; the leaves are opposite one another and slightly toothed.

197

The wild bergamot grows along roadsides, in wastelands, and in dry meadows, often in the vicinity of black-eyed Susan, blazing star, frostflower aster, and gray goldenrod.

PERIOD OF BLOOM: Late July into September.

SOIL: Wild bergamot will grow in slightly acid, sandy, barren soils; fertile sandy loam; and soils that are very fertile. It is not demanding, but in lean soil it forms better and the stems do not become weak and twisted.

LOCATION AND EXPOSURE: Full sun to very light shade. A fine plant for naturalizing in meadows with goldenrods, blazing star, and black-eyed Susans.

PLANTING TIME: Spring, preferably.

ROOT SYSTEM: A mat of fibrous roots and many rhizomes from a large clump.

PLANTING DEPTH AND SPACING: Space 1 to 1½ feet apart. Plant the rhizomes horizontally 1 inch deep with the tip leading to the surface.

PLANTING STOCK AND PROPAGATION: Young nursery-grown plants are best, especially seedlings.

Division of old plants is not always successful. Stem cuttings taken in July give some results, but propagation by seed is the easiest.

Sow seeds as soon as they ripen or in fall. Seedlings often bloom in one year.

COMMENTS: Wild bergamot should always be grown where air circulation is good or it may mildew. When used as a border, cut it back right after blooming.

Three or four dried leaves steeped in a cup of boiling water, with sugar or honey added, makes a pleasing tea. Gather leaves in July.

Monarda didyma • Oswego tea

DESCRIPTION: 2 to 3 feet tall. Brilliant, scarlet-red flowers with lipped florets are found in terminal whorls. Leaves are opposite, toothed, and deep green with occasional red flushes. They are aromatic and have a minty fragrance when crushed.

Oswego tea grows naturally in areas south of Wisconsin, inhabiting moist spots along streams and in rich, open woodland.

PERIOD OF BLOOM: July–August; blooms later in cooler climates.

SOIL: Neutral to slightly acid soil with constant moisture. Water during periods of drought.

LOCATION AND EXPOSURE: Full sun or partial shade in a woodland border. An excellent contrast for bottle gentians and white snakeroots.

PLANTING TIME: Spring preferred.

ROOT SYSTEM: A fibrous rootstock with many branches that form a large mat. To keep this species vigorous, divide and replant every spring.

PLANTING DEPTH AND SPACING: Space 1 to 1½ feet apart. Set the rhizomes about 1 inch deep with the tip leading to the soil surface.

PLANTING STOCK AND PROPAGATION: Nursery-grown field stock or potted cuttings are preferable; also use quality collected stock if available.

Stem cuttings taken in July give fairly good results and must be kept in a cold frame for the first winter in very cold climates.

Sow seeds as soon as they ripen. A few seedlings may bloom in one year.

COMMENTS: In cultivation the monardas are short-lived unless replanted every year or two.

Collinsonia canadensis • stoneroot

DESCRIPTION: 2 to 4 feet tall. This plant has many branches with large ovate light-green leaves. The leaves are quilted and toothed. Panicles of airy, lemon-scented yellow flowers have wine-colored tinges in each blossom. They are somewhat orchidlike.

Stoneroot is usually found in rich soil in moist woodlands where it is protected from early spring frosts. Its foliage especially is sensitive to frost.

PERIOD OF BLOOM: August into September.

SOIL: Fertile garden soil with ample moisture—neutral to only slightly acid woods soil is preferable. The plant will not survive severe drought.

LOCATION AND EXPOSURE: Full sun or very light shade, in protected areas where frost cannot injure its foliage. Should frost damage occur, the plant will send up new shoots and bloom a little later. A deep mulch helps keep it dormant longer in spring.

PLANTING TIME: While dormant in spring or fall.

ROOT SYSTEM: A black, stonelike knotty rhizome like that of blazing star but much harder.

PLANTING DEPTH AND SPACING: Space 1 to 3 feet apart. Set the rhizomes 2 inches deep and mulch, preferably the year round. In cold climates mulch in winter to avoid winter-kill.

PLANTING STOCK AND PROPAGATION: Use nursery-grown stock or quality collected stock.

Divide rhizomes in spring while dormant. Lay the stonelike rootstock on a firm surface and use a clean, sharp chisel and hammer to cut it into pieces. Leave an eye or two on each piece, and plant with the eye upward. Some natural division also occurs.

Seeds rarely ripen and self-sow.

COMMENTS: Stoneroot, often called citronella or horse balm, is rarely grown in the wild garden, but nearly everyone who sees it in one will comment on its beauty and delightful fragrance.

SCROPHULARIACEAE [Figwort Family]

Chelone glabra • white turtlehead

DESCRIPTION: 1 to 3 feet tall. A dense terminal spike of lipped flowers on a leafy stem. The leaves are opposite, lanceolated, and slightly serrated. Plants with very slender leaves have pure white flowers; the flowers of larger plants are often tinted with pink to mauve. Each flower resembles a turtle's head with open mouth.

White turtlehead is found in wet meadows, along streams and lakes, in wet ditches, and in lowlands.

PERIOD OF BLOOM: July into September. Flowers are long-lasting if moisture is ample.

SOIL: Moderately acid to slightly acid soils, from moderate moisture retention to wet. I grow it in a fertile sandy loam with average moisture.

LOCATION AND EXPOSURE: Select a spot in full sun or very light shade. A lovely plant for the open, damp sunny meadow. More interesting when grown in colonies.

PLANTING TIME: While dormant in spring or fall.

ROOT SYSTEM: A coarse fibrous white rootstock with many white branches that will form new plants. The branches can be separated.

PLANTING DEPTH AND SPACING: Space 1½ to 2 feet apart. Set rootstocks upright and spread any branches attached to them horizontally about 1 inch below soil level. Eyes of the rhizomes and the crown should be almost at soil level. Mulch.

PLANTING STOCK AND PROPAGATION: Nursery-grown stock is far superior to collected stock.

To propagate, divide rhizomes, or take stem cuttings taken in July (moderately good results).

Sow seeds when ripe. White turtlehead self-sows in moist areas. Seedlings bloom the second year.

COMMENTS: An excellent companion for the stately red Cardinal flower.

Try cutting a few turtlehead plants back late in June. You will find that they bloom later and are bushier.

Chelone obliqua • red turtlehead

DESCRIPTION: 3 to 4 feet tall. A more robust grower than the white turtlehead. The foliage is a darker green, and the rose-colored flowers with yellow beards are the same shape but larger. They appear later in the year.

Native below the Mason-Dixon Line, it has proved hardy in cold climates.

PERIOD OF BLOOM: Late August into October.

SOIL: Acid to slightly acid soil of good fertility with moderate constant moisture.

LOCATION AND EXPOSURE: A good border plant for its foliage contrast as well as for the color and shape of its flower. Also valuable for naturalizing along a brook or lake or in a damp sunny meadow.

PLANTING TIME: While dormant in spring or fall.

ROOT SYSTEM: The root system is white. A stout rootstock, with fibrous roots, sends out many rhizomes to form a clump.

PLANTING DEPTH AND SPACING: Space 1 to 2 feet apart. Set the rootstock horizontally, carefully covering with about 1 inch of soil. Let the tips of the rhizomes taper upward, almost to soil surface.

Mulch in winter. A continuous mulch helps to retain much-needed moisture.

PLANTING STOCK AND PROPAGATION: Nursery-grown stock is superior, but you may also use quality collected stock.

Propagate by divisions of clumps, preferably in spring, and stem cuttings taken in early July. In my local area seeds do not ripen. If they are available, sow as soon as they ripen and transplant the seedlings in the spring of the second year.

COMMENTS: Red turtlehead is a charming plant with many good qualities and is an excellent addition to the wild garden.

White snakeroot and red turtlehead make an interesting combination grown in protected moist woodlands.

Pink turtlehead (*Chelone Lyoni*) has similar flowers with a medium to light pink color and faint purple streaks. The foliage is broader, but the plant does not grow as tall as either. Originally grown only in cultivation.

Mimulus ringens • monkey flower

DESCRIPTION: 20 to 30 inches tall. Opposite lanceolate leaves are attached to square stems. The tubular flowers resemble frilled snapdragons. The colors range from lavender to violet; a white is quite rare.

The lavender species is usually found along stream beds where it is sunny and the soil rarely dries out. It can even tolerate shallow, standing water if it is not stagnant.

PERIOD OF BLOOM: Late June into September, flowering continuously.

SOIL: The monkey flower grows best where soil is fertile, moist, and only slightly acid to neutral. In the nursery we grow it in average garden soil with constant moisture.

LOCATION AND EXPOSURE: Monkey flower grows best in full sun or partial open shade with constant moisture. When planted near a stone, its roots will run underneath to keep cool and seek moisture.

PLANTING TIME: While dormant in spring or fall.

ROOT SYSTEM: New shoots form from the parent plant, which dies

in fall. The roots are pure white and fibrous, very similar to lobelias. The rootstocks form dense mats and should be separated every year to bloom well.

PLANTING DEPTH AND SPACING: Space about 1 foot apart. Set the plants ½ to 1 inch deep so that the tip of the new shoot is just at soil level. Spread roots evenly, and mulch if planted in fall.

PLANTING STOCK AND PROPAGATION: Use nursery-grown stock or only the strongest offset of quality collected stock.

Divide clumps, preferably in spring; some stem cuttings I took in early July gave good results.

Sow seeds in late fall or early spring. The seed is dust-fine and should only be scattered on top of the soil and covered with an evergreen bough until germination. Some seedlings will bloom the first year.

COMMENTS: Its long blooming period makes this a useful plant. I find that monkey flower does not need continuous wet as it does in the wild and that it still flourishes with only constant moisture. But drought spells disaster! Both the lavender and rarer white monkey flower are lovely companions for the fiery red lobelia.

Veronicastrum virginicum • Culver's root

DESCRIPTION: 2 to 5 feet tall. Whorls of narrow, toothed leaves encircle the stem at intervals. The terminal white flowers, in spirelike wands, are abundant. Close inspection reveals that the flowers have a faint blue tinge. This species grows more vigorously than cultivated veronicas.

Culver's root is found in meadows and open woods with high shade. In a wooded area along the Menominee River it covers a wide expanse up to the water's edge. Looking across the area on a sunny day gives one the feeling of viewing a calm sea of white, slightly tinged with blue. Here sparsely scattered giant oaks and tall Norway pines offer partial shade.

PERIOD OF BLOOM: June into August.

SOIL: Woods or fertile garden soil of moderate acidity and average moisture. The soil can also be damp.

LOCATION AND EXPOSURE: Excellent for planting in a sunny meadow or in high open woodland shade in large colonies. In the meadow,

Joe-pye and swamp milkweed make good companions. Grow Culver's root at the back of a border or along the edge of a woodland.

PLANTING TIME: While dormant in spring or fall.

ROOT SYSTEM: The rootstock is yellow, fibrous and extensive, each small plant forming a clump.

PLANTING DEPTH AND SPACING: Space 1 foot or more apart. Set the plants with eyes about 1 inch deep, spreading the roots carefully. Mulch in winter or year round.

PLANTING STOCK AND PROPAGATION: Nursery-grown stock has a more compact root system, but also use quality collected stock.

Divide clumps in spring or fall. Sow seeds when they are ripe. Stem cuttings are slow to root and do not bloom until the third year.

COMMENTS: The wild veronica is a good flower to use in bouquets; it lasts a long while after being cut. The dried flower-stalks are excellent for dry floral arrangements.

ACANTHACEAE [Acanthus Family]

Ruellia humilis • wild petunia

DESCRIPTION: The leafy flower stalks are about 2 inches high and tend to spread in mats. The light blue to violet flowers (rarely white), are shaped like cultivated petunias but are much smaller, more slender, and do not flare as much. The flowers are borne on short stems, growing in the axils of the hairy, pointed oval leaves.

Wild petunia is native east and south of Wisconsin, but it has proved hardy in our colder climate. It is usually found in dry sandy soil in open fields or at the edge of a woods.

PERIOD OF BLOOM: June into September.

SOIL: Moderately dry to average sandy garden loam that is fertile and only slightly acid.

LOCATION AND EXPOSURE: Full sun or very light shade. It is a charming plant to grow in the niches of a sunny rock garden.

PLANTING TIME: Spring or fall (spring in cold regions).

ROOT SYSTEM: Fibrous, slowly spreading roots.

PLANTING DEPTH AND SPACING: Space 6 to 12 inches apart. Set crowns at soil level. Potted stock, grown from cuttings, should also be planted at soil level.

PLANTING STOCK AND PROPAGATION: Use nursery-grown stock or quality collected stock (spring planted).

Stem cuttings taken late in June or early July and treated with root hormones give almost perfect results. This is the easiest method. Hold the rooted cuttings in a cold frame until spring. Many will bloom the first year.

Seeds are produced in abundance, but germination is poor.

COMMENTS: This dainty creeper is sure to attract attention. The wild petunia is neat and long-lived and blooms for a long time. It even blooms during dry spells, though not so profusely.

RUBIACEAE [Madder Family]

Mitchella repens • partridgeberry

DESCRIPTION: 4 to 10 inch creeping vine. Small, shiny, dark green leaves with some white veins growing on opposite sides of the stem. Pairs of tiny, fragrant, pink or white flowers are followed by red berries in early fall.

In the woodland you will often find colonies of partridgeberry creeping along over decaying white birch and aspen stumps and fallen logs. Where the earth is moist, the plant establishes itself by sending out roots at the nodes as it forks. In damper evergreen forests it grows in the vicinity of twinflower and bunchberry. In some of these areas the shade may be so dense that small masses cover the forest floor.

PERIOD OF BLOOM: June into July.

SOIL: An almost neutral to acid, humus-rich woods soil is preferable. Add some sharp sand.

LOCATION AND EXPOSURE: A partly shaded nook or an area with light to deep shade is ideal. An excellent spot is under evergreens or deciduous trees where the soil is rich in humus and somewhat moist in spring.

To obtain a natural effect, plant partridgeberry among fallen, decaying logs or around old stumps in the woodland. It is an exceptionally neat groundcover among small plants but spreads slowly.

PLANTING TIME: Spring or fall. Potted stock can be planted anytime.

ROOT SYSTEM: Very small, rather short, fibrous roots form where the nodes touch the damp earth. Potted stock develops strong root systems and can be more easily grown in drier areas.

PLANTING DEPTH AND SPACING: Potted stock should be spaced 8 to 12 inches apart, and planted at soil level. Mulch lightly. When working with bareroot stock, be sure to tuck the tiny roots among the decaying humus; mulch lightly. Any bare stems should be covered with ½ inch of soil or humus, and often new roots will develop, especially if the soil is kept moist. Laying a small stone on a longer vine here and there will often encourage new roots to develop.

PLANTING STOCK AND PROPAGATION: Pot-grown nursery stock is best. While bareroot stock requires considerable care to establish, potted stock grows easily with minimum attention.

Quality collected sods are also preferable to bareroot stock.

Cuttings taken in June will give good results. A rooting hormone aids in root formation. In pots, long-stemmed cuttings develop vigorous roots. A good potting mixture is: equal parts of damp peatmoss, sharp sand, leafmold (or compost), plus fertile woods soil. Plants usually do not bear flowers until the second year.

Sow seeds as soon as they are ripe. The hard-shelled seeds are slow to germinate. Seedlings usually appear in the second year if the soil is kept continuously moist.

COMMENTS: The shiny green vine with its bright red, edible berries (which have an insipid taste) is prized for partridgeberry bowls at Christmas time. It can also be grown in a terrarium with other dainty wildflowers and tiny ferns.

The white-berried form is very rare. It does not have white veining in its foliage.

CAPRIFOLIACEAE [Honeysuckle Family]

Linnaea borealis • twinflower

DESCRIPTION: Crawling vine, 3 to 4 inch stems. A dainty, somewhat woody vine with dull greeen, slightly scalloped opposite leaves. Pairs of fragrant pink or white flowers nod gracefully above the reclining vine.

Twinflower grows on decaying, uprooted stumps or fallen moss-covered logs. It is often found along old logging trails in cut-over evergreen forests.

PERIOD OF BLOOM: June into August.

SOIL: Rich, acid to slightly acid, humus-rich woods soil with high to average moisture content.

LOCATION AND EXPOSURE: A cool damp woods is ideal. Plant among rocks where leafmold and humus are deep. Or prepare a bed in shade. A mixture of woods soil, damp peatmoss, and crumbling, rotted pine wood makes a fine growing medium.

Twinflower is not easy to establish. In my wild garden a vine of twinflower volunteered in the shade of a maidenhair fern among pink creeping phlox. The soil in this spot becomes quite dry in summer, yet the plant maintains its green leaves and even adds a few each year along with an occasional pair of blossoms. One would certainly not expect this to be a good spot when one considers the twinflower's natural habitat.

PLANTING TIME: Plant bareroot stock in spring, potted stock anytime.

ROOT SYSTEM: Very short, fine hairy roots that dry almost immediately when exposed to air. Great care is needed to transplant bareroot stock:

PLANTING DEPTH AND SPACING: Space about 1 foot apart. Plants with soil adhering and potted stock should be planted at soil level.

PLANTING STOCK AND PROPAGATION: Nursery-grown potted stock is best. You can also use quality collected sods.

Seeds are hard to collect and slow to germinate. Seedlings are slow to mature.

Cuttings taken in spring when the plants are still dormant give fair results and have proved to be the best method of propagation.

207

Keep potted stock grown from cuttings in a propagating frame two years before moving to a permanent location.

COMMENTS: This flower from the deep woodland, sometimes called deer vine, is a challenge to grow unless ideal conditions are created for it. Sometimes a volunteer persists against all odds.

Triosteum aurantiacum • horse gentian

DESCRIPTION: 2 to 3 feet tall. A coarse wildflower, resembling the common milkweed at first glance. Observed more closely you will note that, unlike the milkweed, the tip of each leaf is pointed and not blunt, that the plant sends up several stalks from each crown, and that it does not travel beneath the ground. Several small starlike purple flowers are borne in the axils of the leaves. In early fall these are followed by orange fruit, resembling rose hips, but smaller and more oblong.

Though rare in my area, horse gentian is occasionally found growing in moist woods in the company of large white trilliums, hepaticas, and red baneberries. Sometimes it may frequent shaded hillsides of drier woods where aspens grow thick.

PERIOD OF BLOOM: May into June.

SOIL: Slightly acid woods soil or fertile garden soil that does not bake dry in summer. Constant moisture is very important.

LOCATION AND EXPOSURE: An excellent plant in open woodland with filtered sunlight or light shade. It is important to remember that horse gentian must have some moisture at all times to flourish.

PLANTING TIME: Very early in spring before new growth appears, or in fall when dormant.

ROOT SYSTEM: A coarse rootstock with extensive fibrous roots, some of which should be pruned before transplanting.

PLANTING DEPTH AND SPACING: Space 2 feet apart. Set the eyes of the crown about 1 inch deep. With age each plant sends up more shoots and forms a clump.

PLANTING STOCK AND PROPAGATION: Young to medium-sized nursery-grown stock is best. You can use young collected stock, but it is scarce.

Divisions have proved unsuccessful. Of fifty stem cuttings I took one July, only one developed and it did not bloom until the third year.

208

I know of no easy way to propagate this species, but sowing seeds seems the best.

Remove the seeds from their pulpy hulls and plant them in fall. Germination is slow, often requiring three years. It takes another two years for the plants to bloom. Filing a nick in the hard-shelled seeds sometimes hastens germination by a year.

COMMENTS: Horse gentian is a novelty in the moist wild garden. Once established, it seems to endure forever.

The long-lasting orange fruit is pretty and for some unknown reason does not attract the ambitious chipmunks who claim most of the other seed crops.

CAMPANULACEAE [Bluebell Family]

Campanula glomerata • clustered bluebell

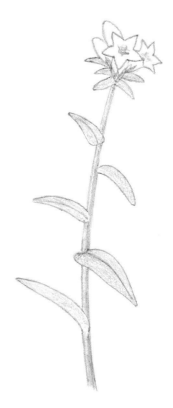

DESCRIPTION: 1 to 2 feet tall. The clusters of intense violet bells are held on erect leafy stems. The basal foliage forms a rosette of ovate leaves. The color of the flowers matches that of Venus's looking-glass.

Originally grown only in cultivation, this bluebell is now found in deserted homestead gardens, along field fence rows, and along open roadsides.

PERIOD OF BLOOM: June into July.

SOIL: Neutral to slightly acid fertile soil. In lean soils bloom is scant.

LOCATION AND EXPOSURE: Full sun or very light shade. Plant bluebells along the border of the woods or in the perennial flower border. The deep green foliage keeps its color all summer and well into fall.

PLANTING TIME: While dormant in spring or fall. May also be transplanted in late August.

ROOT SYSTEM: A fibrous root system with short rhizomes that do not stray far.

PLANTING DEPTH AND SPACING: Space 12 or more inches apart. Set the plants with the attached rhizomes ½ to 1 inch deep, placing

209

the tips of the rhizomes almost at soil level. Each plant will form a neat, compact mat of green.

PLANTING STOCK AND PROPAGATION: Use nursery-grown stock or quality collected stock.

Divide clumps that become too crowded. To keep the plant blooming vigorously, transplant every third year. Few seeds mature. On rare occasions the plant volunteers.

COMMENTS: The shade of violet-purple of this bluebell is so intense that it always draws favorable comments from anyone who sees the plant bloom.

Campanula rotundifolia • harebell

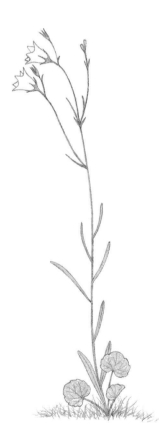

DESCRIPTION: 10 to 15 inches tall. Wiry stems bearing clusters of dainty blue bells grow from a rosette of tiny heart-shaped leaves.

Harebell is found in grassy fields and along sunny roadsides, often where the soil is gravelly. At times I have found it flourishing in pure red sand, especially on roadside shoulders, where other vegetation was extremely sparse.

PERIOD OF BLOOM: June into early August. When the plant is cultivated, the period of bloom often extends into fall.

SOIL: Sandy loam or regular garden soil. Good drainage is very important. Harebells are not demanding otherwise.

LOCATION AND EXPOSURE: Select a sunny spot among grasses, and clear a 12 inch circle. Or select a sunny spot in a rock garden or along the edge of a border.

When the harebell is grown on open ground it is susceptible to rust on the underside of its basal foliage. This does not affect the bloom and is not noticeable until you peek beneath the basal foliage. This problem does not usually arise if the plant is mulched.

PLANTING TIME: Late spring after the basal foliage appears or in late summer into fall. In cultivation or when mulched the plants do not have midsummer dormant spells as they do in grassy areas.

ROOT SYSTEM: A small rootstock with some fibrous roots and many straggly, spreading white rhizomes that are brittle and very easily broken.

PLANTING DEPTH AND SPACING: Space 1 to 2 feet apart. Set the plants with basal foliage at soil level, but any attached offsets should be planted ½ to 1 inch deep. Single-crowned plants will form clumps if not hoed.

PLANTING STOCK AND PROPAGATION: Nursery-grown stock will usually have a more compact root system, especially when grown in sandy soil that is not too fertile. Also use quality collected stock (gather in spring or fall).

Division of clumps in spring gives excellent results. To propagate from seed, scatter the very fine seeds on top of the soil in a flat or in an undisturbed area; germination is variable. Some small seedlings will appear the first year.

COMMENTS: This pretty wildflower is short-lived when grown in cultivation and hoed. I prefer to grow it under mulch.

Harebell is also referred to as the blue bells of Scotland or Scottish bluebells.

Lobelia Cardinalis • Cardinal flower

DESCRIPTION: 15 to 36 inches tall. The lipped flowers are a brilliant fiery red. (There is also a rare white form, *L. Cardialis alba*, which does not grow true from seeds as does the red.) Spikes rise from a neat rosette of lanceolated foliage that becomes smaller as it continues up the leafy stem.

The Cardinal flower is found in wet, sunny meadows and along brooks. Often whole colonies disappear when drainage ditches are dug, only to reappear from seed a few years later.

PERIOD OF BLOOM: July into September, varying with the amount of moisture present and soil fertility.

SOIL: Neutral to slightly acid soil with constant moisture. Soil need not be extremely wet but it must never dry out completely.

LOCATION AND EXPOSURE: Grow the Cardinal flower in full sun or very light shade and mulch to keep the roots moist and cool. It is very much at home growing along a brook with bottle gentians or in a damp meadow among sparse tufts of grasses. It can also grow in a formal border if the soil does not become too dry.

To increase its life span, it is advisable to transplant the Cardinal flower every spring and to cut it back right after it blooms, leaving only a few inches of stalk. As soon as new rosettes form, the parent stalks should be cut back completely.

If you want to collect seed pods, leave only one or two per stalk. Each pod contains an abundance of very fine seed.

PLANTING TIME: Spring planting is best in cold climates. In other areas it can be planted in spring or fall. Potted stock can be planted anytime. In extremely cold regions the plant is best treated as a biennial.

ROOT SYSTEM: The white roots are extensive, coarsely fibrous, and travel far in one year's growth. When transplanting them, cut some of the roots back to about 2½ inches. Potted stock has a more compact root system.

PLANTING DEPTH AND SPACING: Space 8 to 12 inches apart in the garden, or plant at random in a meadow or along a stream.

Set bareroot stock or potgrown stock with crowns at soil level. In fall, before winter mulching, pull a little soil up to the crowns, but do not cover the center.

PLANTING STOCK AND PROPAGATION: Nursery-grown stock is best, though quality collected stock will produce plants also. Stem cuttings taken before the plant blooms can be used too.

Easily grown from seed. Scatter ripe seeds on top of soil in flats and cover with wire mesh. Mulch in the fall and remove mulch in spring. Seedlings should remain in flats until the following spring. For protection, mulch again in the fall using a wire screen to keep from smothering the plants.

COMMENTS: I obtained a specimen of the white variety, *L. Cardinalis alba*, from a New York grower. The plant grew to about 30 inches high and had shiny green, coarsely quilted leaves. A few years later a friend in Missouri gave me a single-crown plant. This lobelia was a division of a lone white plant she had found among many red ones. I was surprised by the difference between the two plants. Hers had narrower, finely quilted dull green leaves. The single crown sent up a lone flower stalk 4½ feet tall; it displayed 74 individual blossoms. What variation within the species!

Lobelia siphilitica • great blue lobelia

DESCRIPTION: 1 to 3 feet tall. The lipped flowers are bright blue with white touches in their throats. Some have a purplish cast, but these do not come true from seed. There is also a pure white form. The entire flower stalk is leafy, with the leaves becoming smaller as they near the top. The basal foliage is a rosette of long, serrated leaves. These are less shiny than those of the Cardinal flower and are not pointed at the tip.

This lobelia is usually found in moist meadows, along stream banks, and often in damp woods at the edge of a swampland.

PERIOD OF BLOOM: August into September; sometimes a few blossoms in October.

SOIL: Neutral to slightly acid fertile soil. Great blue lobelia can be grown in average garden soil if watered during periods of drought. Under such conditions it will not grow as tall. Constant moisture is important if you want to raise ideal specimens.

LOCATION AND EXPOSURE: Full sun or very light shade are equally suitable. This is a good plant to grow with the early white snakeroot in an open moist woodland—for contrast, keep all the lobelias together. When the blue lobelia is grown in a wet area it tends to spread.

PLANTING TIME: In cold climates it is best transplanted in spring when new foliage appears. In other areas, fall or spring planting is satisfactory. Mulch in winter in very cold climates.

ROOT SYSTEM: Stringy white fibrous roots.

PLANTING DEPTH AND SPACING: Space 8 to 12 inches apart or plant at random in a meadow. Set the crowns at soil level. A little soil may be pulled toward the crown before mulching and before the ground freezes. This species is more robust than the red one.

Coarse fibrous white roots should be pruned back to 2¼ inches before transplanting. Divide clumps every spring for good healthy growth.

PLANTING STOCK AND PROPAGATION: Nursery-grown stock is best. Also use quality collected stock.

To propagate, divide clumps in spring; also sow seeds.

Seeds sown as soon as they are ripe germinate readily the following spring. Grow the seedlings in a flat for one year and transfer them to pots or to an open field in the spring of the second year. In moist areas, this lobelia self-sows.

The white form of the great blue lobelia does not come true from seed and is best propagated by division of multiple crowns in spring.

COMMENTS: Occasionally a burgundy-colored plant will appear among the blue lobelia seedlings. It does not set seed and can only be propagated by divisions.

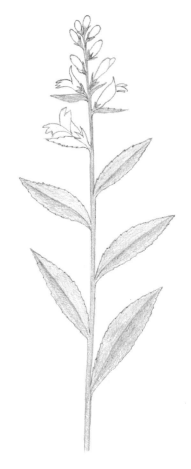

COMPOSITAE [Composite Family]

Vernonia noveboracensis • ironweed

DESCRIPTION: 3 to 5 feet tall. This robust plant has loose, terminal clusters of buttonlike, deep lavender to purple flowers. Lanceolated, toothed leaves alternate along the length of the stem.

Ironweed grows naturally in the eastern half of the United States, inhabiting lowlands and banks of lakes and streams.

PERIOD OF BLOOM: Late August into September and October.

SOIL: Ironweed adapts to a variey of soils with constant moisture, although it always grows in wet soil in the wild.

LOCATION AND EXPOSURE: Ironweed is ideal for naturalizing in a moist meadow or along a stream or lake. But do not hesitate to grow it in a tall border where the soil is fertile and has constant moisture. I grew it from seed in regular garden soil in full sun.

PLANTING TIME: While dormant in spring or fall.

ROOT SYSTEM: A stout, fibrous rootstock. It sends out rhizomes that stay nearby.

PLANTING DEPTH AND SPACING: Space 18 inches apart. Or plant at random. Set the plants with the crown at soil level and mulch.

PLANTING STOCK AND PROPAGATION: Use nursery-grown stock of medium size or quality collected stock.

Propagate by divisions, preferably in spring, or sow seeds as soon as they are ripe. Germination may be uneven. Seedlings are slow to develop, and usually do not bloom until the fourth year. Stem cuttings have proved unsatisfactory.

COMMENTS: Ironweed is an interesting specimen for the wild garden and provides some color in late summer.

Eupatorium maculatum • Joe-pye

DESCRIPTION: 4 to 5 feet tall. Dense convex clusters of lavender to mauve flowers top a stout stem that is tinged with purple at the nodes. White flowers are rare. Large, toothed, ovate leaves line the stem in whorls. They are predominately quilted and have a scent like vanilla.

Joe-pye congregates in large colonies in roadside ditches, moist meadows, and open areas not quite so damp. It often grows in the vicinity of tall meadowrue and boneset.

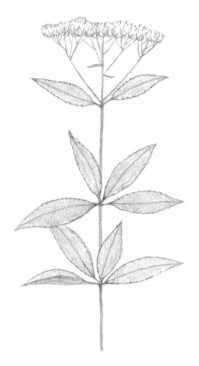

PERIOD OF BLOOM: Late July to September.

SOIL: Any of various soils with reasonably good fertility. In sandy loam soils of only moderate fertility and a minimum of moisture the plant grows much more compactly, not as tall but still pretty and really more refined.

LOCATION AND EXPOSURE: Joe-pye is a bold wildflower best suited for a large moist meadow in full sun. It prefers sunlight, and will tolerate only light shade. Plant in clumps for a more striking display. It contrasts well with Canada goldenrod and tall meadowrue. If the soil has constant moisture it can be grown in a border.

PLANTING TIME: While dormant in spring or fall.

ROOT SYSTEM: A very tough, fibrous rootstock. It is very hard to break up. The purplish eyes are barely visible when the plant is dormant.

PLANTING DEPTH AND SPACING: Space 2 or more feet apart or plant in colonies. Set the rootstock slightly below the soil. Mulch if you wish.

PLANTING STOCK AND PROPAGATION: Medium-sized nursery-grown stock is best, or use quality collected young stock.

Divide the clumps in spring or fall. It is difficult to divide the roots, as they are very intermatted. Trim the wiry roots to a few inches. Vigorous new roots soon develop if ample moisture is available.

The little winged seeds must be covered only lightly when sown. Cover them with an evergreen bough to keep the wind from carrying them away. Joe-pye self-sows.

COMMENTS: Joe-pye is only one of the large group of *Eupatoria*. The white snakeroot is its very charming cousin.

Eupatorium perfoliatum • boneset

DESCRIPTION: 2 to 4 feet tall. Flat-topped dull white flowers, sometimes with a faint bluish cast, form upright clusters. Lance-shaped leaves, prominently veined and heavily quilted, grow opposite each other along the stem. The foliage is quite unusual and very different from any other in this family.

Boneset frequents damp ditches, meadows, and river bottoms, often in the company of tall meadowrue and Joe-pye.

PERIOD OF BLOOM: July into August.

SOIL: Any of various soils with very high to average moisture content.

LOCATION AND EXPOSURE: Grow boneset in the meadow with Joe-pye as a companion. An excellent plant for foliage contrast in full sun or light shade.

PLANTING TIME: While dormant in spring or fall.

ROOT SYSTEM: A coarse fibrous rootstock that forms a clump which is difficult to divide.

PLANTING DEPTH AND SPACING: Space about 1 foot apart. When grown in fertile soil each plant forms a clump. Set the crowns at soil level and trim off any excess straggly roots; new roots will grow.

PLANTING STOCK AND PROPAGATION: Use nursery-grown stock of medium size or quality collected young stock.

Divide the clumps in spring or fall. Seed germination has proved poor. Boneset rarely self-sows.

COMMENTS: Boneset is not a pretty flower in itself, but when grown in masses its color and foliage contrast well with other wildflowers.

Eupatorium rugosum • early white snakeroot

DESCRIPTION: 1 to 3 feet tall, often taller in very moist areas. Buttons of dense long-lasting white flowers form showy terminal clusters on rigid leafy stems. The branches have many divisions, giving the plant the appearance of a round bush. The thin petiolate leaves are toothed, tapering to a gradual point. This species is better adapted to cold than the late-flowering *Eupatorium aromaticum*.

Early white snakeroot is found in open damp rocky woods, along streams, and in moist meadows. It grows and blooms profusely in thickets and in the shade of tall hardwoods where the soil is moderately moist and rich in humus.

PERIOD OF BLOOM: July into August, sometimes September.

SOIL: Humus-rich fertile soil that is slightly acid to neutral. Snakeroot needs constant moisture to bloom well. Soil need not be wet, although the plant can tolerate standing water admirably.

LOCATION AND EXPOSURE: Grow early white snakeroot in a sunny spot or in a rocky woods where leafmold is deep, or interplant with tall and medium ferns in a shady nook. It is particularly beautiful when reflected in a pool or a slow-running brook, and is also a fine plant for a formal border.

PLANTING TIME: While dormant in spring or fall.

ROOT SYSTEM: A compact, wiry, fibrous rootstock. The eyes of new growth are slow to appear in spring. The roots may seem dead but are very much alive. This is a common trait of the eupatoria.

PLANTING DEPTH AND SPACING: Space 2 to 3 feet apart. Set the eyes of the crowns barely ½ inch below soil level. The late emergence of shoots in spring protects the foliage, which is sensitive to frosts.

PLANTING STOCK AND PROPAGATION: Use nursery-grown stock or quality collected young stock.

Divide clumps in spring or fall; use only the vigorous portions. Seed germination is unreliable. The plant self-sows under ideal conditions.

COMMENTS: A colony of white snakeroot in bloom resembles a blanket of down settling on a meadow. This is my favorite eupatorium.

The juices of the snakeroots are poisonous to man and cattle, and it presented problems to the pioneers.

Liatris scariosa • blazing star

DESCRIPTION: 2 to 3 feet tall. One or two sturdy leafy stalks rise from a rosette of linear basal foliage. Spikes of many buttonlike, feathery flower disks bloom at intervals along the entire length of the stalk. The flower spike blooms from the top downward. This is characteristic of all the liatris. The violet-lavender to rosy-purple variety is the most common. Sometimes a rare white one appears among them.

Blazing star is found in open sandy country, along roadsides, in wastelands, and among sparse prairie grasses—often covering huge areas with splendid color. On wastelands it often grows with early goldenrod, which blooms at the same time.

PERIOD OF BLOOM: August into September, sometimes as early as late July.

SOIL: Blazing star seems to be indifferent to soil pH. Lean soils or moderately fertile soils encourage the best flowers with the straightest stalks. In rich soil the plant loses its stature and the spikes become limp, bending at odd angles. Good drainage is very important.

LOCATION AND EXPOSURE: Blazing star is a choice plant for sandy problem areas where little else will grow. Once established, the plant endures drought well. Full sun all day and fairly lean soil will ensure straight flower spikes and abundant bloom.

In sandy prairielike areas it is best planted among sparse grasses. Or interperse it with birdfoot violets, butterfly flowers, blue-eyed grass, pussy-toes, goldenrods, and wild asters.

PLANTING TIME: Spring or fall. If the plant is moved during the growing season the flower stalk should be cut off, leaving some of the leafy stem. The top may die, but it will usually appear the next spring.

ROOT SYSTEM: Young seedling corms are cinnamon-colored; they turn dark with age. A black warted corm that increases in size produces many warts when cultivated. In the wild there is rarely more than one stalk.

PLANTING DEPTH AND SPACING: Space about 6 inches apart or scatter. Set the corms 1 inch deep. Deeper planting will encourage the corm to send up extra stalks to form an attractive plant. If the stalks become too crowded the corm should be dug up in the spring and cut into pieces, leaving one or two eyes in each portion.

PLANTING STOCK AND PROPAGATION: Use nursery-grown stock or quality collected stock.

For division of large corms, cut the corm into pieces like potatoes, leaving one or two eyes in each portion. Dry for an hour before planting, or dust with fungicide. Plant 1 inch deep. Mulch in winter only to protect the corm in very cold climates, but remove the mulch in spring.

Seeds are slow to germinate, usually waiting until the second year. One-year-old seedlings can be moved to their permanent home.

COMMENTS: The blazing star is hardy and easy to cultivate. The flowers, opening at the top and working down the stalk, are ideal for floral arrangements. Snip off the wilted flowers and there are no bare stalks to hide.

The blazing star is decidedly a sun lover.

Just a few years ago while hiking in an area where sand dunes and prairie grasses alternated I came upon a colony of liatris—many hundreds of them. In their midst grew a small colony of delicate mauve-pink plants. It is not an easy color to describe, but they were outstanding. My botany books do not list this color phase. Is it a rare form, or a new variety?

Liatris pycnostachya • Kansas gayfeather

DESCRIPTION: 2 to 4 feet tall. Tall wands of closely set florets top sturdy stems with linear foliage. The flowers are violet-lavender to rosy purple, and rarely white. Basal foliage is also linear but broader. It tends to become less prominent as the flowers bloom. This plant is another reserved bloomer.

Kansas gayfeather is found among grasses in damp open prairies, usually in the vicinity of goldenrods.

PERIOD OF BLOOM: August into September.

SOIL: Moderately fertile soils.

LOCATION AND EXPOSURE: Full sun is necessary to grow straight spikes. In shade the plant grows rampantly and produces abundant leaves and crooked, sparsely flowered spikes. Grow Kansas gayfeather in a sunny border or in an open prairielike place.

PLANTING TIME: Spring or fall, preferably spring.

ROOT SYSTEM: A blackish to dark-gray warted corm with many eyes. It increases in size with age.

PLANTING DEPTH AND SPACING: Space about 1 foot apart or plant at random in colonies. Set the corms 1 inch deep. Corms produce more spikes when planted deeper, but require transplanting more often. The first year after transplanting, do not expect well-formed flower spikes. It seems that the plant must adapt itself to its new environment. Mulch in winter only in cold climates.

PLANTING STOCK AND PROPAGATION: Use nursery-grown stock or quality collected medium-sized corms.

The division of large corms is the quickest and surest method of propagation. Cut the corms as one would potatoes for spring planting, leaving one to two eyes in each piece. Dry for an hour or dust with fungicide.

Seeds are slow to germinate, often requiring two years. Seedlings bloom the second and third year.

COMMENTS: Kansas gayfeather is very easy to grow and soon forms large clumps when cultivated. There is a white form but it does not increase as rapidly.

Solidago canadensis · Canada goldenrod

DESCRIPTION: 3 to 4 feet tall. Feathery, rich yellow sprays of florets atop sturdy stems. Narrow medium-green foliage alternates along the entire length of the stem.

This goldenrod is found along roadsides and fence lines, in dry open fields, or in dampish meadows that dry out in summer.

PERIOD OF BLOOM: August into September.

SOIL: Adaptable to most soil conditions. Its height is determined mostly by the fertility and moisture content of the soil.

LOCATION AND EXPOSURE: Goldenrods are sun lovers, but tolerate very light open shade. Lovely for the back of a border and very showy when grown among old fence rails or next to a stone wall with wild blue asters.

PLANTING TIME: Spring or fall.

ROOT SYSTEM: Short slender rhizomes with a touch of rose at the tip. They form large clumps. To produce beautiful plants, the roots must have ample growing room.

PLANTING DEPTH AND SPACING: Space about 2 feet apart. Set rhizomes horizontally about 1 inch deep with the tip leading to the surface. The outer rhizomes produce the strongest plants. Divide clumps and transplant every third year for showy plants that bloom profusely.

PLANTING STOCK AND PROPAGATION: Use nursery-grown stock or quality collected young stock.

Propagate by division of clumps, using only the strong outer rhizomes and discarding the center growth. The plant self-sows readily where soil is open.

COMMENTS: If the goldenrod were not so easily cultivated and not so abundant, perhaps we would prize it more highly. It combines beautifully with many of the late summer and fall flowers, especially in a tall border. The association of goldenrod pollen with hay fever has been discredited.

The galls that form on goldenrods in wastelands are interesting to the dry-flower arranger, and the insects inside the galls provide good bait for the ice fisherman.

220

Solidago rigida • prairie goldenrod

DESCRIPTION: 3 to 4 feet tall. Large flat topped flower heads of rich golden yellow, atop sturdy stems. Most of the foliage is basal—often 8 inches long and several inches wide, and forming neat, gray-green rosettes. True leaves are scant.

The prairie goldenrod, also called stiff goldenrod, frequents lean meadows, rocky pastures, and hillsides in full sun.

PERIOD OF BLOOM: Late August until frost. The flowers remain yellow for a long time, even after frosts have damaged the leaves.

SOIL: Prairie goldenrod is adaptable. It forms large clumps in the sandy fertile loam of our garden. Good drainage is important.

LOCATION AND EXPOSURE: A showy plant for a large sunny border. Grow it with purple or rose-colored New England asters.

PLANTING TIME: While dormant in spring or fall.

ROOT SYSTEM: A coarse fibrous rootstock with many pinkish to rose-colored shoots. It has long white roots that reach far into the ground for food and moisture.

PLANTING DEPTH AND SPACING: Space 2 or more feet apart since the plants form large clumps. Set the crowns at soil level and spread the roots evenly. Roots should be trimmed back to 3 or 4 inches. Divide the clumps every third year.

PLANTING STOCK AND PROPAGATION: Nursery-grown stock is best; the rhizomes are divided more often, which makes for more vigorous plants. Also use quality collected young stock.

Propagate by division of clumps. Use only the strong outer plants, and discard the center growth. The plant will also volunteer where soil is open.

COMMENTS: "Plume o' gold" is a more fitting name for this lovely plant. It is a good wildflower to grow in colder climates, as early frosts do it no harm.

Prairie goldenrod is very different in appearance from other goldenrods, and I consider it one of the best for late blooming.

Solidago graminifolia • grass-leaved goldenrod

DESCRIPTION: 2 to 4 feet tall. A leafy stalk with many alternate willowlike leaves is topped by a flat open cluster of numerous small yellow flowers.

221

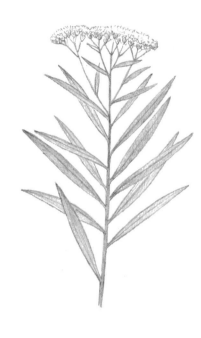

This goldenrod often forms a gold blanket over moist thickets, meadows and roadside ditches.

PERIOD OF BLOOM: Late July into September.

SOIL: A moist, fertile to average garden soil with constant moisture. PH is not important, but the plant is usually found in a somewhat acid soil.

LOCATION AND EXPOSURE: The grass-leaved goldenrod is best suited for naturalizing in a moist open meadow with Joe-pye, swamp milkweed, tall meadowrue and flat-topped white aster. If you prefer a lone specimen in a wild garden, plant it in a bottomless gallon can and bury it at soil level.

PLANTING TIME: While dormant in spring or fall.

ROOT SYSTEM: A slender rhizome that wanders and sends up new shoots at frequent intervals, especially when grown in fertile soil or when mulched.

PLANTING DEPTH AND SPACING: Space 2 feet apart, as rhizomes spread to form colonies. Set rhizomes horizontally 1 inch deep with eye almost at soil level.

PLANTING STOCK AND PROPAGATION: Nursery-grown stock is rarely available. Use quality collected young stock.

Divide rhizome clumps while plant is dormant. It self-sows sparsely.

COMMENTS: Grass-leaved goldenrod is a good plant to grow in the open meadow if you want a mass of yellow to cover a large expanse or to contrast with other wildflowers.

Aster macrophyllus • large-leaved aster

DESCRIPTION: 2 to 3 feet tall. An open cluster of rayed light-blue flowers with darker centers. The basal foliage is large and heart-shaped; the leaves on the stems are smaller and sparse.

Found in dry open woods and moist thickets where the soil is humus-rich, this wildflower rarely blooms in deep shade, but it spreads to make good groundcover.

PERIOD OF BLOOM: August into September.

SOIL: Slightly acid, fertile woods soil, either damp or somewhat dry in midsummer. Constant moisture is important if you want the best foliage.

LOCATION AND EXPOSURE: Grow the large-leaved aster in colonies in high open shade where some sun filters through, or as ground-cover in a more deeply shaded area. The foliage withstands very severe frosts.

PLANTING TIME: While dormant in spring or fall.

ROOT SYSTEM: Many short rhizomes form a large rootstock with fibrous roots.

PLANTING DEPTH AND SPACING: Space 2 to 12 inches apart. Set the crowns at soil level and mulch lightly overall.

PLANTING STOCK AND PROPAGATION: Nursery-grown stock is rarely offered. Use quality collected stock.

To propagate, divide clumps or sow seeds as soon as they are ripe. In barren areas it sometimes self-sows in a moist shady area.

COMMENTS: This particular species of aster is best used as a ground-cover; the foliage is showier than the flowers.

Aster novae-angliae • New England aster

DESCRIPTION: 3 to 4 feet tall. Many fine-rayed terminal clusters of purple-violet flowers. The flowers are usually very uniform in color, but the rose-pink kind has some variation. All have prominent yellow centers. The leaves are long and narrow, somewhat sticky, and cling to the entire length of the hairy stem.

New England aster springs up naturally in open meadows, along roadsides, and in thickets. In central Wisconsin, it blankets road-sides and fields each autumn with splashes of color.

PERIOD OF BLOOM: Late August into October.

SOIL: Neutral to slightly acid fertile soil with constant moisture. The plant grows vigorously under these conditions.

LOCATION AND EXPOSURE: New England aster is an excellent plant to grow in colonies in full sun or very light open shade. Use it in a border with cultivated perennials, or grow it among taller wild-flowers. Mulch this plant heavily to keep the roots cool and the soil moist. When the plant is mulched the leaves grow along the entire length of the stem for the whole season and the flowers are of better quality.

PLANTING TIME: Fall, spring, or late summer after the rhizomes have formed. Late fall is best.

223

ROOT SYSTEM: Short white rhizomes, often tinged with pink, radiate from the blooming stalk and form a neat clump. Each clump has many fibrous roots that grow extremely long, especially in heavily mulched fertile gardens. Divide the rhizomes often to keep the plant growing vigorously.

PLANTING DEPTH AND SPACING: Space 1 to 2 feet apart, depending on the fertility of the soil and effect wanted. Set the plants horizontally with the roots 1 inch deep and the tips of the rhizomes just below soil level. The extensive fibrous roots should be trimmed back to 3 or 4 inches. Mulch heavily for winter. Remove some of the mulch in spring, then replace it when the new growth has hardened.

PLANTING STOCK AND PROPAGATION: Nursery-grown stock is best and most vigorous. Also use quality collected stock.

Division of rhizomes gives true colors not obtained from seeds. Divide clumps, using only the rhizomes with the strongest tips, and replant often. It self-sows readily in open soils and roadsides.

COMMENTS: For a spectacular color contrast, grow New England aster with late goldenrods and fall sunflowers.

Aster laevis • smooth aster

DESCRIPTION: 2 to 3 feet tall. Violet-blue to deep-sky-blue rayed flowers with large open heads atop smooth stems. The foliage is smooth and lanceolate and the leaves grow along the entire stem.

Smooth aster is found in old hayfields, in open woods, along roadsides where soil is fertile, and at times volunteering in cultivated flower beds. Each autumn it sends a welcome splash of blue across fields and meadows.

PERIOD OF BLOOM: September into October.

SOIL: Smooth aster is not demanding; it will bloom in lean soils as well as fertile ones. When cultivated in fertile soil and mulched, one small plant will grow to the size of a bushel basket within two years. Care, fertile soil, and constant moisture will produce abundant bloom.

LOCATION AND EXPOSURE: Plant this aster at random in an open meadow or along a sunny woodland border for a final splash of blue against the more somber autumn colors. Or grow it in the background of a border of annual or perennial wildflowers. Good air circulation is important to prevent mildew on the foliage.

PLANTING TIME: While dormant in spring or fall; spring is preferable in very cold climates.

ROOT SYSTEM: A compact rootstock with fibrous roots and many pinkish rhizomes. In an open meadow where it competes with other plants or where the soil is lean, the smooth aster rarely sends up more than two stalks. If the roots become crowded cultivated plants quickly die.

PLANTING DEPTH AND SPACING: Space 2 or more feet apart if grown with a heavy mulch in fertile soil. Set the rhizomes horizontally 1 inch deep, with the tip of the rhizome tapering upward.

PLANTING STOCK AND PROPAGATION: Use nursery-grown stock or quality collected stock. Do not divide plants that have only two or more flowering stalks.

Divide large clumps from the garden, using only the stronger outer rhizomes. Seeds scattered in a sparse grassland gave excellent results.

COMMENTS: I have a special fondness for this aster—in my area it is the last splash of blue for the year.

Aster ptarmicoides • frostflower aster

DESCRIPTION: 12 to 18 inches tall. The flat-topped flower heads bear rayed white petals and have yellow centers. When the flowers begin to bloom, the outer petals appear first. The basal as well as the stem foliage is shiny dark green, narrow, and willowlike.

Frostflower aster is usually found scattered in tufts among early yellow goldenrods and blazing stars in dry open fields, wastelands, and prairies.

PERIOD OF BLOOM: July into September.

SOIL: Neutral to slightly acid garden soil or sandy loam. In very fertile soil this aster grows more robust and loses some of its daintiness.

LOCATION AND EXPOSURE: Full sun is preferable, but the plant will tolerate light partial shade. It is best grown in the dry, prairielike garden with early goldenrod, blazing star, harebell, or blue-eyed grass. A neat little plant for edging a perennial border in full sun.

225

PLANTING TIME: While dormant in spring or fall.

ROOT SYSTEM: Many short rhizomes with fibrous roots form a neat clump. The rootstock becomes woody with age, and the plant loses its vitality.

PLANTING DEPTH AND SPACING: Space 8 to 12 inches apart. Set the rhizome about 1 inch deep with crown at soil level. This aster grows best without mulch. Where the soil is moderately fertile the plant should be separated and transplanted every third year. Otherwise it grows so dense that it chokes itself out.

PLANTING STOCK AND PROPAGATION: Nursery-grown stock is hard to find. Use quality collected young stock.

Divide vigorous young plants in spring or fall, using only the plants with fine fibrous roots. Seeds are slow to germinate, but the plant self-sows under prairie conditions.

COMMENTS: Frostflower aster is a charming wildflower and easy to cultivate. I especially value its shiny, dark green leaves in the wild garden. It is also known as the upland white aster.

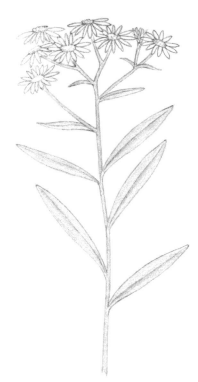

Aster umbellatus • flat-topped aster

DESCRIPTION: 3 to 5 feet tall. The flat-topped flower heads consist of many sparsely rayed white flowers with pale yellow centers. The centers fade to a rust color. Many alternating lanceolate leaves grow along the entire length of the stalks.

This aster is usually found in damp meadows growing among Joe-pye, blue vervain, and swamp milkweed. It is also found along fence lines, in thickets, and along the borders of open woods.

PERIOD OF BLOOM: July into October.

SOIL: Neutral to slightly acid soil with constant moisture is preferable, but I find that this plant will grow in wetter or drier soils if it is mulched.

LOCATION AND EXPOSURE: This long-lasting perennial is easily established. Plant it in colonies in sunny moist meadows among other wildflowers. Individual specimens are not so impressive.

PLANTING TIME: While dormant in spring or fall.

ROOT SYSTEM: A coarse rootstock with fibrous roots, usually sending up only one stalk per plant.

PLANTING DEPTH AND SPACING: Space 1 or more feet apart, or plant in colonies with other wildflowers. Set the crowns at soil level and spread the roots evenly. If roots are extra long, trim to 3 or 4 inches.

PLANTING STOCK AND PROPAGATION: Use nursery-grown stock if available, or quality collected stock of medium size.

Seeds sown in fall will produce blooms by the second year. The plant self-sows, especially where land is open, and often volunteers in the cultivated border.

COMMENTS: Flat-topped asters look best when planted in masses.

There are many other species of wild asters, though some have unimpressive flowers. Often new species appear in the prairie garden, their seeds evidently carried in on the wind.

Antennaria plantaginifolia • pussytoes

DESCRIPTION: 4 to 6 inches tall. The flower stems bear white woolly flower heads that resemble a kitten's paw. The oblong, round-tipped, gray-green leaves are mostly basal. They have an overall silvery sheen.

Pussytoes is found in most of the eastern half of the United States. In Wisconsin it frequents dry open pastures, wastelands, and sandy roadsides where the soil is very lean. You might find endless stretches of pussytoes carpeting the earth along the edges of reforested prairielands. As the trees mature, they shade the patches, which then get scrawny and gradually disappear. I am sure that some seeds must remain dormant because a year or two after reforested areas are cut over, open areas are again covered with pussytoes.

PERIOD OF BLOOM: May into June.

SOIL: Poor sandy soils to moderately fertile sandy loam soils, all with good drainage. In more fertile soils it grows more robust and is not as pretty.

LOCATION AND EXPOSURE: Give pussytoes a spot in full sun with moderately fertile soil and it will spread, becoming denser each season. It can be used instead of grass in sunny barren sandy areas where nothing else will grow. It makes a remarkable carpet.

Pussytoes is fine for a sandy bank to help hold the soil in place. Also grow it in scattered patches in a prairie garden.

PLANTING TIME: Early spring or late August into fall.

ROOT SYSTEM: Each parent plant with fibrous roots sends out several

stolons which take root to form new plants. The stolons divide frequently as they creep, eventually forming dense mats.

PLANTING DEPTH AND SPACING: Space 4 to 8 inches apart, depending on the size of the plants and the desired density. Carefully tuck in the roots and set them with the crown at soil level. Where stolons are attached to the parent plant, carefully cover all small roots with soil, and firm.

PLANTING STOCK AND PROPAGATION: Nursery-grown stock is preferred, but seldom offered. Use quality collected stock that is vigorous. The easiest method of propagation is by stolons from an overcrowded patch in the garden, spring is best. Seeds volunteer on open soils.

COMMENTS: Few other plants can make a more suitable groundcover for a sunny barren area.

Heliopsis helianthoides • ox-eye

DESCRIPTION: 3 to 5 feet tall. A stout stalk with multiple branches bears an abundance of 2 inch flower heads. These heads have many broad-rayed golden-yellow petals, and slightly raised centers peppered with brown. The opposite ovate foliage is toothed and rather coarse. It tends to stick to the skin.

Ox-eye is found in open sunny spots—usually roadsides, railroad beds, and wastelands. The flowers form a maze of yellow so dense that scarcely any of the green foliage shows through.

PERIOD OF BLOOM: Late July into September.

SOIL: Neutral to slightly acid garden soil, or the gritty gravelly soil found along roadsides and railroad crossings. Ox-eye seems to grow in any soil. In very fertile soil it grows rampantly.

LOCATION AND EXPOSURE: Full sun or very open shade along a woodland border. Ox-eye is a fine plant to naturalize in large areas; it is long-lasting and quite drought-resistant.

PLANTING TIME: While dormant in spring or fall.

ROOT SYSTEM: A stout, somewhat rhizomous rootstock with fibrous roots, forming a heavy woody clump with age. Many sturdy stalks arise from the clump, but diminish in size as the roots become crowded.

PLANTING DEPTH AND SPACING: Space 1 to 3 feet apart. Set plants with the eyes just below soil level. Trim back long roots to 3 or 4 inches. Divide cultivated plants every few years; in the wild this does not seem necessary.

PLANTING STOCK AND PROPAGATION: Nursery-grown stock if available, or quality collected stock with strong eyes. Roots may appear dormant and the eyes inconspicuous.

Propagate by division of strong clumps (not easy to divide) and sow seeds in fall or early spring. Ox-eye self-sows, though not abundantly.

COMMENTS: Ox-eye is a coarse wildflower with an exceptionally long blooming period. Cut flowers last long in floral arrangements. This is an excellent plant to use where you want a golden color over a long period of time.

Achillea Millefolium • common yarrow

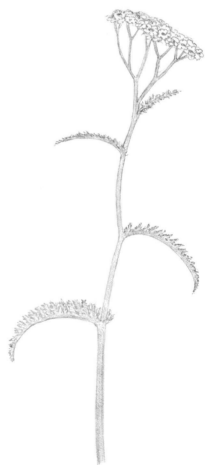

DESCRIPTION: 1 to 2 feet tall. Each leafy stem divides abruptly at the top to form a flat-topped umbel. The umbel is composed of many small individual white florets with light yellow centers. The fernlike foliage is a lovely shade of dark green.

Originally from Eurasia, this plant has readily adapted to its new environment. It inhabits roadsides and fields, and colonizes in wastelands if the soil is reasonably fertile.

PERIOD OF BLOOM: June into September.

SOIL: Sandy loams, gritty roadside soils, or rich garden soil (where it will grow luxuriantly). The plant is very adaptable.

LOCATION AND EXPOSURE: Common yarrow is best grown in full sun. It is a good plant to grow on slopes, as its extensive rhizomes spread and form mats that hold the soil. It can take more abuse than grass, but do not step on the plants until they are well-established.

PLANTING TIME: Spring, August into fall. The plant will soon make a neat patch of green.

ROOT SYSTEM: Strong white rhizomes. Parent plants produce many rhizomes that fork and make large colonies.

PLANTING DEPTH AND SPACING: Space 6 to 12 inches apart, depending on the desired effect. Set the rhizomes ½ to 1 inch deep with the tip almost at soil level.

PLANTING STOCK AND PROPAGATION: Use nursery-grown stock or quality collected stock.

Divide clumps, using the strong rhizomes. Common yarrow does not readily self-sow.

COMMENTS: To encourage common yarrow to bloom for a longer period of time, the faded blossoms should be picked regularly. Although sometimes called a weed, its cool white blossoms and lush green foliage provide a welcome relief in summer heat. Its cousin, cultivated rose-pink yarrow, makes an interesting companion flower.

In difficult areas where yarrow is grown to hold down the soil or to replace grass, set the lawn mower a little higher than you would for cutting the regular lawn. Yarrow rarely requires more than one cutting after blooming.

Chrysanthemum Leucanthemum • ox-eye daisy

DESCRIPTION: 1 to 2 feet tall. Each stem displays a daisy with single snow-white petals and a compact golden disk. The dainty foliage is dark green and deeply cut. It is sparse on the stem, but forms a neat clump at the base.

Ox-eye daisy is found along roadsides and in abandoned hayfields, where it makes a lovely display.

PERIOD OF BLOOM: June into July.

SOIL: These daisies grow nicely in any soil, though fertility does affect the height of the stem, the size of the flower, and the quality of the foliage. They are pretty in all instances, however. I grow them in sandy loam with superb results.

LOCATION AND EXPOSURE: When grown in full sun and reasonably good soil they bloom luxuriantly. They even bloom well in very light open shade. Ox-eye daisy is a fine and easily grown plant to naturalize in large meadows.

PLANTING TIME: Spring or fall. Clumps may be divided in late August.

ROOT SYSTEM: A compact rootstock with fibrous roots.

PLANTING DEPTH AND SPACING: Space 6 to 12 inches apart, depending on the size of the plants or clumps. Spread the roots evenly and set the crown at soil level. Large clumps should be divided every second or third year, especially when grown in cultivation.

PLANTING STOCK AND PROPAGATION: Use nursery-grown stock or quality collected young stock.

Seeds sown as soon as ripe germinate quickly and make small blooming plants the following year. Ox-eye daisy self-sows readily, but unwanted seedlings soon die when dug under. (Cut back all faded flowers promptly if no seed is wanted.)

COMMENTS: To walk through fields of pure white daisies on a summer's day is to know an indescribable serenity. In some states the ox-eye daisy is classified as a weed—how wonderful that it is so common!

Tanacetum vulgare • common tansy

DESCRIPTION: 18 to 36 inches tall. This plant has a flat-topped umbel composed of many distinct yellow buttons without petals. The stout leafy stems have coarse fernlike foliage.

Common tansy grows vigorously in old pastures, among rocks, and along roadsides. I have seen acres taken over by this somewhat weedy plant.

PERIOD OF BLOOM: July into September.

SOIL: Neutral to slightly acid garden soil, or rocky grit along roadsides and railroad crossings. Common tansy grows readily in most soils, but rampantly in fertile ones.

LOCATION AND EXPOSURE: Full sun is best. Because it is too coarse and large for a small garden, common tansy is suited for naturalizing in large wasteland areas or in unused meadows. If you wish to grow it in the garden, however, you can restrict its growth by planting it in a bottomless gallon container sunk at soil level.

PLANTING TIME: Spring or fall.

ROOT SYSTEM: A creeping rhizome, pinkish at the tip, with many fibrous roots. It forks often.

PLANTING DEPTH AND SPACING: Space 2 feet apart. Set the rhizomes ½ to 1 inch deep with the shoot or eye pointing upward almost to soil level. It spreads to form colonies.

PLANTING STOCK AND PROPAGATION: Nursery-grown stock is rarely offered. Use quality collected young stock.

Tansy self-sows readily. When grown in out of the way places

231

the seeds may be left to ripen—some birds will feast on them.

COMMENTS: Flowers cut just when they are about to bloom are excellent for dried floral arrangements.

Tansy is also used as a tea and as a flavoring in cookies. It has a bitter aftertaste, however. This plant is also called golden buttons and bitter buttons.

The cultivated tansy, *Tanacetum vulgare* (forma *crispum*) is much preferred to the wild species. The foliage is more crinkled and fernlike and the whole plant has a neater appearance.

Senecio aureus • golden ragwort

DESCRIPTION: 10 to 18 inches tall. Several stems rise from a rosette of round, dark green, toothed leaves. The stems bear flat-topped clusters of 1 inch daisylike golden flowers with brown centers. Stem leaves are scant.

Golden ragwort is often found in rocky deciduous woods, along low stream beds in deep shade, and on hummocks in swamplands. In such areas continuous moisture is available. To my surprise it volunteered and flourished in my garden where the soil had only an average moisture content.

PERIOD OF BLOOM: May into June.

SOIL: Slightly acid to neutral soils. The earth may be very damp to wet or only moist. The plant is quite adaptable to average growing conditions.

LOCATION AND EXPOSURE: It is not necessary to duplicate exactly the ragwort's natural environment, since it grows readily both in full sun and in open shade. It is a good plant for a tulip bed. The lovely rosette of dark green leaves remains all season as a groundcover.

PLANTING TIME: Spring or fall.

ROOT SYSTEM: A compact rhizome with short basal offshoots that form a neat compact clump. Roots are white and fibrous.

PLANTING DEPTH AND SPACING: Space 10 to 15 inches apart. Set the crowns at soil level and spread the roots evenly. Each plant forms a neat clump which should be divided every other year. When this flower is cultivated it grows vigorously.

PLANTING STOCK AND PROPAGATION: Nursery-grown stock is much

huskier and stronger than stock from wild plants. But quality collected stock may also be used.

To propagate, divide clumps in spring.

Golden ragwort self-sows under favorable conditions.

COMMENTS: Golden ragwort is rarely offered in wildflower catalogs. It is a good plant to grow in cultivation.

Cichorium Intybus • chicory

DESCRIPTION: 1 to 4 feet tall. The linear basal foliage is much like that of the dandelion. The lanceolate foliage becomes smaller and quite sparse near the top of the much-divided, branching stem. The rayed flower heads of brilliant copen blue (rarely, white or pink), remain open only a few hours in the forenoon and then quickly close to set seed.

Chicory was brought to North America by colonists. On sunny summer mornings the bright blue flowers decorate old meadows, wastelands, and roadsides.

PERIOD OF BLOOM: Flowers continue to open from July into September. Each blossom lasts only a few hours and then quickly fades. Chicory flowers have the shortest life span of any wildflower I know.

SOIL: Chicory grows readily in any of various soils, but it does require good drainage. It even seeds on gravelly shoulders along the highway.

LOCATION AND EXPOSURE: It is best to naturalize chicory in large open spaces; it is too aggressive for a garden. Grow it in full sun in a meadow—its intense blue flower provides a welcome bit of color.

PLANTING TIME: While dormant in spring or fall.

ROOT SYSTEM: A stout, forked, fleshy root with some spreading fibrous roots. It is very resistant to drought.

PLANTING DEPTH AND SPACING: Space 1 to 2 feet apart. Dig quite a deep hole to accommodate the taproot. Set the crown at soil level. It is best to select young plants.

PLANTING STOCK AND PROPAGATION: Use young nursery-grown stock or quality collected young plants.

Chicory self-sows. If you do not wish to have it spread, pick the flowers as they fade.

COMMENTS: In pioneer days the root of the chicory plant was dried, roasted, and ground to use with coffee or as a coffee substitute. I find that ground chicory gives beef gravy a good brown color without altering the taste if used sparingly.

Actinea herbacea • lakeside daisy

DESCRIPTION: The daisylike flowers with rather narrow, showy rays are only a few inches tall. They have very showy butter-yellow petals and large disklike yellow centers. The short-stemmed flowers vary in size according to the growing conditions. The narrow willowlike foliage makes neat mats that remain green all through the summer and into the winter.

Originally found in a very limited area in states bordering the Great Lakes, this rare wildflower was introduced commercially by a Michigan nurseryman and has since spread across the continent. The first stock was rescued from an area which was about to be opened as a limestone pit, and thus lakeside daisy was saved from extinction.

PERIOD OF BLOOM: May into June, but can be extended if the plants are grown in well-drained soil with mulch to conserve moisture.

SOIL: The original stock was found where limestone lay beneath the soil layer, and the soil presumably had a high pH. The nurseryman who introduced them grows the flowers in a well-drained clay soil with wood-shavings mulch, and also under ordinary conditions. He exploded the old supposition that the plant should be left in the wilderness because it was impossible to grow under ordinary garden conditions.

I grow lakeside daisy in full sun in a sandy loam soil with a pH of 6. It usually has constant moisture.

LOCATION AND EXPOSURE: For best bloom, full sun is preferable. Grow the lakeside daisy along the border as an edging or use it in a sunny wildflower garden. It is very versatile indeed.

PLANTING TIME: Spring or fall. I prefer spring planting in very cold climates. When planting in fall, mulch.

234

ROOT SYSTEM: White, stringy, fibrous roots very much like those of the lobelias. Offsets form around the parent plant to make a neat clump.

PLANTING DEPTH AND SPACING: Plant the crown at soil level and space about 6 to 10 inches apart.

PLANTING STOCK AND PROPAGATION: Use nursery-grown stock.

Propagate by divisions in spring. Sow seeds in fall for spring germination. Blooms appear the second year from seed.

COMMENTS: The lakeside daisy is easy to cultivate, and long-lasting.

Appendix I

Wildflowers to Choose for Special Conditions

Over the years I have found that many wildflowers will grow in environments that differ greatly from their native ones. Some wildflowers from a moist and fertile habitat will grow in lean, dry soils, and vice versa. Some adapt their sun and shade requirements and some do not. Allegheny Mountain gentian is a good example: it is native to moist woods and uplands from Kentucky to Florida, where the climate is mild. Yet this flower has adapted nicely to the climate of northeastern Wisconsin with its extreme winters, and has adapted to lean sandy soil, sandy loam, and fertile garden soil. I have grown it in full sun and in high open shade with equal success.

Other wildflowers, however, must have their native requirements met exactly or they will not flourish. The lady's-slippers are good examples: They must have high open shade and humus-rich woodlands soil that contains mycorhizal fungus or they will soon perish.

The following is a listing of varying conditions of soil, light, and weather, and the wildflowers that are suitable for them—both the wildflowers that grow naturally under such conditions and the wildflowers that can adapt to them. (For detailed growing instructions, see the individual plant.) Plants marked with an asterisk (*) go dormant after blooming—either naturally or under the conditions described.

ANNUALS AND BIENNIALS

The wildflowers listed here are very easy to grow in almost any type of soil, and give a quick splash of color.

Wildflowers for Good Garden Soil in Full Sun

These may be grown along a border, in a flower bed, or in a garden row as well as to fill in bare spots until perennial wildflowers take over.

Black-eyed Susan: *Rudbeckia hirta*
California poppy: *Eschscholtzia californica*
Indian mallow: *Abutilon Theophrasti*
Pale corydalis: *Corydalis sempervirens*
Prickly poppy: *Argemone intermedia*
Queen Anne's lace: *Daucus Carota*

Spiked Lobelia: *Lobelia spicata*
Smooth false foxglove: *Gerardia virginica*
Strawberry blite: *Chenopodium capitatum*
Venus's looking-glass: *Specularia perfoliata*
Yellow goatsbeard: *Tragopogon pratensis*

Wildflowers for a Rock Garden in Full Sun

Black-eyed Susan: *Rudbeckia hirta*
California poppy: *Eschscholtzia californica*
Pearly everlasting: *Anaphalis margaritacea*
Spiked lobelia: *Lobelia spicata*

Strawberry blite: *Chenopodium capitatum*
Venus's looking-glass: *Specularia perfoliata*

Wildflowers for High Open Shade in a Rich, Moist Woodland

Allegheny vine: *Adlumia fungosa*
Herb-Robert: *Geranium Robertianum*
Jewelweed: *Impatiens capensis*
Wild cucumber: *Echinocystis lobata*

Wildflowers for Lean Soils in Full Sun

These are usually used to naturalize large areas.

Black-eyed Susan: *Rudbeckia hirta*
Common mullein: *Verbascum Thapsus*
Pearly everlasting: *Anaphalis margaritacea*
Queen Anne's lace: *Daucus Carota*

Wildflowers for Damp, Grassy Meadows in Full Sun

Cow parsnip: *Heracleum maximum*
Fringed gentian: *Gentiana crinita*
Indian paintbrush: *Castilleja coccinea*

Wildflowers for River Bottoms, Damp Thickets, and Along Streams

Cow parsnip: *Heracleum maximum*
Jewelweed: *Impatiens capensis*
Wild cucumber: *Echinocystis lobata*

Weedy Wildflowers

Cut the blossoms before the plants set seed.

Common mullein: *Verbascum Thapsus*
Indian mallow: *Abutilon Theophrasti*
Prickly poppy: *Argemone intermedia*
Queen Anne's lace: *Daucus Carota*
Yellow goatsbeard: *Tragopogon pratensis*

PERENNIALS

Wildflowers for a Very Early Spring Display near the Home

These plants will bloom while snow still lingers in patches in the deep woodland.

Grape hyacinth: *Muscari botryoides*
Purple corydalis: *Corydalis bulbosa*
Snow trillium: *Trillium nivale*

Wildflowers for a Late Fling of Autumn Color

When frost has claimed all the other wildflowers these plants will still boldly display their colorful blooms.

Allegheny Mountain gentian: *Gentiana decora*
Prairie goldenrod: *Solidago rigida*

Wildflowers for a Wild Garden in Full Sun Along a Border or in the Open Yard

Any soil that will grow good vegetables is highly satisfactory.

Amsonia: *Amsonia Tabernaemontana*
Aster, New England: *Aster novae-angliae*
Aster, smooth: *Aster laevis*
Blazing star: *Liatris scariosa*
Blackberry lily: *Belamcanda chinensis*
Blue-eyed grass: *Sisyrinchium angustifolium*
Blue flag: *Iris versicolor*
Blue salvia: *Salvia azurea*
Boneset: *Eupatorium perfoliatum*
Butterfly flower: *Asclepias tuberosa*
*Camass, eastern: *Camassia scilloides*
*Camass, western: *Camassia esculenta*
Celandine poppy: *Stylophorum diphyllum*
Columbine: *Aquilegia canadensis*
Common yarrow: *Achillea Millefolium*
Cranesbill: *Geranium maculatum*
Crested dwarf iris: *Iris cristata*
Culver's root: *Veronicastrum virginicum*
False dragonhead: *Physostegia virginiana*
False blue indigo: *Baptisia australis*
False spikenard: *Smilacina racemosa*
Gentian, Allegheny Mountain: *Gentiana decora*
Gentian, bottle: *Gentiana Andrewsii*
Gentian, soapwort: *Gentiana Saponaria*
Golden ragwort: *Senecio aureus*
Goldenrod, Canada: *Solidago canadensis*
Goldenrod, prairie: *Solidago rigida*
Great blue lobelia: *Lobelia siphilitica*
Greek valerian: *Polemonium reptans*
Harebell: *Campanula rotundifolia*
Hoary puccoon: *Lithospermum canescens*
Joe-pye: *Eupatorium maculatum*

Kansas gayfeather: *Liatris pycnostachya*
Lakeside daisy: *Actinea herbacea*
Meadowrue, early: *Thalictrum dioicum*
Meadowrue, tall: *Thalictrum polygamum*
Monkey flower: *Mimulus ringens*
Musk mallow: *Malva moschata*
Nodding wild onion: *Allium cernuum*
Oswego tea: *Monarda didyma*
Ox-eye: *Heliopsis helianthoides*
Ox-eye daisy: *Chrysanthemum Leucanthemum*
Pasque flower: *Anemone pulsatilla*
Phlox, blue: *Phlox divaricata*
Phlox, prairie: *Phlox pilosa*
Pink bleeding heart: *Dicentra eximia*
Prairie smoke: *Geum triflorum*
*Purple corydalis: *Corydalis bulbosa*
Purple loosestrife: *Lythrum Salicaria*
Pussytoes: *Antennaria plantaginifolia*
Queen of the prairie: *Filipendula rubra*
Rose verbena: *Verbena canadensis*
Shooting star: *Dodecatheon Meadia*
Skullcap, blue heaven: *Scutellaria baicalensis*
Skullcap, downy: *Scutellaria incana*
Skullcap, early blue: *Scutellaria ovata*
Skullcap, mad-dog: *Scutellaria lateriflora*
Skullcap, pink: *Scutellaria integrifolia*
Skullcap, showy: *Scutellaria serrata*
Star-of-Bethlehem: *Ornithogalum umbellatum*
Stoneroot: *Collinsonia canadensis*
Swamp milkweed: *Asclepias incarnata*
Tiger lily: *Lilium tigrinum*
Turtlehead, red: *Chelone obliqua*
Turtlehead, white: *Chelone glabra*
Wild bergamot: *Monarda fistulosa*

Wildflowers for a Wild Garden in Full Sun Along a Border or in the Open Yard (*continued*)

Wild blue lupine: *Lupinus perennis*
Wild petunia: *Ruellia humilis*

Wild senna: *Cassia marilandica*
Woodland strawberry: *Fragaria vesca*

Wildflowers for Groundcover in High Open Shade under Tall Trees

The area should be reasonably free of underbrush. Deciduous woodlands.

Barren strawberry: *Waldsteinia fragarioides*
Bishop's-cap: *Mitella diphylla*
Bloodroot: *Sanguinaria canadensis*
Bluebead lily: *Clintonia borealis*
Bugleflower: *Ajuga reptans*
Canada mayflower: *Maianthemum canadense*
Cranesbill: *Geranium maculatum*
Foamflower: *Tiarella cordifolia*
Ginseng: *Panax quinquefolium*
Golden seal: *Hydrastis canadensis*
Goldthread: *Coptis groenlandica*

Hairy alumroot: *Heuchera villosa*
Hepatica: *Hepatica americana*
Mayapple: *Podophyllum peltatum*
Moneywort: *Lysimachia Nummularia*
Partridgeberry: *Mitchella repens*
Pink bleeding heart: *Dicentra eximia*
Trillium, large white: *Trillium grandiflorum*
Trillium, purple: *Trillium erectum*
Trillium, yellow: *Trillium luteum*
Wild ginger: *Asarum canadense*
Wintergreen: *Gaultheria procumbens*
Woodland strawberry: *Fragaria vesca*

Wildflowers for Sandy Loam Soil (or sandy, gritty soils) as well as for Naturalizing in Lean Prairielike Areas. Full Sun All Day.

In prairielike areas the soil may be lean but there is always a thin layer of humus on top.

Birdfoot violet: *Viola pedata*
Blazing star: *Liatris scariosa*
Blue-eyed grass: *Sisyrinchium angustifolium*
Blue salvia: *Salvia azurea*
Butterfly flower: *Asclepias tuberosa*
Chicory: *Cichorium Intybus*
Common milkweed: *Asclepias syriaca*
Common yarrow: *Achillea Millefolium*
False blue indigo: *Baptisia australis*
Frostflower aster: *Aster ptarmicoides*
Harebell: *Campanula rotundifolia*
Hoary puccoon: *Lithospermum canescens*
Kansas gayfeather: *Liatris pycnostachya*

Ox-eye daisy: *Chrysanthemum Leucanthemum*
Pasque flower: *Anemone pulsatilla*
Prairie goldenrod: *Solidago rigida*
Prairie phlox: *Phlox pilosa*
Prairie smoke: *Geum triflorum*
Pussytoes: *Antennaria plantaginifolia*
Rose verbena: *Verbena canadensis*
Seneca snakeroot: *Polygala Senega*
Shooting star: *Dodecatheon Meadia*
Smooth aster: *Aster laevis*
Wild bergamot: *Monarda fistulosa*
Wine cups: *Callirhoe involucrata*
Wood lily: *Lilium philadelphicum*

Wildflowers for a Rock Garden in Full Sun

Reasonably fertile soil that does not get bone dry.

Barren strawberry: *Waldsteinia fragarioides*
Birdfoot violet: *Viola pedata*
Blue-eyed grass: *Sisyrinchium angustifolium*
Blue salvia: *Salvia azurea*
Bugleflower: *Ajuga reptans*
Columbine: *Aquilegia canadensis*
Common cinquefoil: *Potentilla canadensis*
Cypress spurge: *Euphorbia Cyparissias*
*Grape hyacinth: *Muscari botryoides*

Lakeside daisy: *Actinea herbacea*
Pasque flower: *Anemone pulsatilla*
Prairie phlox: *Phlox pilosa*
Prairie smoke: *Geum triflorum*
*Purple corydalis: *Corydalis bulbosa*
Pussytoes: *Antennaria plantaginifolia*
Shooting star: *Dodecatheon Meadia*
Silverweed: *Potentilla anserina*
*Star-of-Bethlehem: *Ornithogalum umbellatum*
Wine cups: *Callirhoe involucrata*

Wildflowers for the Rock Garden in High Open Shade

Humus-rich soil.

Barren strawberry: *Waldsteinia fragarioides*
Bishop's-cap: *Mitella diphylla*
Bloodroot: *Sanguinaria canadensis*
Canada mayflower: *Maianthemum canadense*
Celandine poppy: *Stylophorum diphyllum*
Columbine: *Aquilegia canadensis*
Cranesbill: *Geranium maculatum*
*Dutchman's-breeches: *Dicentra Cucullaria*
Foamflower: *Tiarella cordifolia*
Golden ragwort: *Senecio aureus*
Golden seal: *Hydrastis canadensis*
Goldthread: *Coptis groenlandica*
Greek valerian: *Polemonium reptans*
Hairy alumroot: *Heuchera villosa*
Hepatica: *Hepatica americana*
*Grape hyacinth: *Muscari botryoides*

Moneywort: *Lysimachia Nummularia*
Partridgeberry: *Mitchella repens*
Phlox Laphamii: *Phlox divaricata Laphamii*
Phlox, blue: *Phlox divaricata*
Phlox, mountain: *Phlox ovata*
Pink bleeding heart: *Dicentra eximia*
Rock geranium: *Heuchera americana*
Shooting star: *Dodecatheon Meadia*
*Spring beauty: *Claytonia virginica*
*Squirrel corn: *Dicentra canadensis*
Starflower: *Trientalis borealis*
Violet, American dog: *Viola conspersa*
Violet, downy yellow: *Viola pubescens*
Violet, sweet white: *Viola blanda*
Virginia bluebell: *Mertensia virginica*
Wild ginger: *Asarum canadense*
Woodland strawberry: *Fragaria vesca*
Yellow stargrass: *Hypoxis hirsuta*

Wildflowers to Grow along Lakes and Streams or in High Open Shade or Where There Is Sunshine for Most of the Day

The soil is usually moist and always fertile.

Canada lily: *Lilium canadense*
Cardinal flower: *Lobelia Cardinalis*
Crested dwarf iris: *Iris cristata*
False dragonhead: *Physostegia virginiana*
Forget-me-not: *Myosotis scorpioides*
Gentian, bottle: *Gentiana Andrewsii*
Gentian, soapwort: *Gentiana Saponaria*
Golden ragwort: *Senecio aureus*
Grass of Parnassus: *Parnassia glauca*
Great blue lobelia: *Lobelia siphilitica*
Ironweed: *Vernonia noveboracensis*
Joe-pye: *Eupatorium maculatum*

Lakeside daisy: *Actinea herbacea*
Monkey flower: *Mimulus ringens*
Oswego tea: *Monarda didyma*
Ox-eye: *Heliopsis helianthoides*
Purple loosestrife: *Lythrum Salicaria*
Queen of the prairie: *Filipendula rubra*
Skullcap blue heaven: *Scutellaria baicalensis*
Swamp candles: *Lysimachia terrestris*
Swamp milkweed: *Asclepias incarnata*
Turtlehead, red: *Chelone obliqua*
Turtlehead, white: *Chelone glabra*

Wildflowers for Bogs, Marshes, and Lowlands Where Water Often Stands in Spring

Soil is always fertile. Full sun.

Boneset: *Eupatorium perfoliatum*
Canada lily: *Lilium canadense*
Common cattail: *Typha latifolia*
Flat-topped aster: *Aster umbellatus*
Ironweed: *Vernonia noveboracensis*
Joe-pye: *Eupatorium maculatum*

Marsh marigold: *Caltha palustris*
Skunk cabbage: *Symplocarpus foetidus*
Swamp candles: *Lysimachia terrestris*
Swamp milkweed: *Asclepias incarnata*
Wild calla: *Calla palustris*

Wildflowers for Moist Meadows in Full Sun

The soil is fertile and moisture is always ample, but there is some tolerance to short periods of summer drought.

Blue flag: *Iris versicolor*
Boneset: *Eupatorium perfoliatum*
*Camass, eastern: *Camassia scilloides*
*Camass, western: *Camassia esculenta*
Canada anemone: *Anemone canadensis*

Cardinal flower: *Lobelia Cardinalis*
False dragonhead: *Physostegia virginiana*
Flat-topped aster: *Aster umbellatus*

Wildflowers for Moist Meadows in Full Sun (*continued*)

Gentian, bottle: *Gentiana Andrewsii*
Gentian, soapwort: *Gentiana Saponaria*
Goldenrod, Canada: *Solidago canadensis*
Goldenrod, grass-leaved: *Solidago graminifolia*
Grass of Parnassus: *Parnassia glauca*
Great blue lobelia: *Lobelia siphilitica*
Ironweed: *Vernonia noveboracensis*
Joe-pye: *Eupatorium maculatum*
Lily, Canada: *Lilium canadense*

Lily, Michigan: *Lilium michiganense*
Lily, Turk's-cap: *Lilium superbum*
Monkey flower: *Mimulus ringens*
Purple loosestrife: *Lythrum Salicaria*
Queen of the prairie: *Filipendula rubra*
Swamp candles: *Lysimachia terrestris*
Swamp milkweed: *Asclepias incarnata*
Tall meadowrue: *Thalictrum polygamum*
Turtlehead, red: *Chelone obliqua*
Turtlehead, white: *Chelone glabra*

Wildflowers for Cool, Moist Woodlands in Deep Shade

The lower branches of deciduous trees and evergreens are about at head level. Soil is rich, often somewhat acid. This type of woodland usually supports ferns as well as native wildflowers.

Bluebead lily: *Clintonia borealis*
Bunchberry: *Cornus canadensis*
Canada mayflower: *Maianthemum canadense*
Creeping snowberry: *Gaultheria hispidula*
Dwarf ginseng: *Panax trifolium*

Partridgeberry: *Mitchella repens*
Trillium, nodding: *Trillium cernuum*
Trillium, painted: *Trillium undulatum*
Twinflower: *Linnaea borealis*
Violet, sweet white: *Viola blanda*
Wintergreen: *Gaultheria procumbens*

Wildflowers for Sphagnum Bogs and Moss-covered Rotting Logs and Stumps

There is always moisture present except in periods of extreme summer drought. Acid soil.

Creeping snowberry: *Gaultheria hispidula*
Dwarf ginseng: *Panax trifolium*
Goldthread: *Coptis groenlandica*
Partridgeberry: *Mitchella repens*
Pink lady's-slipper: *Cypripedium acaule*
Twinflower: *Linnaea borealis*

Wildflowers for Moist, Rich, Sometimes Rocky Woodlands; Humus-rich Soil in the Shade of Buildings or Trees; Open Deciduous Woodland Where Leafmold Is Plentiful and Existing Shade Is High; Well-drained River Bottoms

Allegheny Mountain gentian: *Gentiana decora*
American bugbane: *Cimicifuga americana*
Amsonia: *Amsonia Tabernaemontana*
Aster, large-leaved: *Aster macrophyllus*
Baneberry, red: *Actaea rubra*
Baneberry, white: *Actaea pachypoda*
Barren strawberry: *Waldsteinia fragarioides*
Black cohosh: *Cimicifuga racemosa*
Bishop's-cap: *Mitella diphylla*
Bloodroot: *Sanguinaria canadensis*
Bluebead lily: *Clintonia borealis*
Blue cohosh: *Caulophyllum thalictroides*
Boneset: *Eupatorium perfoliatum*
Bowman's root: *Gillenia trifoliata*
Bunchberry: *Cornus canadensis*
*Camass, eastern: *Camassia scilloides*
*Camass, western: *Camassia esculenta*
Canada mayflower: *Maianthemum canadense*
Celandine poppy: *Stylophorum diphyllum*
Cranesbill: *Geranium maculatum*
Culver's root: *Veronicastrum virginicum*
*Dutchman's-breeches: *Dicentra Cucullaria*
Dutchman's-pipe: *Aristolochia macrophylla*
Dwarf ginseng: *Panax trifolium*
Early meadowrue: *Thalictrum dioicum*
Early white snakeroot: *Eupatorium rugosum*
Foamflower: *Tiarella cordifolia*
Galax: *Galax aphylla*

Ginseng: *Panax quinquefolium*
Golden ragwort: *Senecio aureus*
Golden seal: *Hydrastis canadensis*
Grass-leaved goldenrod: *Solidago graminifolia*
Greek valerian: *Polemonium reptans*
Green dragon: *Arisaema Dracontium*
Hairy alumroot: *Heuchera villosa*
Hepatica: *Hepatica americana*
Horse gentian: *Triosteum aurantiacum*
Indian cucumber: *Medeola virginiana*
Jack-in-the-pulpit: *Arisaema triphyllum*
Lady's-slipper, mountain: *Cypripedium montanum*
Lady's-slipper, showy: *Cypripedium reginae*
Lady's-slipper, small white: *Cypripedium candidum*
Lady's-slipper, yellow: *Cypripedium Calceolus pubescens*
Lily, Canada: *Lilium canadense*
Lily, Michigan: *Lilium michiganense*
Mayapple: *Podophyllum peltatum*
Nodding mandarin: *Disporum maculatum*
Nodding wild onion: *Allium cernuum*
Oswego tea: *Monarda didyma*
Partridgeberry: *Mitchella repens*
Phlox Laphamii: *Phlox divaricata Laphamii*
Phlox, blue: *Phlox divaricata*
Phlox, mountain: *Phlox ovata*
Pink bleeding heart: *Dicentra eximia*
*Purple corydalis: *Corydalis bulbosa*
Rock geranium: *Heuchera americana*
Rose mandarin: *Streptopus roseus*

Moist, Rich Woodlands; Humus-rich Soil in Shade (*continued*)

Skullcap, downy: *Scutellaria incana*
Skullcap, early blue: *Scutellaria ovata*
Skullcap, mad-dog: *Scutellaria lateriflora*
Skullcap, pink: *Scutellaria integrifolia*
Skullcap, showy: *Scutellaria serrata*
Solomon's seal: *Polygonatum biflorum*
Spikenard: *Aralia racemosa*
*Spring beauty: *Claytonia virginica*
*Squirrel corn: *Dicentra canadensis*
Starflower: *Trientalis borealis*
Stoneroot: *Collinsonia canadensis*
Toothwort, cut-leaved: *Dentaria laciniata*
Toothwort, two-leaved: *Dentaria diphylla*
Trailing arbutus: *Epigaea repens*
Trillium, large white: *Trillium grandiflorum*
Trillium, nodding: *Trillium cernuum*

Trillium, Ozark: *Trillium ozarkanum*
Trillium, prairie: *Trillium recurvatum*
Trillium, purple: *Trillium erectum*
Trillium, rose: *Trillium stylosum*
Trillium, snow: *Trillium nivale*
Trillium, toadshade: *Trillium sessile*
Trillium, yellow: *Trillium luteum*
Trout lily: *Erythronium americanum*
Twinleaf: *Jeffersonia diphylla*
Violet, American dog: *Viola conspersa*
Violet, Canada: *Viola canadensis*
Violet, downy yellow: *Viola pubescens*
Violet, early blue: *Viola palmata*
Violet, smooth yellow: *Viola pensylvanica*
Virginia bluebell: *Mertensia virginica*
Wild ginger: *Asarum canadense*
Wild oats: *Uvularia sessilifolia*
Woodland strawberry: *Fragaria vesca*
Yellow stargrass: *Hypoxis hirsuta*

Wildflowers for Dry, Open Woodlands Where Sunlight Filters Through Leafless Trees in Spring

Leafmold is plentiful and moisture abundant at time of blooming. These wildflowers may also be grown in the shade of tall buildings and trees where soil is humus-rich.

Aster, large-leaved: *Aster macrophyllus*
Aster, New England: *Aster novae-angliae*
Bloodroot: *Sanguinaria canadensis*
Bunchberry: *Cornus canadensis*
Canada mayflower: *Maianthemum canadense*
Cranesbill: *Geranium maculatum*
Culver's root: *Veronicastrum virginicum*
Early meadowrue: *Thalictrum dioicum*
False Solomon's seal: *Smilacina stellata*
False spikenard: *Smilacina racemosa*
Fringed polygala: *Polygala paucifolia*
Hepatica: *Hepatica americana*

Merrybells: *Uvularia grandiflora*
Partridgeberry: *Mitchella repens*
Phlox, blue: *Phlox divaricata*
Pink bleeding heart: *Dicentra eximia*
Pink lady's-slipper: *Cypripedium acaule*
*Purple corydalis: *Corydalis bulbosa*
Rock geranium: *Heuchera americana*
Shinleaf: *Pyrola virens*
Skullcap, downy: *Scutellaria incana*
Solomon's seal: *Polygonatum biflorum*
Trailing arbutus: *Epigaea repens*
Trillium, Ozark: *Trillium ozarkanum*
Trillium, large white: *Trillium grandiflorum*

Dry, Open Woodlands, Filtered Sun (*continued*)

Trillium, purple: *Trillium erectum*
Trillium, yellow: *Trillium luteum*
Violet, American dog: *Viola conspersa*
Violet, broad-leaved wood: *Viola latiuscula*
Violet, downy yellow: *Viola pubescens*

Wild sarsaparilla: *Aralia nudicaulis*
Wintergreen: *Gaultheria procumbens*
Wood anemone: *Anemone quinquefolia*
Yellow lady's-slipper: *Cypripedium Calceolus pubescens*

Weedy Wildflowers that Have Colorful Blossoms

The spent blossoms of these plants should be cut right after blooming to prevent them from setting seed. Those marked with a dagger (†) also spread by stolons and are best grown in a bottomless gallon can sunk into the earth to within one inch of soil level.

*Bugleflower: *Ajuga reptans*
Canada anemone: *Anemone canadensis*
Chicory: *Cichorium Intybus*
†Clustered bluebell: *Campanula glomerata*
†Cypress spurge: *Euphorbia Cyparissias*

†Gill-over-the-ground: *Glechoma hederacea*
Ox-eye daisy: *Chrysanthemum Leucanthemum*
Queen Anne's lace: *Daucus carota*
*Swamp candles: *Lysimachia terrestris*

Wildflowers for Very Lean Soils or Even Ash Piles

These plants are aggressive and will spread to hide an otherwise ugly site.

*Bugleflower: *Ajuga reptans*
Common cinquefoil: *Potentilla canadensis*
Gill-over-the-ground: *Glechoma hederacea*

Silverweed: *Potentilla anserina*
Toadflax: *Linaria vulgaris*
Violet, common blue: *Viola papilionacea*
Violet, Confederate: *Viola Priceana*

Wildflowers for Soils Containing Some Lime

Soils should be neutral and rarely only slightly acid. Under a high canopy of trees such as maples and birches.

Grass of Parnassus: *Parnassia glauca* (prefers sun)
Green dragon: *Arisaema Dracontium*
Merrybells: *Uvularia grandiflora*
Showy lady's-slipper: *Cypripedium reginae*

Small white lady's-slipper: *Cypripedium candidum*
Twinleaf: *Jeffersonia diphylla*

247

Wildflowers for Acid Soils

Soil is humus-rich and there is a high canopy of shade, usually offered by oaks and evergreens.

Bearberry: *Arctostaphylos Uva-ursi* (prefers sun)
Bunchberry: *Cornus canadensis*
Creeping snowberry: *Gaultheria hispidula*
Dwarf ginseng: *Panax trifolium*

Fringed polygala: *Polygala paucifolia*
Galax: *Galax aphylla*
Pink lady's-slipper: *Cypripedium acaule*
Painted trillium: *Trillium undulatum*
Trailing arbutus: *Epigaea repens*
Wintergreen: *Gaultheria procumbens*

Wildflowers for Climates Where Winters Are Severe and the Soil Freezes

Must have winter mulching.

Butterfly flower: *Asclepias tuberosa*
Early white snakeroot: *Eupatorium rugosum*
Skullcaps: *Scutellariae*
Stoneroot: *Collinsonia canadensis*

Appendix II

Successful Lady's-slipper Cultivation

When you decide to bring lady's-slippers into your garden, be sure that you can provide for their needs. If you start them under the proper conditions, they will take care of themselves thereafter.

Select a woodland spot in open shade; try to arrange the plantings so that filtered sunlight can reach the plants while they are blooming. The steps in cultivation—preparing the soil, planting the wildflower, fertilizing, and mulching—are discussed below.

1. Preparing the Soil

Brought-in soil. If you do not have a spot with suitable soil, you can bring in woodland soil to prepare a bed. Mix the soil with a generous amount of damp peatmoss and add some bonemeal if you wish. First take out about a foot of the old soil and replace it with an equal amount of the new soil and peatmoss mixture, otherwise you will have a high mound and the earth will dry out. Pack the soil down lightly. Mulch it with oats, straw (or leafmold), water thoroughly, and leave it to "mellow" for a year or more.

Virgin soil. When digging up virgin woods soil for a bed, discard the layer that does not contain humus. Remove heavy roots, live plants, and large stones. Do *not* remove small twigs, partly decayed forest litter, and other organic matter. Put the soil in a wheelbarrow and break it up thoroughly. Mix in an equal amount of damp peatmoss.

Peatmoss. Always use damp peatmoss. Dry peatmoss draws moisture out of the surrounding soil, leaving little for the plants' roots to absorb.

pH. The exact pH of the soil is not very important. All our lady's-slippers, even the pink variety, thrive in a soil with a pH of 6.

Mycorhizal fungus. Lady's-slippers, especially the pink variety, require mycorhizal fungus in the soil. This is a threadlike fungus, webbing the woodland earth. You will be able to see the fungus as it forms a lacework on the fine roots of trees and shrubs that penetrate the forest floor. Whenever I find any mycorhizal or other fungus in the woods, I always take some back to my lady's-slipper beds. Fungi can mean the difference between life and death for these plants, which are themselves partially parasitic. (A method for increasing fungi is given in Paragraph 5 below.)

2. Planting

Rake away all the dry forest litter from the selected site and reserve it for future mulching. Dig a hole 1 to 1½ feet wide and from a few inches to a foot deep, depending on the type of lady's-slipper (see individual plant instructions in Perennial Wildflowers for Permanence).

Return at least half of the soil to the hole, and build a shallow mound to within an inch of the top of the hole.

Set the rhizome on the mound of earth, with the roots gradually extending downward until the tips of the roots are 1 to 1½ inches lower than the crown. Cover the roots with the lady's-slippers soil mixture until you have almost filled the hole. The line where the new shoots meet the roots should be about ½ to 1 inch below soil level.

3. Bonemeal

Sprinkle a tablespoonful of bonemeal over the bed as food for future use. Bloodmeal is fine too.

4. Sphagnum moss

Cap the new shoots with a mound of damp-to-wet sphagnum moss. Use just enough to cover the tips and form a 4 inch circle around them. The moss will keep the tips from drying out and will protect them from rodents.

5. Mulch Containing Mycorhizal Fungus

Spread an inch of oak leafmold and old weathered straw or decaying marsh hay (at the stage where it is beginning to turn dark). Make a raised bed of the mixture, about a foot high. If you have a natural woodland setting where there are pockets and depressions in deep shade, try filling them with the mixture. Make a reasonably high mound; the pile will settle as it begins to decompose.

Keep the area moist, but not dripping wet. Introduce some of the mycorhizal fungi on the outer edges and center of the leaf–straw bed. The fungi will gradually run through the entire bed.

Later, portions of this fungi-laden humus can be buried where wanted. Often two years will elapse before the entire bed is filled with fungi.

When you transfer fungi-laden mulch, always cover it with a layer of some other mulch to keep it from drying out.

6. The Top Layer of Mulch

Summer. Fresh lawn clippings used as soon as the grass is cut make a very good mulch in summer. They become part of the soil and provide food for the plant. Dried clippings are useless. Spread 1 inch of clippings over the entire root area. It may be necessary to remove some of the top layer of dry humus, and this can be put aside for reuse in fall. Fresh grass clippings should be added each time the lawn is cut and throughout the entire growing season. Dampen the grass mulch between mulching periods to hasten decay.

Winter. For extra protection during the first winter, mulch with old marsh hay or weathered old straw. Place a twig or small stick as a marker near each plant bud or group of buds so that you will know where to push aside some of the mulch in spring. If the lady's-slippers have too much mulch while they are actively growing, the stalks will be weak and will topple. After the plants bloom, tuck some of the mulch around the stalks.

When lady's-slipper roots are exposed to the air, new roots are stimulated to form at the base of the new root buds so that the plant can survive. The old roots continue to function for a year or two, and then they disappear. If the new roots have not established themselves enough to take over, the plant will die. This is why it is so important to introduce the plant under ideal conditions. Once the plants have grown new roots and established themselves, they grow stronger every year. Do not divide the clumps.

Always keep lady's-slipper beds moist by good mulching. Water deeply when necessary, but do not water them every day. Overwatering may drown the plants; it also washes away valuable nutrients in the soil.

The method I have described has made it possible for lady's-slippers to adapt and grow into beautiful specimens in my gardens. I hope it will work as well for you.

251

Appendix III

Wildflower Nurseries

All of these nurseries sell wildflower stock through the mail, and most have catalogs worth writing for.

Allgrove
Box 459H
Wilmington, Mass. 01887

Alpenglow Gardens
13328 Trans-Canada Hwy.
North Surrey P.O.
New Westminster, B.C.
Canada

Baldwin Seed Co. of Alaska
Anchorage, Alaska

Claude A. Barr
Prairie Gem Ranch
Smithwick, S.D. 57782

Gardens of the Blue Ridge
Ashford, N.C. 28603

Griffey Nursery
Rt. 3, Box 17A
Marshall, N.C. 28753

Jamieson Valley Gardens
Rt. 3B
Spokane, Wash. 99203

Leslie's Wildflower Nursery
30 Sumner St.
Methuen, Mass. 01844

Lousenberry Gardens
Oakford, Ill. 62673

Midwest Wildflowers
Box 64B
Rockton, Ill. 61072

Mincemoyers
R.D. 5, Box 397-H
Jackson, N.J. 08527

Orchid Gardens
Rt. 3
Grand Rapids, Minn. 55744

The Three Laurels
Marshall, N.C. 28753

Vick's Wildflower Gardens
Box 115
Gladwyne, Pa. 19035

Woodland Acres Nursery
Marie Sperka
Rt. 2
Crivitz, Wis. 54114

Appendix IV

Perennial Wildflowers by Color

The wildflowers listed here are grouped according to the color or colors in which they occur most commonly. For a complete description of a particular flower and its color, the reader can refer to the individual entry for that plant.

Blue to Violet

Allegheny Mountain gentian
American dog violet
Amsonia
Birdfoot violet
Blue-eyed grass
Blue flag
Blue salvia
Bottle gentian
Broad-leaved wood violet
Bugleflower
Chicory
Clustered bluebell
Common blue violet
Crested dwarf iris
Downy skullcap
Early blue skullcap
Early blue violet
Eastern camass
False blue indigo
Forget-me-not
Gill-over-the-ground
Grape hyacinth
Great blue lobelia
Greek valerian
Harebell
Hepatica
Horse gentian
Ironweed
Kansas gayfeather
Large-leaved aster
Mad-dog skullcap
Monkey flower
New England aster
Pasque flower
Prairie phlox
Shooting star
Showy skullcap
Skullcap blue heaven
Smooth aster
Soapwort gentian
Virginia bluebell
Western camass
Wild bergamot
Wild blue phlox
Wild lupine
Wild petunia

Brown

Dutchman's-pipe
Jack-in-the-pulpit
Skunk cabbage
Wild ginger

Green

Bluebead lily
Blue cohosh
Golden seal
Green dragon
Indian cucumber
Jack-in-the-pulpit
Rock geranium
Skunk cabbage
Solomon's seal
Wild sarsaparilla

Orange

Blackberry lily
Butterfly flower
Canada lily
Michigan lily
Tiger lily
Turk's-cap lily
Wild columbine
Wood lily

Pink to Red

Bearberry
Blazing star
Bowman's root

Cardinal flower
Common milkweed
False dragonhead
Fringed polygala
Jessie's red violet
Joe-pye
Kansas gayfeather
Mountain phlox
Musk mallow
Nodding wild onion
Oswego tea
Partridgeberry
Pink bleeding heart
Pink lady's-slipper
Pink skullcap
Prairie phlox
Prairie smoke
Prairie trillium
Purple corydalis
Purple trillium
Queen of the Prairie
Red turtlehead
Rose mandarin
Rose trillium
Rose verbena
Rue anemone
Shooting star
Spotted cranesbill
Spring beauty
Swamp milkweed
Toadshade
Trailing arbutus (turns pink
    with age)
Twinflower
Two-leaved toothwort
Western bleeding heart
Wild ginger
Wine cups

White

American bugbane
Bearberry
Bishop's-cap
Black cohosh
Bloodroot
Boneset
Bowman's root
Bunchberry
Canada anemone

Canada mayflower
Canada violet
Common yarrow
Confederate violet
Creeping snowberry
Culver's root
Dutchman's-breeches
Dwarf ginseng
Early white snakeroot
False spikenard
Flat-topped aster
Frostflower aster
Galax
Ginseng
Golden seal
Goldthread
Grass of Parnassus
Hairy alumroot
Hepatica
Large white trillium
Mayapple
Mountain lady's-slipper
Musk mallow
Nodding mandarin
Nodding trillium
Ox-eye daisy
Ozark trillium
Painted trillium
Partridgeberry
Purple loosestrife
Pussytoes
Red baneberry
Rock geranium
Rue anemone
Seneca snakeroot
Shinleaf
Shooting star
Showy lady's-slipper
Small white lady's-slipper
Snow trillium
Spikenard
Spring beauty
Squirrel corn
Starflower
Star-flowered false Solomon's
    seal
Star-of-Bethlehem
Sweet white violet
Tall meadow rue
Trailing arbutus

Twinflower
Twinleaf
Two-leaved toothwort (turns
    pink with age)
White baneberry
White mertensia
White phlox
White turtlehead
Wild calla
Wintergreen
Wood anemone
Woodland strawberry

Yellow

Barren strawberry
Blue cohosh
Bluebead lily
Canada goldenrod
Canada lily
Celandine poppy
Common cinquefoil
Common tansy
Cypress spurge
Downy yellow violet
Ginseng
Golden ragwort
Grass-leaved goldenrod
Hoary puccoon
Indian cucumber
Lady's mantle
Lakeside daisy
Large yellow lady's slipper
Marsh marigold
Merrybells
Moneywort
Nodding mandarin
Ox-eye
Prairie goldenrod
Silverweed
Smooth yellow violet
Solomon's seal
Stoneroot
Swamp candles
Trout lily
Wild oats
Wild senna
Yellow stargrass
Yellow trillium

Glossary

ALTERNATE LEAVES Leaves growing at regular intervals at different levels along the stem, but not opposite each other.

ANTHER The pollen-bearing portion of the stamen.

AXIL The space formed between any two plant parts, usually between the leaf and the stem or between two veins in a leaf.

AXILLARY BUD The bud growing in the axil of a plant.

BRACT A modified or rudimentary leaf growing near the calyx (outer envelope) of a flower or at the base of the flower stalk; bracts may be green and leaflike or colored.

BUD The rudimentary state of a stem or a branch; an unopened flower.

BULB The complete plant at a resting stage of growth; a fleshy leaf-bud with scales or coats formed underground.

BULBIL A small bulb; also a bulblike organ, especially when found on the stem.

CALYX The outer envelope of a flower, usually green, though it can be colored; found below the corolla.

CARUNCLE An outgrowth on the protective outer covering of some seeds.

COROLLA The whorl of colored petals above the calyx.

CORONA The crown of a flower, such as the cup of a narcissus or daffodil.

CORM The fleshy, underground part of a stem, which furnishes reserve material for bud growth; also a solid bulb.

INFLORESCENCE The flowering part of a plant above the last stem leaves; it includes the branch, stem, stalk, bract, and actual flower.

LAYERING A method of inducing a shoot to root before being detached from the parent plant.

NODE A knoblike enlargement on a stem, which normally bears a leaf or whorl of leaves; buds appear at this spot and roots form most readily from it when cuttings are taken.

OFFSET New bulbs, corms, or short runner roots typical of the parent plant which may be detached and used to produce new plants.

257

OPPOSITE LEAVES   Leaves growing directly opposite each other on the stem, usually at regular intervals.

PANICLE   A pyramidal, loosely-branched flower cluster; a raceme that branches.

PETIOLE   A leaf support; a leaf stalk.

RACEME   A simple growth of flowers on short stems on a common, usually elongated, axis.

RADIX   A plant root; also its base.

RAY   The branch of an umbel or similar inflorescence.

RHIZOME   Any horizontal or subterranean stem that produces shoots and roots; it differs from a true root in possessing buds, nodes, and usually scalelike leaves.

ROOT   The underground part of a plant that absorbs moisture and carbon dioxide and stores food material; it differs from the stem in that it lacks nodes, buds, and leaves.

ROSETTE   A cluster of leaves or other plant parts in a circular pattern.

RUNNER   A shoot trailing on the ground which roots at the end to form a new plant.

SCALE LEAF   One of the rudimentary leaves which enclose and protect winter buds.

SPADIX   A floral spike with a fleshy axis usually enclosed in a type of large bract known as a spathe.

SPATHE   A large bract enclosing one or more flowers.

STALK   A stem or support of a particular plant organ; for example, a flower stalk.

STEM   The plant part that supports the leaves and buds and, in the case of flowering plants, the flowers.

STOLON   A horizontal-growing branch, low on the plant, which roots at the tips and nodes; a runner.

SWALE   A low-lying stretch of land, such as a small meadow, swamp, or marshy depression.

TAPROOT   A primary root that grows directly downward and gives off small lateral roots.

TERMINAL   Located at the end of a shoot; not lateral or axillary.

TUBER   A swollen underground stem, bearing buds or eyes from which new plants may grow.

UMBEL   An umbrellalike growth of stalked flowers rising from a common point.

WHORL   A circular arrangement of leaves or flowers on the stem.

Index of Common Names

Index of Botanical Names